HUMAN RIGHTS WATCH BOOKS

PERU

River
Highway

DEPARTMENT
PUNO Name
.... Boundary
★ Capital

Regions in
State of
Emergency
July, 1991
Source:
Instituto de Defensa Legal

Detail of Middle and
Upper Huallaga Valley

A

Rioja
Moyobamba ★
Tarapoto

Bellavista
Juanjuí
Huallaga

**SAN
MARTIN**

Santa
Lucia
Uchiza
La Morada

LA LIBERTAD

ANCASH

Tingo
Maria

HUANUCO

Huánuco ★

COLOMBIA
QUITO ★
ECUADOR

Putumayo

BRAZIL

LORETO

Amazonas

Iquitos

Marañon

Ucayali

Tumbes

TUMBES

PIURA
Piura

CAJAMARCA

AMAZONAS

**SAN
MARTIN**

Moyobamba

Chachapoyas

Cajamarca

Chiclayo

LAMBAYEQUE

LA LIBERTAD

Trujillo

ANCASH

Huaraz ★

HUANUCO
Huánuco ★

Pucallpa

BRAZIL

UCAYALI

PACIFIC

OCEAN

Cerro
de ★
Pasco

PASCO

LIMA

JUNIN

Huancayo

B

**MADRE
DE
DIOS**

Puerto ★
Maldonado

LIMA

Callao

Huancavelica ★

CUSCO
Cusco

Detail of Pasco,
Junin and Ayacucho

Constitución

Iscozacin
Pichis
Palcazu

PASCO

Puerto Prado
Centro Sanibeni
Satipo

JUNIN

Huancayo

Chongos
Alto
Huancavelica

HUANCAVELICA

Ica

Ayacucho

Abancay

APURIMAC

Santo
Tomás

PUNO

Anapati
Ene

CUSCO

B

Uchuraccay
Ccano
Huanta

Santa
Barbara
Soccos
Cangallo
Accomarca
Cayara
Chilcayoc

ICA

AYACUCHO

Ayacucho
Apurimac
Abancay

APURIMAC

AYACUCHO

AREQUIPA

Puno ★

Arequipa

BOLIVIA

MOQUEGUA
Moquegua

TACNA
Tacna

CHILE

© 1991 Michael S. Miller

0   kilometers   250

0   miles   200

(Scale of detail maps 150% of main map)

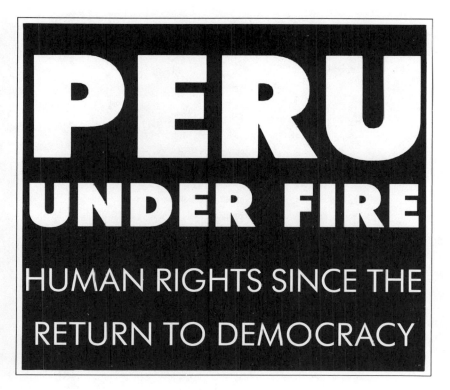

PERU
UNDER FIRE

HUMAN RIGHTS SINCE THE
RETURN TO DEMOCRACY

AMERICAS WATCH

HUMAN
RIGHTS
WATCH
BOOKS

Yale University Press   New Haven and London

Americas Watch was established in 1981 to monitor and promote observance
of internationally recognized human rights in Latin America
and the Caribbean. Human Rights Watch also includes Africa Watch,
Asia Watch, Helsinki Watch, Middle East Watch, and the
Fund for Free Expression.
Set in Times Roman type by
The Composing Room of Michigan, Inc.
Printed in the United States of America by
Vail-Ballou Press, Binghamton, New York.

Library of Congress Cataloging-in-Publication Data

Peru under fire : human rights since the return to democracy /
Americas Watch.
    p.   cm. — (Human rights watch books)
Includes bibliographical references and index.
ISBN 0-300-05237-5
1. Human rights—Peru.   2. Civil rights—Peru.
3. Violence—Peru.   4. Peru—Politics and government—1980–
I. Americas Watch Committee (U.S.)   II. Series.
JC599.P4P485   1992
323.4'9'0985—dc20   91-42500
                              CIP

The paper in this book meets the guidelines for permanence and
durability of the Committee on Production Guidelines for Book
Longevity of the Council on Library Resources.

10 9 8 7 6 5 4 3 2 1

CONTENTS

FOREWORD

There are occasions when societies seem to reach their breaking points and contradictions brewing within suddenly explode. This would seem to be the case today in Peru, a country struck by a political violence so serious that it has cost the lives of more than 23,000 Peruvians since 1980.

Peru's problems are clearly rooted in unresolved conflicts that have prevented the construction of a democratic society—in the true sense of the word—and made it impossible to improve the economic conditions of the population. The relative modernization of Peruvian society in previous decades has only maintained these contradictions under different guises. The severe gap between the state with its institutions on the one hand, and civil society on the other, make formal channels for conflict resolution or even for the functioning of the economy inoperable or simply overwhelmed by reality.

As the institutional crisis has deepened, it has become more evident with each setback that society, with its frustrations and hopes, has exceeded the capacity of formal institutions to cope. These institutions, in turn, appear ever closer to fiction than reality. In this context, the state—gradually but consistently—ceases to regulate social dynamics and becomes increasingly irrelevant. At the same time, the crisis of the fragmented civil society and its organizations worsens.

The effects of the economic crisis and of structural adjustment policies on the already miserable quality of life for the overwhelming majority of Peruvians must be added to the mix. The cold and terrible statistics indicate that more than half of all Peruvians live in extreme poverty. It is difficult to imagine a more dramatic and complex picture—one that abundantly exceeds even the circles in Dante's Inferno.

As if the combination of these calamities were not enough, there is another component crucial in explaining the deterioration of the situation in Peru and the dark clouds gathering in its future: *political violence*. This violence is so acute and extensive that it should be characterized as an internal conflict or war, with the logical militarization of certain institutions and behaviors and, as *Peru under Fire* demonstrates, the violation of human rights. What has taken place in Peru in recent years is described and analyzed in this book by Americas Watch, and I refer the reader to its contents.

This book and my own experience present questions that I would like to raise. First, why have so many atrocities taken place in a country that in recent years has been under constitutional rule, without any interruption to the spiral of violence and abuse? Second, if solutions exist to this situation, what are they? I do not know if a complete answer to either question is possible, and it is certainly far more difficult to answer the second. I do not intend, therefore, to answer them here but to offer instead a few general observations.

The first question can be answered on two levels. One level refers to certain essential elements of the Peruvian society and state: those elements that make Peruvian institutions inoperable, such as the profound tragedy of a multi-ethnic society that is not clearly reflected in its judicial, political, or even educational structures. It is neither by chance nor irrelevant that bilingual education has never been part of the national educational policy. The institutional structure has never matched the essential character of Peruvian society. Therefore, it can hardly operate efficiently, much less respond adequately to an acute crisis.

These problems manifest themselves in matters concerning, for example, the administration of justice and maintenance of public order—right down to the enforcement of traffic laws or running of public transportation. In different forms and varying magnitudes, the state could almost be dispensed with and yet chaos would not necessarily result. Over the past several decades, Peruvians have referred to the judicial system, which is characterized by inefficiency and corruption, with the saying *más vale un mal arreglo que un buen pleito* (better a bad settlement than a good litigation), which expresses their general distrust. This is, by the way, a "democratic" distrust, because it is shared by both rich and poor. The ineffectiveness of official judicial mechanisms has spurred the development or consolidation of unofficial mechanisms that eventually go against the text and spirit of the law. The scope and reach of extralegal procedures is broad: from prearranged arbitration stipulated in many contracts between companies to physical punishment—including extrajudicial execution —against those from certain poor neighborhoods who have committed offenses. In all cases it illustrates one aspect of reality: individuals need to take matters into their own hands to solve what in theory should be handled by the state.

It was in this context that Sendero Luminoso got its start. Sendero is a political and military force with a clear strategy of total rupture with state institutions and of seizing power through violent revolution. Sendero's actions exacerbated many of the worst aspects of Peruvian society. It attacked the very weaknesses of the state, and its political regime—both its political and its military actions, which are predominantly terrorist in nature—targeted the weakest links of the state's presence, especially in rural areas. Without great effort at first, but making implacable use of violence and terror, Sendero easily swept away the already minimal state presence. Gradually, Sendero created gaps and absences, and eventually filled them itself.

The state's response has varied through the years, and it has combined few successes with many errors. In spite of their differences, all three constitutional governments that have ruled since the military regime stepped down in 1980 have—pathetically—shared one element: they attempted to solve militarily what was and is both a military and a political problem. These fundamentally flawed counterinsurgency strategies no doubt originated in the limitations presented by state and political structures with minimal presence or legitimacy. The reestablishment of public order has come to be understood not as the reinstatement of normal functions of the state but in a more limited way, as the affirmation of a police or military presence. This, of course, does not reinforce the state in all its components: judges, civilian officials, mayors, teachers, and security forces. Although it is the state defined in this way that must be defended, in practice only one of its necessary components is unilaterally affirmed: the action of security forces and, specifically, that of their repressive element.

One of the greatest paradoxes of Peru today results from this perception. The state's adversary is the especially bloody Sendero, a profoundly antipopular force that stands against all imaginable forms of grass-roots democracy. But in spite of that, and as a consequence of the state's own errors and deficiencies, the authorities do not generally obtain public support in the struggle against Sendero. We should ask ourselves whether the logic behind the state's policies is leading to the very militarization of society and state that Sendero Luminoso aims for. Contrary to the authoritarian option, it can undoubtedly be said that the human rights violations committed by members of the security forces are not conducive to the public order, which they claim to protect, but rather support Sendero's Manichaean logic. Human rights abuses are instrumental to Sendero terrorism, not to the struggle for the defense of human rights and democracy.

I do not wish here to analyze Sendero Luminoso. It is enough to keep in mind that most of the deaths in the present situation are attributable to Sendero, and that nine out of every ten of its victims are peasants or popular leaders. It is enough to verify that the terror and the authoritarian, violent imposition of Sendero's ideas are its principal political tools. It would be wrong to characterize this group as an expression of the poor or, even less, as speaking for or leading the oppressed. On the contrary, Sendero has become yet another factor in their impoverishment and oppression.

In facing the challenge from Sendero, the state has exhibited its weaknesses more than ever, resulting in this paradox: it has yielded territory while abetting or overlooking gross violations of human rights. What makes matters worse is that little has been done to break the vicious circle of impunity, thus increasing the sense of vulnerability among the citizens without politically isolating Sendero.

The Peruvian state has both historical and current responsibilities. Even if Sendero Luminoso generates the violence, the state can no longer present itself as its victim, because the state has acted with the skill and prudence of a bull in a china shop. A country's economic situation of course determines in part its alternatives. But even if difficulties exist in this area, there should be no question of falling into economic determinism. Some responses are not bound by economic limitations and have yet to be seriously explored by the state in Peru. The crisis of the state and its role in the administration of justice and, more generally, in how it deals with social conflict and armed subversion, are specific problems that require specific responses.

Among other plans of action, it is necessary to guarantee the democratic institutionality of Peru as a whole, certainly without impairing the military-police component of the state. Yet, with the extent to which the legal framework for resolving conflicts is overstepped and the military option is applied unilaterally, the state's capacity to consolidate itself and to survive is weakened. That consolidation and survival demands an energetic action to prevent and, where applicable, to investigate and sanction all human rights violations, particularly disappearances, extrajudicial executions, and the corrosive activities of paramilitary groups. To discourage impunity—which contributes to the destabilization of democracy—the citizens must have access to the mechanisms for the investigation, prosecution, and conviction of those who commit illegal acts. This must be done not to place institutions under fire but rather to implement an elementary requirement of justice and to strengthen democratic checks and balances.

It is imperative that legitimate use of force by the state be exercised within the limits of the constitution and the laws. To that end, it is critical to prepare an adequate pacification strategy and, more specifically, to adopt democratic and humanitarian concepts in the training and operation of the military. In this sense, it is essential to promote respect for international humanitarian law, in order to set minimum standards to be respected in the internal conflict.

Democratic order is formed not only by democratic institutions but also by the different components of civilian society in dynamic interaction. The organizations that promote and protect these rights have, in this context, a special significance, especially in situations where the official institutions are precarious. In a context of severe violence—as in Peru today—these organizations tend to be especially vulnerable. For that reason there must be clear guarantees and respect for nongovernmental organizations as well as for persons who are committed to the defense, promotion, and investigation of human rights.

Part of the knot of contradictions to be unraveled will be found in considerations like the ones I have offered. Something along these lines can serve as a backdrop for the opportunity to promote effective and consistent proposals to construct peace and to achieve respect for human rights—two sides of the same coin.

Diego García-Sayán
Executive Director
Andean Commission of Jurists

PREFACE

Political violence in Peru comes from more than the proverbial "two sides." The essential conflict is between a flawed democratic state and an insurgent challenge, but neither the state nor its challenger is homogeneous. Not only are there two well-established guerrilla groups that compete with each other, killing one another's combatants as well as civilians and the state's security forces, but the state's own agents of repression are various, ranging from military and police personnel to paramilitary groups and village militias, all of whom also prey on civilians as well as attacking legitimate targets. The drug traffic that corrupts political and social institutions and encourages crime also finances the insurgencies, lines the pockets of uniformed personnel, and foments violence against anyone who strays into its path. This book describes the perpetration of political violence by all "sides" and attempts to convey its extraordinary cost.

It is worth noting three recent developments since *Peru under Fire* was written. Chronologically, they are, first, a firm stance by the U.S. Congress on military aid to Peru; second, President Alberto Fujimori's mixed reaction to that stance; and third, the Peruvian leader's issuance of a series of decrees that at long last articulate his government's vision of a counterinsurgency plan.

American aid for antinarcotics activity and counterinsurgency training in Peru was debated in Washington during September 1991, and the Peruvian government, called to account for human rights violations, saw $10 million in aid to the army cut from that package, including training funds. This, in spite of consistent apologies for the military by the State Department, in particular its Human Rights Bureau. As of the end of 1991, a handful of U.S. Special Forces trainers were giving instructions to police, a program that had been underway since 1987 and as yet has not received sufficient oversight regarding abuses by police; but no trainers for the army were expected in the immediate future. The $24 million in military aid that remained in the package for Peru was destined primarily for ground support equipment, spare parts and equipment for aircraft and their crews, police antinarcotics training, and equipment for army civic action, according to the State Department.

Cutting back U.S. assistance to the army, the most intransigent force of repression associated with the Peruvian state, was a victory for supporters of strong human rights legislation and oversight in the granting of military aid. The debate over aid had other salutary effects as well. A congressional decision to freeze the aid temporarily in August, before taking it up in detail, had the effect in Peru of reawakening public and press interest in human rights, and after years of declining attention to the issue, abuses again became front-page news, as did proposals for police reform and calls for legal progress in human rights cases. Fujimori and military officials were forced to take the human rights issue seriously, despite the State Department's evident lack of commitment to it. Peruvian human rights organizations, through the Coordinadora Nacional de Derechos Humanos, had expressed their fear that military aid would be used to victimize civilians; Americas Watch took the same position. And in Peru the aid program caused other suspicions, too: as one expert on the insurgency wrote for a prominent magazine, "The North American aid is not oriented toward helping to fight our antidrug war. What they want is for Peruvians to fight the antidrug war of the United States more efficiently and considerably more cheaply."[1]

Criticism of Peru's official forces by the U.S. Congress nonetheless provoked nationalistic reactions in much of the Peruvian press and defensive rhetoric from senior government officials. President Fujimori himself had visited the United States to lobby for the aid, involving his personal prestige in an effort that was, by its nature, uncomfortable. Since 1989 Peruvian political leaders and the highly nationalistic armed forces had hesitated and thought hard before accepting offers of military aid that the Bush administration had insisted they needed, and having taken the plunge, these officials were, as they saw it, rewarded with humiliation.

They had had little choice but to submit to this exercise; the United States is inclined to help Peru with international lending agencies and development agencies inasmuch as Peru accepts the U.S. plan for fighting the insurgents and the drug traffic together, taking American money and advice. And the Peruvian military needs aid. An independent national stance had become a luxury, given the nation's crippled economy and the insurgents' continued expansion. In the end, for the aid to be awarded, Fujimori had to accept the force of human rights complaints and promise concrete reforms.

The bitterness of this process may partially explain why, since his setback in the U.S. Congress, President Fujimori has lashed out at Peruvian and international human rights organizations with unprecedented fervor. In speeches before the military leadership in September and October, he referred generically to some human rights organizations as the legal arms of subversion and excoriated them for what he said was their defense only of the human rights of terrorists. These were words his audience evidently wished to hear after its embarrassment in Washington, but they do not accurately describe the work of Peru's serious human rights organizations. And although broad and aggressive language about defenders of human rights may indirectly affect their safety,

Fujimori has so far ignored requests for clarification. Similarly misleading attacks by Fujimori were made against Americas Watch and Amnesty International in November. The president told a San Francisco audience, with no basis whatever in fact, that Americas Watch fails to report on Sendero Luminoso atrocities, and soon after addressed complaints about the organization to an air force audience in Peru.

Whatever the political aim behind such speeches, Fujimori's promised reforms, instituted at the insistence of Congress, reflect concerns set out in this book, such as the need for prosecutors to have thorough and unrestrained access to military detention centers in emergency zones. To Fujimori's credit, he ordered some changes immediately; at least one, access by the International Committee of the Red Cross to military and police detention centers, was working well in the months that followed, although the government would commit itself only to six months' worth of such cooperation. On the other hand, of the nine cases on which Congress had specifically demanded legal progress, one suffered a setback and in seven no action had been taken by year's end.

Ultimately, U.S. aid may be endangered as much by Peruvian corruption as by human rights abuses: collaboration with the drug traffic is so rife among military and police that in November U.S. officials were acknowledging that they could not confidently release antidrug aid to Peru. Those statements also echo concerns we express here, although U.S. officials appear determined to make a flawed plan function.

As 1991 ended, the country in which U.S. officials are so determined to invest military aid faced the possibility of a major legal transformation, the product of more than 120 extraordinary decrees on economic and military policy, instituted by Fujimori and subject to congressional review. In his customarily abrupt style, Fujimori laid before the nation a design for the militarized state, the state adapted to conditions of internal war by, for example, subordinating the practical authority of the Defense Ministry, Interior Ministry, and police to the armed forces; concentrating decision-making in a new National Defense Council; creating a new National Intelligence Service to coordinate all political intelligence, and making its structure, facilities, personnel, and budget secret, its agents empowered to conduct searches and seizures without judicial warrant.

In the strategy expressed through these decrees, the Fujimori government has sought to expand dramatically the military's legal sphere of action. One decree makes it a crime to disclose information the army considers secret—a crime that could extend to exposés of human rights abuses. The Political Military Commands of the emergency zones would be in charge of developmental programs in their areas of authority; and in areas not under state of emergency, a serious disturbance of public order or even an imminent danger of same would be, under one new decree, sufficient cause for the armed forces to intervene and supersede police authority, while another decree gives the military the authority to enter prisons, and a third empowers it to reestablish order by invading universities, which in Latin America have a long tradition of autonomy.

Drawing the population into the counterinsurgency effort—through a decree that punishes nonparticipation with fines and even imprisonment—is termed National Mobilization. Young campesinos will likely pay the highest price if this aspect of the plan is not amended: through three decrees, the plan envisages expanding and further arming the civil defense patrols, which are defined misleadingly in one decree as spontaneous and freely formed. Especially innovative is the decree that provides that youths of military age may replace their military service with time served in a civil patrol. This tactic renders the patrols unequivocally subordinate to military orders; the response of Sendero Luminoso is not hard to anticipate.

On December 6, 1991, fifteen political parties of all persuasions wrote a public letter to the president that described the package of decrees as implying "an extraconstitutional change in the political regime" and as adopting "forms of internal control that are damaging even for the military organizations directly involved in the task of counterinsurgency." At year's end the Chamber of Deputies had passed an alternative to Fujimori's plan that awaited Senate action. But whether or not the government's militarization decrees survive, they illuminate the thinking of Peru's most powerful men.

A moment that could have led to improvements—when a democratically elected government had the possibility to institute meaningful reforms, albeit under pressure—quickly passed. Political violence, its figures fluctuating month by month, continues as before, and so does the administrative breakdown that affects human rights. In September 1991, because of an undeclared slowdown by prosecutors protesting abysmal wages, some one hundred cases a day could not be attended to, in a system where trial delays of several years are already the norm. On October 2, a civilian court ordered the release of senior police officials implicated in the murders of three young men in Callao in June: one more instance of the court's failure to prosecute vigorously in a nationally publicized human rights case. Paramilitary agents killed sixteen people, including children, in a Lima neighborhood called Barrios Altos on November 3, but no adequate investigation has been carried out and President Fujimori has not demanded one; during recent months Sendero has murdered peasants in Cajamarca, members of the Ashaninka tribe in Junin, and civil patrollers in Ayacucho and Huancavelica.

In the first ten months of 1991, more than 2,600 Peruvians lost their lives to political violence. How to humanize the conflict remains an enormous challenge in a nation where there are so many sources of violence, where, willing or not, so many citizens have become accomplices. In *Peru under Fire,* Americas Watch makes *some* basic recommendations. We are aware that the problems of Peru go well beyond the scope of one book to describe or of one administration to solve. But the fifteen parties' letter to Fujimori suggests a basic Peruvian consensus that "maintaining the constitutional democracy in effect may be a difficult task, but it is, at the same time . . . the surest and certainly the most correct road to final victory." To expand militarization, on the other hand, "endangers . . . the very viability of the nation."

Cynthia Brown
Americas Watch Representative
Santiago, Chile

ACKNOWLEDGMENTS

Human Rights Watch and Yale University Press express their appreciation to the J. M. Kaplan Fund for making this joint publishing program possible.

This book was written and researched by Cynthia Brown, Americas Watch representative in Santiago, Chile, and editor of *With Friends Like These: The Americas Watch Report on Human Rights and U.S. Policy in Latin America* (Pantheon, 1985). The author wishes to acknowledge the work of Juan E. Méndez, executive director of Americas Watch, whose reporting on Peru from 1984 through 1988 is cited frequently. Allyson Collins of Human Rights Watch assisted with analysis of the congressional debate over U.S. aid to Peru, and Patricia Sinay of Americas Watch provided research assistance.

Peruvian human rights monitors deserve particular thanks. Their findings form the basis for parts of this book, and their generous cooperation is much appreciated.

INTRODUCTION

After more than a decade of expanding internal conflict, Peru has entered the 1990s weakened on all fronts. The nation's economy is crippled, .and its democracy—overcentralized and unresponsive for generations—is resorting to desperate measures to survive. A new administration inherited this crisis in 1990, a government elected largely as a protest against traditional leadership and as perhaps the last hope for moderating the violence that grips Peruvian society. But the new government appears as overwhelmed as its predecessors.

A brutal insurgent movement, Sendero Luminoso, attacks the state, its representatives, and its supporters through terrorism, victimizing not only its armed enemies but any persons not perceived as allies. Since 1980 Sendero Luminoso has expanded steadily and, pursuing its so-called popular war against the government, is active in most of the national territory. As a result, more than half of Peru's twenty million citizens live under a sustained state of emergency, effectively governed by the military and lacking basic protections against arbitrary arrest, disappearance, and extrajudicial execution by the armed and police forces or the paramilitary groups they tolerate.

The nation's elected leadership, faced with an unparalleled economic crisis, has lacked the capacity or will to confront subversion with reforms that could reduce the economic, racial, cultural, and regional divisions feeding the insurgency. Nor has it been able to curb the corruption that undermines confidence in the rule of law. The conservative government of Fernando Belaúnde Terry (1980–85) ignored Sendero for two years, then relied primarily on repression as its response to the insurgency, creating a model for the expansion of military authority. Belaúnde's successor tried but failed to do better: at first seeking to control human rights abuses in the emergency zones, the government of Alan García (1985–90) gradually ceded authority to the military; abuses not only continued but notably increased after 1988, even spreading outside the zones of conflict. Alberto Fujimori, the current president, was elected largely because he was not tied either to the traditional right or to García's discredited populism. Peruvians who voted for Fujimori—predominantly the poor—evidently hoped not only for a miracle of economic recovery but that he would relieve them of the scourge of political violence.

As a major producer of coca leaf, the basis for cocaine, Peru also suffers from the criminality and violence that the drug traffic engenders. This aspect of the national crisis has now become internationalized and may be further militarized, as the United States has determined to train army and marine forces for drug interdiction in the coca-producing Upper Huallaga region. Though not engaged in the refinement or distribution of cocaine, peasants in the Upper Huallaga jungle areas already feel the effects of the war against drug traffic and Sendero; human rights violations, by both Sendero Luminoso and the official forces, have increased substantially since 1988.

These problems emerge from the poverty in which most Peruvians live and the state's historical failure to respond to the needs of this majority. With the brief exception of Gen. Juan Velasco's military regime (1968–75), Peruvian governments of the past forty years have avoided addressing the problems of land tenure that have embittered Peru's rural, largely Indian population and have led many to abandon the countryside for the capital. Social advances that the urban and rural poor achieved under Velasco were diminished or eliminated under succeeding governments, even after Peru returned to democracy in 1980. And although García was elected in 1985 on a platform of social progress, his government instead presided over an economic crisis that has brought Peru to the edge of bankruptcy.

Thoughtful Peruvians of varied political views, including some members of the armed forces, argue that the spread of Sendero, the cultivation of coca, and the unhealthy expansion of military power within a democratic state are problems that cannot be resolved without a coherent strategy for development and national integration. At a seminar in Lima in April 1990, analysts as diverse as human rights advocate Diego García-Sayán, executive director of the Andean Commission of Jurists, and Sinesio Jarama, retired army general and former commander of the military region that comprises Lima and the central rain forest areas, agreed on the dangers of a policy that meets Peru's political challenges only with force and rhetoric.

Speaking of the challenge to the state to legitimize itself in the battle against Sendero, General Jarama spoke of the need for "projects for development, for administration of justice, for elimination of corruption, for solving the ancestral problems of land tenure, [and] . . . for integration into the country's political, social and economic life of the sectors that are marginalized and segregated; only in this way can social organization be achieved around concrete projects for development and defense, as a prior step toward the national popular mobilization that is so much talked of and of which nothing has been realized."[1] García-Sayán, noting the human costs of the military policy, suggested that advances need to be made in five areas: the democratization of state machinery, to encourage popular participation; an increased presence of the state and its authority throughout the country; the protection of human rights, including outreach to the population; respect for international humanitarian law; and the promotion of developmental alternatives in the coca-producing areas.[2]

Peru enjoys important democratic freedoms, including freedom of the press and of union organization. Indeed, the media play an important role in a society where the normal policy-making structures and judicial entities are frequently inefficient or corrupt. Newsmagazines have pursued the issue of human rights, sometimes at extraordinary risk for the journalists involved. And the government permits even the organ of one major guerrilla group to publish without hindrance.[3] Union activists are rarely punished for organizing, but they may suffer pressure from paramilitary groups, official forces, or the insurgency for their views and influence or for public demonstrations while on strike. A few members of the National Congress have been active in the defense of human rights, and on occasion their work has saved lives or, in the case of penal code reform, has made unbearable lives less unbearable. Yet, although human rights abuses skyrocketed in the late 1980s and have continued to climb since then, the issue of human rights rarely appeared on the nation's front pages until U.S. aid to Peru was briefly withheld in 1991 because of human rights abuses. The recommendations of the most important congressional commission on violence—presided over by Sen. Enrique Bernales—have not been followed, and to date no military officer has been successfully prosecuted on charges of human rights abuse. Human rights were barely discussed by the candidates in the presidential campaign of 1990.

Indeed, as Peruvians grow ever more desperate for relief from economic and political instability, there is a danger that public opinion will grow to tolerate official violence as a "solution" to Sendero. Americas Watch is concerned by the overall decline of public debate about human rights, especially when it accompanies a worsening human rights situation. The conflict with Sendero has been costly, both economically and in terms of human life. But as great a threat as the insurgency poses for the democratic state, the legitimacy of that state rests on its refusal to adopt cruel methods of response.

It is difficult to be hopeful about Peru. Sendero enjoys a mystique of discipline and cruelty, while the state appears at best a leaky boat, at worst a shipwreck. The "national popular mobilization" of which Jarama spoke at the seminar in Lima remains elusive; its bases still are not agreed upon, and the people whose participation is essential to its success, predominantly the urban poor and peasants in the rural emergency zones, continue to be targets of official as well as insurgent violence.

The Fujimori government faces a combination of problems unique in Latin America. But it also may benefit from the lessons of the conflict. In this book Americas Watch reviews what we believe to be those lessons, with particular emphasis on the escalation of human rights violations in recent years.

VITAL STATISTICS

Official Name: Republic of Peru

Area: 496,222 square miles; shares borders with Ecuador, Colombia, Brazil, Bolivia, and Chile

Population: 21,904,000

Ethnic Groups: Indians, 45 percent; Mestizos, 37 percent; Caucasians, 15 percent; blacks, Asians, 3 percent

Religious Group: Roman Catholic, 90 percent

Languages: Spanish and Quechua (official); Aymara (30 percent speak no Spanish)

Government: Constitutional republic with president and prime minister; twenty-four departments; one province; eleven regional assemblies recently formed

Major Political Parties and Recent Coalitions: American Popular Revolutionary Alliance (APRA); Change 90 (CAMBIO 90); Democratic Front (FREDEMO); Liberty Movement (LIBERTAD); Popular Action (AP); Popular Christian Party (PPC); and United Left (IU) and Socialist Left (IS) coalitions

The Insurgency: Sendero Luminoso, or Shining Path; Túpac Amaru Revolutionary Movement (MRTA)

Economy: GDP, $19 billion (1990); annual real growth rate, −4.6 percent (1990); average annual real growth rate, −9 percent (1985–90); per capita GDP, $1,377 (1990); rate of inflation, 7,650 percent (1990); foreign debt, $20 billion (1990)

Peru is party to the following international human rights treaties:

Convention on the Prevention and Punishment of the Crime of Genocide; signed December 11, 1948; ratified February 24, 1960

Convention Relation to the Status of Refugees; accession December 21, 1964

International Convention on the Elimination of All Forms of Racial Discrimination; signed July 22, 1966; ratified, September 29, 1971

Convention on the Political Rights of Women; accession July 1, 1975

International Covenant on Civil and Political Rights; signed August 11, 1977; ratified April 28, 1978

International Covenant on Economic, Social and Cultural rights; signed August 11, 1977; ratified April 28, 1978

International Convention on the Suppression and Punishment of the Crime
of Apartheid; accession November 1, 1978

Convention on the Elimination of All Forms of Discrimination against
Women; signed July 23, 1981; ratified September 13, 1982

Protocol Relating to the Status of Refugees; accession September 15, 1983

Convention against Torture and Other Cruel, Inhuman or Degrading Treatment or Punishment; signed May 29, 1985

ABBREVIATIONS

ANAP Association of Native Peoples of Pichis (Asociación de Nativos del Pichis)

APRA American Popular Revolutionary Alliance (Alianza Popular Revolucionaria Americana)

APRODEH Association for Human Rights (Asociación Pro-Derechos Humanos)

CeaPaz Center for Study and Action for Peace (Centro de Estudios y Acción para la Paz)

CEAS Commission on Social Action (Comisión de Acción Social)

CECONSEC Headquarters of Native Communities of the Central Jungle (Central de Comunidades Nativas de la Selva Central)

CODEH Human Rights Committee (Comité de Derechos Humanos)

COMISEDH Human Rights Commission (Comisión de Derechos Humanos)

CRF Rodrigo Franco Democratic Squad (Comando Democrático Rodrigo Franco)

DEA U.S. Drug Enforcement Agency

DESCO Center for the Study and Promotion of Development (Centro de Estudios y Promoción del Desarrollo)

DIRCOTE Antiterrorism Bureau (Dirección Contra el Terrorismo)

FREDEMO Democratic Front (Frente Democrático)

ICRC International Committee of the Red Cross

IDL Legal Defense Institute (Instituto de Defensa Legal)

ILD Institute of Liberty and Democracy (Instituto Libertad y Democracia)

IMET International Military Education and Training

INE National Statistics Institute (Instituto Nacional de Estadísticas)

INPE National Penitentiary Institute (Instituto Nacional Penitentiario)

IUS United Socialist Left (Izquierda Unida Socialista)

MIR Revolutionary Left Movement (Movimiento de Izquierda Revolucionaria)

MRTA Túpac Amaru Revolutionary Movement (Movimiento Revolucionario Túpac Amaru)

OAS Organization of American States

PMC Political Military Command

PPC Christian Popular Party (Partido Popular Cristiano)

SEREAL Servicio Especiales de Apoyo Logístico (subsidiary of Mobil Oil)

SERPAJ Justice and Peace Service (Servicio Paz y Justicia)

UMOPAR Mobile Rural Patrol Unit (Unidad Móvil de Patrulla Rural)

1

THE SOURCES AND SCOPE OF
VIOLENCE IN PERU

Peru, a nation of twenty-two million, has traditionally been two countries: one
coastal, centered in Lima, dominated by whites, the other rural and predominantly Indian. Within that basic division there are others, as between the
characters of different regions, different economic classes within regions, and
different ethnic groups. In the cities Spanish is spoken, while in many rural
areas the inhabitants speak the indigenous language, Quechua. Traditionally,
and up to the present, there has been little interaction between the coastal
centers of political power and wealth and the population of the rain forests and
highlands. With few exceptions—notably, the agrarian reform of the Velasco
military regime (1968–75)—the political and economic programs of successive governments have failed to respond to the needs of the urban and rural
poor. These facts are not in dispute in Peru; what absorbs Peruvians is how to
solve the problems that this history and ongoing social fragmentation have
produced, and how to do so in the context of an unprecedented economic crisis
and more than a decade of escalating political violence provoked by an
insurgency.

Peru faces a daunting complex of economic, political, and social ills. United
Nations data show that in 1986, before the worst of the current economic crisis,
70.7 percent of Peruvians were classified as poor.[1] The portion of the population then living in extreme poverty approached 20 percent, concentrated in the
rural highlands and rain forests; meanwhile, in the more populated rural areas
and cities, 2.5 million persons had been impoverished only shortly before, as a
result of economic recession.[2] In following years this situation worsened
dramatically.

A large foreign debt and declining production after mid-1987, inflation that
surpassed 2,700 percent in 1989, and the resulting collapse of real wages were
combined with severe economic losses due to insurgent sabotage and the cost of
the counterinsurgency effort. As of September 1989, a basic family basket of

1

food cost fourteen times the minimum wage.[3] Official statistics put under-employment, at the end of 1989, at 73.9 percent, a more accurate reflection of real conditions than the relatively low acknowledged unemployment level of just under 8 percent.[4] In the final year of Alan García's administration, July 1989 to July 1990, inflation surpassed 4,600 percent. Meanwhile four of five houses in Peru lack water, sewage, or electricity. Life expectancy in low-income areas is less than fifty years. Nationwide, one in eight infants dies before completing one year of life, and in the Andean highlands this figure is even higher.[5]

President Alberto Fujimori took office in July 1990 and confronted inflation with "shock" measures that sent it soaring a month later. Gasoline prices increased 3,000 percent from one night to the following morning, and the prices of staple foods also rose several times over. These measures, which con-tradicted Fujimori's campaign promises, increased the economic agony of the poor; social relief was little and late in coming. Though the "Fuji-shock" later reduced inflation—indeed, by September 1991 the rate was 5.6 percent a month[6]—it would seem that all options open to Peru require a heavy sacrifice, especially for those who already have almost nothing. Lima had become the most expensive city in Latin America by early 1991, but the minimum wage was worth only sixty U.S. dollars a month.

Physical evidence of the crisis is everywhere, in deteriorating buildings and roads, in lack of public services. During 1990, most traffic lights in Lima did not function due to cost-cutting measures and traffic was entirely self-regulating, with a predictable increase in street accidents. The educational sector is so underfinanced that 90 percent of university professors face either unemployment or some degree of underemployment.[7] Health workers and other public service employees commonly engage in strikes that last several months—though they gain little or nothing by these protests—because their salaries barely pay for food and transport. In such conditions the relative calm and fatalism of Peruvians is more surprising than is the pervasiveness of crime. When the prices of staple foods skyrocketed in August 1990 as result of the shock measures, many observers expected riots in the slums and violent raids on food stores. Some markets hired sharpshooters to stand on their roofs and discourage the hungry hordes, but such force was unnecessary.

In Lima's slum neighborhoods, among the poorest in Latin America, the epidemic of cholera that broke out in 1991 is only one of several potentially fatal daily conditions, ranging from violent crime to impotable drinking water. Cholera, a disease transmitted through human feces—contaminated drinking water, irrigation water, and raw fish and shellfish are the common carriers—claimed more than 100 lives in Peru by February 1991 and led to more than 5,000 hospitalizations. More than 23,000 people had been infected in some measure by then. That number is testament to the lack of sanitation in impoverished areas and, given that cholera is easily treatable, to the crisis of Peru's health care system and public-information strategies. Ironically, the emergency improved conditions slightly for some of the poor; according to a community leader in Lima's Villa El Salvador slum, with the official concern to prevent additional cases of cholera the neighborhood finally got the clean drinking water that residents had demanded for years, and as a result the rate of infant deaths from gastric infections and diarrhea fell dramatically.

The political system of Peru returned to democracy in 1980, guaranteeing all adults a large measure of free expression and the opportunity to vote. Political debate is lively, and the ideological range of legal political parties is broad, although electoral apathy is also widespread. The media play an important role not only as channels for opinion and information but as investigators and informal ombudsmen for the society. But Peru's is a system debilitated by corruption, lack of judicial independence, intense partisan rivalries, and the enormous distance between Lima-based government and much of the population. Moreover, the economic importance of narcotics and the easy money they promise have exacerbated the corruption and violence that permeate Peruvian society. Although estimates vary on the nation's income from drugs and that income has fluctuated in recent years, a moderate annual estimate for 1988–89, a high-income year, is half a billion dollars.[8]

The economic desperation of the poor, intensified during the 1980s by austerity programs and uncontrolled inflation, has led to the development of an informal or underground economy, which by 1986 accounted for 38.9 percent of the Gross National Product (GNP) and saves millions of Peruvians from starvation.[9] The same combination of factors—austerity and inflation—has contributed to a notable rise in violent crime. The state's failure to solve the economic crisis or to deal effectively with crime, or even to clean its own house of corruption, further weakens respect for the rule of law.

Two urban situations vividly illustrate the crime problem and the quality of much Peruvian law enforcement. On Lima's outskirts, to drive at night on the principal highway is dangerous because one's car is likely to be assaulted—as often as not, by gangs of off-duty police. Their criminal activity is widely taken for granted, the byproduct of salaries too low to support a family. Similarly, in a Lima prison visited by Americas Watch in 1990, a prisoner had been assigned by the resident doctor to "guard" the hospital dispensary; this was to prevent the police guards from robbing the few available medicines. As Hernando de Soto, adviser to President Fujimori told the *New York Times*, "This society is collapsing, without a doubt. There is no respect for the state, the parliament, the laws, the judicial system. . . . Nothing works here."[10]

In this context Peru is confronting an insurgent movement, the Partido Comunista del Perú–Sendero Luminoso, which declared war on the Peruvian state in 1980 and since then has not ceased growing. The organization, whose name translates as Shining Path, follows a messianic leader, Abimael Guzmán, and operates with exemplary discipline as well as exceptional cruelty. Official estimates of Sendero's fighting strength hover around three thousand combatants, men and women; unofficial estimates are up to double that figure. During 1990 the organization suffered reverses and defections, but that did not affect its continued expansion of fighting territory. Now active nearly throughout the nation, Sendero also has ambitions to expand its influence beyond the nation's borders, and there has been speculation about support for the organization in Bolivia, whose border with Peru is long and virtually uncontrolled.

Sendero Luminoso has publicized its overall Maoist strategy: a gradual expansion of control from the south-central highlands, where it first became established, into the northern and central departments, and finally to encircle Lima and choke off the capital's lines of supply and communication. The progress of the war to date reflects this strategy to near-perfection. The initial zones of conflict have spread steadily to include, in recent years, departments and provinces of special economic and political importance as supply centers for Lima, and the capital has now become the scene of much political violence. Sendero is established in the coca-producing area of the Upper Huallaga River valley in the north-central rain forests—and secures financing for its operations nationwide from its activities there—while in the central department of Junín during part of 1990 it reportedly controlled a territory the size of Kuwait and it habitually uses river transport for easy access to other strategic areas.

The departments of Ayacucho, Apurímac, and Huancavelica, where Sendero began, are among the poorest in Peru, with a population that is predominantly Quechua-speaking, undernourished, illiterate, and historically ignored by the central government. The rise of Sendero in these areas had much to do with social and ethnic aspirations—even, notes one Peruvian analyst, with Andean peasants' concept of education as a means to control knowledge, the beginning of freedom from manipulation by whites. Sendero grew out of a university movement, and Abimael Guzmán was a professor at the University of Huamanga in Ayacucho during a decade when Indian peasants first gained significant access to secondary and higher education.[11]

That these students' hopes for empowerment would be frustrated only fed the ideology of Sendero, which advocates complete demolition of the state and its replacement with "the radical and definitive new society . . . , without exploiters or exploited, without oppressed or oppressors, without classes, without a state, without parties, without democracy, without arms, without wars."[12] Without many things, including, as it happens, dissent. Still, the state's failure to represent most of its citizens had created a frustration from which it was a small step to *senderista* nihilism.

As the 1980s began, the group enjoyed a measure of popular support in the Andean sierra, and Guzmán—Presidente Gonzalo to his followers—became the center of a cult of personality. The appeal of Sendero's authoritarianism is hard to define, but that authoritarianism has been present, in ideological documents and in the insurgents' actions, since the beginning. Indeed, it is partly from its antidemocratic methods that Sendero Luminoso derives its aura of invincibility. Sendero lacks a sentimental view of human life.

A much smaller rebel group, the Movimiento Revolucionario Túpac Amaru (MRTA), is also active and competes with Sendero for influence; its own tactics have become increasingly violent, but unlike Sendero it appears concerned with international opinion and with building a traditionally leftist image among the poor, factors that mitigate its violence against civilians. Sendero is unconcerned by either of these issues.

To a degree unprecedented among insurgencies in Latin America, Sendero uses terror to establish and maintain control, attacking both persons and public property with an aim to destroying the fragile Peruvian state. During 1989, according to Peruvian human rights organizations, Sendero was responsible for some 1,400 killings, of which 80 percent were assassinations of the defenseless. The Senate's commission on political violence credited the group with over 1,500 killings the following year, of which fewer than 200 were of police or military personnel.[13] Official figures show that the economic damage attributable to political violence—principally Sendero—between 1980 and 1990 was over $18 billion; this is six times the value of total annual exports, or the equivalent of 80 percent of Peru's foreign debt.[14] During 1991 Sendero continued to target any persons conceived to be enemies or merely unsupportive; journalists and human rights monitors joined the categories of citizens that Sendero excoriated for "collaboration." Sendero's savagery and uncanny expansion have taken on a certain mythic force in the Peruvian public consciousness. Correspondingly, faith in the state's ability to defeat Sendero is in danger of giving way.

THE STATE'S RESPONSE

It is evident that the insurgency finds adherents in large part because of the economic hardships and state neglect endured by most Peruvians. This chapter is concerned with the consequences of those pressures, and of the insurgency itself, as they relate to the state's protection or violation of human rights.

In various reports on Peru, Americas Watch has traced the development of two governments' legal and military responses to the insurgency: the government of Fernando Belaúnde Terry (1980–85), which followed on twelve years of military dictatorship, and the successor government of Alan García, the charismatic populist who is widely blamed for Peru's present desperation. The rise of Sendero Luminoso coincided with the reestablishment of civilian government, as Belaúnde was elected president in 1980 under a new constitution that guaranteed basic rights and liberties. Rather than meet the threat of Sendero with measures to gain popular support, Belaúnde's administration dealt with increasing social unrest, including labor strikes as well as Sendero sabotage, by imposing and reimposing temporary states of emergency. Political violence—then centered in the department of Ayacucho, with manifestations in neighboring Apurímac and Huancavelica—was met with the imposition and persistent renewal of the state of emergency in the most affected departments or provinces within those departments.

Belaúnde's response, a military answer to complex social and political conditions, became the model for the Peruvian state's response to Sendero throughout the 1980s, though criticized by presidential candidates before their election and by diverse authorities on political violence. The state of emergency, which the president has sole authority to impose, may last sixty days and may be renewed; it permits security forces to enter private homes and make arrests without warrants. The rights to public assembly and freedom of movement are suspended. Other rights, such as the right of detainees to know the charges against them and to obtain legal representation, are not legally suspended, but as Americas Watch noted in a 1984 report reviewing the Belaúnde years, these rights were routinely violated in practice during states of emergency imposed by his government.

Between December 1981 and May 1985, Belaúnde decreed twenty-four states of emergency affecting part or all of Ayacucho, fifteen affecting part or all of Apurímac, twelve affecting part or all of Huancavelica, and seven for Peru as a whole. The capital and provinces within several other departments were also placed under state of emergency, briefly or for the full period permissible under law.[15] In Lima the state of emergency typically left authority in the hands of the executive, such that the central government would not be rendered meaningless, while elsewhere the military became the ultimate authority with the creation of Political Military Commands (PMCs) in each emergency zone.

The effectiveness of the state of emergency in stemming violence was widely debated in Peru as the numbers of deaths and disappearances registered in emergency zones climbed sharply in 1982–84 and Sendero continued to grow and expand its areas of operation. Official figures indicate that during 1984 more Peruvians died in political violence than in any other year of the decade—

although 1989 was a close second and 1990 was more violent than the preceding year.[16] Of particular concern to Americas Watch was the Belaúnde government's abdication of civilian authority in the emergency zones, such that the government ignored and even justified persistent abuses of human rights by the armed forces and police.

While the military's power expanded, the Belaúnde government attempted to restore credibility to the judicial system through disciplinary actions against judges and judicial assistants for corruption. This campaign, though manifestly necessary, was ineffective for several reasons, among them the chronic underfinancing of the court system and the courts' inability to handle their enormous caseloads. The repressive tendency evident in Belaúnde's pacification approach was also evident in the legal sphere. An antiterrorist law, Decree 46, which defined the crime of terrorism in terms both vague and overly broad,[17] severely prejudiced the rights of persons detained on terrorism charges and was widely used by the security forces in zones of emergency to arrest opposition political activists, labor unionists, and campesino leaders who were critical of the system but were not linked with Sendero. Torture, which was and is systematically used on both political and nonpolitical detainees in Peru, was facilitated by the law's provision that police officers control the investigative stage of the legal process against accused terrorists.

After the election of APRA (Alianza Popular Revolucionario Americana) candidate Alan García as president in April 1985, changes were immediately noticeable. The new government stated its commitment to human rights and rejected a purely military solution to Sendero Luminoso, which so evidently drew support from the dispossessed. In García's first year, disappearances decreased, as did extrajudicial executions and indiscriminate killings by the security forces in the emergency zone. The military appeared to respond to García's human rights posture and to assume a more development-conscious attitude in its counterinsurgency strategy, seeking to win the population's support. Village civil-defense patrols created by the navy in Ayacucho after the emergency was first declared in 1982 were allowed to fall into passivity after 1985, and their members were permitted to return to full-time farming. Yet, abuses continued to occur and were rarely investigated, while the power of the military grew apace with the continued spread of Sendero and the MRTA.

García was forced to maintain the state of emergency in Ayacucho, Apurímac, Huancavelica, and Huánuco and later to expand the area of the emergency into part or all of the departments of Lima, Pasco, San Martín, and Junín by the end of 1988. In some cases the state of emergency was a short-term measure, but in others it was repeatedly renewed. This militarization of a large portion of the national territory had little perceptible success against Sendero, but in 1988 the number of politically related deaths tripled over the year before.

In the emergency zone peasants were trapped between the complementary violence of the military and Sendero Luminoso. Although Sendero performed more outright executions, the military engaged with impunity in killings and disappearances that increased the population's long-standing distrust of central authority.

Nor, for practical political reasons, could the government realistically hope for near-term success in the counterinsurgency campaign. Both the Interior Ministry and a special Senate commission concluded in 1988 that the different armed and security forces lacked effective coordination and a coherent counterinsurgency strategy. García's early proposals for economic development of the highlands had not been implemented, however; in effect, the situation had not changed. By the end of 1988, Peruvians were being governed under a state of emergency in eight departments and part of a ninth. The increasingly hard-line policy of the armed forces after 1988 was due in part to a redoubled effort by Sendero, which determined to push ahead toward what it calls "strategic equilibrium" with the state—the second of three projected phases of its war—by stepping up military actions in all its zones of activity. The reinforcement of militarism, meanwhile, was reflected in migrations of peasants from both highland and rain forest areas, more than half of them to Lima. Migration, a steady feature of Peruvian demographics for several decades, increased markedly after 1983–84 due to political violence, and after 1987 another surge in migration was impelled by Sendero's punitive actions, the army's counterinsurgency sweeps, and the social and economic disintegration of areas of conflict. The state has made no national study of this situation, but the Catholic church and various private institutions have offered estimates of 50,000–200,000 for residents of emergency zones who became internally displaced during the decade, with about 60 percent of these settling in the capital. The northern provinces of Ayacucho, cradle of Sendero and the counterinsurgency campaign, lost two-thirds of their inhabitants between 1980 and 1985, according to a university study, and the trend has continued.[18]

Just as the state has failed to study and address the plight of the displaced, it has failed to protect its representatives in the emergency zones. Judges and prosecutors have joined the thousands forced to leave for security reasons, and local authorities such as mayors and governors, favorite targets of Sendero, have been lucky if they could live long enough to emigrate. Their flight, in turn, reduces the jobs available in the areas under greatest military pressure and generates further economic migration.

As conditions hardened in the countryside toward the end of the 1980s, the reporting of human rights violations became more difficult. Journalists were forbidden to travel in the emergency zones and human rights monitors, as well as witnesses to abuses, faced serious threats to their lives. Those threats came from both sides: Sendero has no special respect for Peruvian human rights organizations, which systematically report on its abuses along with those of the military. The press was treated with hostility by some military commands, better by others, but press credentials did not guarantee safety, as is evident from several well-known cases of disappearance and murder.

By 1988 paramilitary aspects had been added to the war. A group calling itself the Comando Democrático Rodrigo Franco began to operate, first as a revenge squad against Sendero and later widening its targets. There was strong evidence to suggest, though it was never proven, that elements of President García's APRA party were linked to the commando's operations. Other death squads, evidently linked to the security forces but not seeking notoriety, would become active briefly and then sink from sight. The military, meanwhile, had revived its promotion of paramilitary self-defense patrols in rural communities under a state of emergency, a tactic that converted civilians into targets for insurgent reprisals. The patrols themselves were frequently guilty of human rights abuses, acting independently or in concert with military units. And although they purportedly served a purely defensive function, the patrols sought out guerrillas, engaged them in combat, and thus converted patrol members—including women and minors—into legitimate military targets. The elements of political violence multiplied.

The quandary facing the abandoned peasants of the emergency zones, victimized by both sides, is that neither side will permit neutrality. Case after case demonstrates that communities that have sought to remain aloof from the conflict have been punished by either one or both of the opposing forces. Many have been forced to become in effect unpaid auxiliaries to the armed forces by forming civil defense patrols against their will and under military tutelage that weakens or destroys communal traditions. Others, for lack of an alternative to Sendero terror, have embraced the patrols as a potential solution. The formation of the patrols, however, has been linked since the early 1980s with grave abuses. To the extent that they form part of a larger, repressive military design of counterinsurgency, it was perhaps inevitable that the patrols would not be limited to defensive activity but would become in many cases another predatory force. Since 1988 these patrols have proliferated, voluntarily or not, in the traditional zones of Sendero activity and in the central rain forest, among other areas.

In the north-central region of the Upper Huallaga River valley, where coca is produced for processing in Colombia and sale in the United States and Europe, the violence that accompanies the drug trade was also taking on a political component in the 1980s, as Sendero sought to establish itself and act as go-between in coca transactions. The inhabitants of the region, many of them immigrants from other parts of Peru, did not always support Sendero but, as elsewhere in the country, had little reason to trust the central government. Police corruption made a mockery of efforts to interdict shipments. As the U.S. Drug Enforcement Administration (DEA) worked with little success, the government faced a central contradiction—if it pursued the drug traffic, under police authority, it would alienate peasants by destroying their livelihood; if it went after Sendero, a task for the army under emergency powers, then it would need the coca growers' help, and would have to leave coca alone. García actually provided few developmental benefits to the region, but he took a nationalist, prodevelopment stance with the United States on antidrug policy, a position that found much support in Peru even while Sendero's advances in Upper Huallaga provoked an all-out military campaign. The combination of drugs and insurgency in the Upper Huallaga valley would become one of Peru's unique and most complex characteristics.

Unlike Belaúnde, García did not cede civilian authority to the military without resistance, and on occasion he displayed political courage in acknowledging military abuses. Massacres of peasants in Accomarca and Pucayacu, both in Ayacucho department, in 1985 met with public condemnation from García, though this was not enough to ensure full and impartial investigations.[19] Especially at the outset of García's term in office, the issues of human rights, judicial responsibility, and civilian authority were intensely debated. And even as the economic and security situation worsened, there still seemed reason to hope that positive signs might translate into broader improvements. For example, although Americas Watch found the overall situation bleak in 1988, we noted in a report that year that the Office of the Prosecutor General (Fiscalía de la Nación), an arm of government independent of the executive and judiciary, had begun to fulfill its role as public defender against government abuses. In particular, we were heartened by the Fiscalía's appointment of a tenacious special prosecutor to investigate disappearances in Ayacucho. We were also encouraged in 1988 by revisions in the antiterrorist legislation, which strengthened the role of judicial authorities and provided basic protections for detainees.

The courts' inefficiency and subservience to political pressure did not change, however; nor did the systematic torture to which political detainees were subject while under interrogation by police. Military courts continued to absolve uniformed personnel implicated in violations of human rights, making a mockery of civilian attempts at investigation.

In this context, Americas Watch observed with deep concern in 1988 that the various branches of government, with few exceptions, exhibited a passive attitude in the face of human rights abuses, including the standing committees of Congress and some of the special committees formed by Congress to investigate abuses. As the government grew resigned and tolerant of violence by the military, the representatives of the ruling party in Congress ignored or actively impeded investigation of serious allegations, such as those surrounding a massacre in Cayara, Ayacucho, in May 1988. This failure to provide ethical leadership, we concluded, was largely responsible for a growing public tolerance of abuses and opened the way for a further increase in the violence that had already claimed some fifteen thousand lives and produced over two thousand disappearances since 1980. Sadly, human rights conditions became bleaker and the García government's attitude even more defensive in 1989 and early 1990, an intensely violent period.

There was tolerance, too, of a form of cruelty less visible than political violence: the conditions of confinement in Peru's penal institutions for both security-related and common-crime detainees. Such is the economic crisis in Peru, and such is the lack of oversight caused by bureaucratic confusion, that conditions in the prisons of Lima and Callao are among the worst anywhere. Not only do prisoners wait years to face trial, but those who cannot afford bribes are likely to endure harsher treatment both in court and in prison. Overcrowding, violence, unsanitary conditions, and a near-complete lack of food—these hardships have contributed to riots led by security-related prisoners and in 1990 to hunger strikes and other unrest. Some prisoner protests have had tragic results; the quelling of Sendero-led riots in 1986 took a larger toll than any other instance of political violence during the decade, with more than two hundred inmates killed in two prisons.

Because the police function as guards controlling the interior of the prisons and fail to maintain even a semblance of order, common prisoners in particular are subjected to a regime of intimidation, robbery, and undernourishment against which they have no recourse. Security-related prisoners fare slightly better than common inmates in these conditions, enjoying an internal discipline and external support that common inmates lack. Alberto Fujimori, stunned by what he saw on a prison visit during his presidential campaign, has made some small advances possible; but in the absence of consistent state concern, the prisons remain filthy, abusively managed, and anarchic.

By the time Fujimori was elected president in mid-1990, Sendero was active in twenty-one of Peru's twenty-four departments. The 1990 elections suggested both the limits of Sendero's popular support and the extent of traditional politicians' failures—including those of the legal left. Hitherto unknown, and lacking a consolidated political party base, Fujimori was elected in large part by rural voters, those most affected by the counterinsurgency and most disaffected with traditional central government. That population defied Sendero's electoral boycott and credible threats of reprisal when it voted, against all predictions, for Fujimori. That he is nonwhite, part of a cultural minority, undoubtedly played a role in Fujimori's appeal to the marginalized majority. And his background as an agricultural specialist suggested, as he promised, an emphasis on development in the provinces, if the economic situation would permit it. Voters sought an alternative to what they knew and apparently had had enough of.

Fujimori's lack of traditional alliances could be viewed in two ways. He enjoyed unprecedented freedom of action when he took office, but the heterogeneity of his Cambio 90 party and its lack of a majority in Congress were weaknesses. He compensated by allying himself with the army and adopting an autocratic style of government that sidesteps Congress on many issues. One of his first actions was to force some 250 police officials into retirement because of their alleged corruption and ties to paramilitary groups, and not incidentally their allegiance to the former governing party. As unorthodox as this style may be, its results, in his initial year as president, reveal him as more traditional than he first appeared, at least as regards management of the counterinsurgency campaign. Active-duty army generals hold the two top posts at the Interior Ministry—a change Fujimori made at the start of his administration—and shielding the army from human rights prosecutions was the aim of a controversial presidential decree in December 1990, later repealed by Congress. Fujimori's administration has given new impetus to an old idea, the creation of civil defense patrols, and has supported the counterinsurgency campaign without appreciably changing the military character of the state's response. An early promise to create a national human rights commission has remained in the "planning" stage, as has a proposal to unify the commands of the counterinsurgency zones to foster a more coherent policy. Although President Fujimori rejected a U.S. aid agreement early in his administration, a new framework agreement was signed in May 1991, paving the way for U.S. antinarcotics aid, and by August Fujimori was in Washington lobbying hard for military and economic assistance. The U.S. package included more economic assistance than the old one, but this did not transform the U.S.-Peruvian plan into a developmental alternative. On balance, Fujimori's continuation of earlier pacification strategies during his first year was more notable than the occasional departures he made from standard practice.

An exploration of alternatives to the current strategy has never been more urgently required. In May 1991, political violence claimed an average of seventeen Peruvians a day, double the level of 1989.[20] As a 1990 congressional report on violence pointed out, criticism of "an exclusively military conception of antisubversive strategy" is shared not only by "intellectuals, specialists in the subject, and politicians but also by military authorities, who have stated that it is not correct to concentrate in the 'military domain' activities and operations that correspond to other domains, such as the political, the economic, and the psychosocial. . . . It is obvious that the validity of the critique just described requires a complete review of the countersubversion plans now in operation and their substitution by others."[21] A year later, having gone unheeded, the same congressional commission would produce another report, reiterating those opinions and noting that their relevance had become even "more urgent."[22]

The commission that made those statements has also contributed greatly to the understanding of Peru's current crisis. Its reports are the most widely cited authority on the incidence of political violence in Peru, and the analysis contained therein provides a framework for discussion of how that violence is carried out, promoted, and often covered up.

THE FINDINGS OF THE BERNALES COMMISSION

The Peruvian Senate in May 1988 created a commission to study and analyze violence and propose solutions to the crisis. The commission has produced three reports in the three years since, under the leadership of Sen. Enrique Bernales Ballesteros. Brief and concise, the reports are most often quoted for their figures on deaths from political violence and the economic cost of that violence to the nation, but they also contain analysis of the spread and nature of violence from all quarters.

The work of this commission has been meticulous, within the limits imposed by emergency conditions. Its reports, particularly the two most recent, provide a sound basis for examining political violence in Peru, although, as the commission reports admit, members were not always able to carry out investigations based on witness complaints where these involved travel to emergency zones. The commission was often forced to depend on military sources for information about the emergency zones, such as numbers of subversives killed in combat. But in keeping with the intellectual honesty of its presentation, the commission's reports take note of the serious questions that have arisen as to whether those dead whom the military has denominated "subversive" can confidently be considered combatants.

The commission follows up witness statements with requests for official investigation, but it does not always get the information it has demanded. In another sense, too, the commission's profile of political violence in Peru is incomplete, as it does not analyze disappearances, a practice discussed in the following section. To the commission's figures on violence from 1980 to 1989, it is necessary to add 2,400–3,000 disappearances. For 1990 alone must be added at least 200 more.

Sources of the commission's figures include press accounts, direct testimony, material provided by human rights organizations and research institutes, and, in large measure, the Defense and Interior ministries.[23]

The 1980s

The Bernales Commission's 1989 report traces violence in Peru through the 1980s. Some of these comparative figures put recent developments in useful perspective. With regard to attacks on persons and property by Sendero Luminoso, the MRTA, and paramilitary groups, for example, the report indicates that between May 1980 (when Sendero declared the beginning of its prolonged popular war against the state) and the July 1985 inauguration of Alan García, 5,880 attacks occurred. In the four and a half years from July 1985 to December 1989, that number nearly doubled, to 10,621. This brings the total for the decade to 16,501, of which 2,117 occurred during 1989.

Aside from the numbers, the commission followed the geographical distribution of violent actions, noting that in 1989 more than half occurred in urban areas. This represents a shift from the early 1980s, when violence was concentrated in the rural departments of Ayacucho, Huancavelica, and Apurímac. Attacks on electrical towers alone, including those that affected northern industries such as mining, involved repair costs and lost work hours amounting to $600 million in 1989. During the decade, the economic cost of terrorism to Peru, according to the commission, was over $15 billion—equal to almost 83 percent of the GNP.

The report also quantifies the dead and wounded, although it cautions that its numbers may be low by as much as 10 percent, owing to difficulties in confirming oral testimonies. By year, its figures on deaths are as follows:

1980	3	1985	1,359
1981	4	1986	1,268
1982	170	1987	697
1983	2,807	1988	1,986
1984	4,319	1989	3,198

The total number of deaths is 15,811. With a 10 percent variable, it is up to 17,500.

Based on its lower, confirmed figure, the report categorizes the dead: 6,386 civilians, 8,079 subversives, 1,197 members of the forces of order, and 149 persons (all killed during 1989) labeled narcotraffickers.

With regard to the deaths of those defined as subversives, the report questions whether all can be construed as combatants. In particular, given the especially high number of supposed subversives killed in 1983 and 1984—4,428, or more than half of the total for the decade—the commission recalls that in October 1988 it requested investigations into these deaths, referring to the "probability that a part of this high number corresponds to persons who, according to some sources, are considered 'disappeared.'"[24]

As these figures indicate, violence increased substantially between 1988 and 1989, and 1989 produced the second-highest death toll of the decade. Seen another way, during 1989 an average of 8.76 Peruvians died every day in political violence. This represented an increase of more than 60 percent over the number of killings in 1988, according to the commission's figures. The report also notes that, as between 1984 and 1989, the years with the highest number of deaths, 1989 may represent the larger social cost, as violence had spread throughout the nation. For 1989, the report breaks down killings by attribution to those responsible. Of 3,198 deaths in 1989, 1,526 are attributed to Sendero Luminoso, 161 to the MRTA, 11 to the Comando Democrático Rodrigo Franco, 153 to unidentified terrorist groups, 127 to narcotraffickers, 342 to the police forces, and 886 to the armed forces.

Breakdowns by month show that more than one-fourth of the killings in 1989 occurred in June (470) and October (398). In June security forces carried out their most intensive campaigns against Sendero in the north-central region of the Upper Huallaga valley (see chapter 9). Violence in October was linked to approaching municipal elections, which Sendero sought to undermine through terror.

Total civilian deaths in 1989 were 1,450, only slightly lower than the number of civilians killed in 1984 (1,758). The principal victims, as always, were peasants, with 700 killed and 129 wounded. The report attributes this in part to inadequate police protection in rural areas, adding that although peasants interviewed by the commission requested a stronger and more constant police presence, this demand was combined in some cases with complaints that police "dedicate themselves to acts of pillage and intimidate campesinos, accusing them falsely of being senderistas."[25]

In rural areas the commission encountered special difficulties in ascertaining the names, ages, and genders of the victims, especially in the cases of supposed subversives. But from the information it was able to gather, young people appeared to be the primary targets. The numbers are significant among the age group 15 to 19 years old, ascend in the group aged 20 to 24 years, and peak with the group aged 25 to 29.

Second-most affected were the urban poor, reflecting the overall shift of violence to the cities (260 dead, 223 wounded), and third came workers (148 dead), followed by representatives of government authority (144 killed, including 52 mayors, as well as governors, judges, and provincial prosecutors—these being targets mainly of Sendero). The armed forces lost 105 members, the national police 243. For the combined forces of order, 1989 was the year of heaviest casualties in the decade, with deaths most numerous in June.

As to woundings, which totaled 1,033 in 1989, the commission observed especially how few they were in relation to deaths. This is attributed to two factors: the Sendero practice of killing all wounded, and the way in which the forces of order report on confrontations with subversives. The commission pointed out that there have been cases in which information is given on both dead and wounded soldiers but on subversives only dead and an undetermined number of those who allegedly fled; in other words, the armed forces have registered neither wounded nor detainees. Human rights organizations in Peru fear that this lack of reporting may conceal executions of innocent civilians.

1990–91: Starting the Next Decade

According to Senator Bernales, the week preceding the April 8, 1990, presidential and parliamentary elections and the week beginning April 16 were "the most violent of the decade." Bernales stated that, according to his commission's sources, political violence in the first four months of 1990 had claimed the lives of 1,080 Peruvians, as compared to 904 during the same period the previous year. In April 1990 alone, 301 persons were killed for political reasons.[26]

Bernales's predictions for a bloody year were borne out. By the end of December—that is, less than six months into the present government—the number of deaths from political violence under Fujimori amounted to 15 percent of the total deaths in the five years under García.

The commission's report on 1990 speaks of the steady pace of violent attacks against persons and property, with a total of 2,049, only slightly fewer than in 1989, when 2,117 attacks occurred. A majority of the insurgents' violent actions took place in the highlands (869) and metropolitan Lima (774). The trend toward urbanization of political violence remained evident; 27 percent of Sendero Luminoso's violent attacks occurred in Lima, and the MRTA devoted even more of its energy (68 percent of attacks) to the capital. Fully three times as many of the attacks during the year took place in urban areas (1,549) as in rural zones (500).

In analyzing the slight decline in number of attacks, the commission cautions against viewing the numbers superficially. The somewhat lower figure "should not be interpreted as a lesser volume of subversive action but rather as a tendency to regroup and concentrate that action"—on Lima and the central rain forest areas in Sendero's case and on the high forest (Central Huallaga) and also Lima in the case of the MRTA.[27] The report notes that the change of government in 1990 had no perceptible effect on rebel activity.

From 1980 through 1990, the commission recorded a total of 18,550 politically motivated armed attacks. The total cost of these, in terms of economic damage, is $18 billion, equal to 80 percent of the nation's foreign debt. For 1990 alone, the economic cost is estimated at $3 billion.

What the commission calls the "social cost"—the cost in human life—is more devastating still. In 1990, 3,452 Peruvians died from political violence, an average of 9.46 people a day. The breakdown of these killings, which include combat deaths, is as follows: 1,512 by Sendero Luminoso; 68 by the MRTA; 5 by the Comando Democrático Rodrigo Franco; 259 by campesino organizations (the civil defense patrols); 106 by narcotraffickers; 284 by unidentified groups; 369 by police forces; and 849 by the armed forces. Again, the commission notes the low proportion of wounded reported. Without assigning responsibility to either side, the 1990 report states: "According to testimonies that the commission gathered in 1989 and that have been reinforced by cases produced in 1990, situations have occurred in which wounded have been executed."[28] This is, of course, a violation of all international norms of behavior in armed conflict.

The most violent month of 1990 was June, the final month of the outgoing government and a month of intensified conflict in the central rain forest of Junín and in the Huallaga River region. Of the victims, as in the past, the largest category was civilians (1,584), the second-largest presumed subversives (1,542), third was the armed forces (258), and finally narcotraffickers (68). The category of presumed subversives, as the report notes, must be regarded with caution, "since there are cases in which there is lack of proof, of personal identification and judicial verification to establish the situation and real condition of the persons who have died."[29] It is quite possible, notes the report, that some of the dead in this category were not members of subversive groups but were forced to participate in guerrillas' military actions.

That half of the civilian dead were known to be peasants led the commission to comment on the multiplication of civil defense patrols, which are created to repel Sendero but which, ill-equipped and often unable to count on support from the armed forces, "are exposed to brutal punishment by the subversive groups."[30] A significant number of deaths are attributed to those patrols, however, reflecting a level of activity that, as we describe later, goes beyond the purely defensive. Fewer victims were registered among government authorities, including the forces of order, but more were reported among urban residents. And although it was impossible to establish identity in two out of three deaths, a profile of identified victims shows the same age curve as previously: the victims are most likely to be between the ages of 25 and 29.

Provisional information on the first four months of 1991, given to Americas Watch by the commission, indicated that Sendero had staged over fifty attacks, nearly forty of these in urban areas, suggesting an even stronger push into Lima. The MRTA lagged far behind, with fewer than fifteen attacks, but it, too, had concentrated its actions in the cities. These numbers are (with the exception of February 1991) notably lower than those for 1990. Likewise, the number of politically related deaths, at somewhat under 760 and averaging about 5 per day, represent a notable decline from 1990 levels. When we interviewed several sources for their views on the reason for this apparent decline in violence, opinion was divided as to whether the downturn in reported deaths was genuine or the result of manipulation by military sources. Even two members of the Bernales Commission had differing views on this question.

Americas Watch is not in a position to verify one position or the other. The commission, however, was forced on more than one occasion during early 1991 to suspend its investigations because of difficulties in gathering data. The problems of access affecting the press, human rights organizations and even state prosecutors translate into limited sources of information for the commission.

Nonetheless, and more impressive because it is probably under-reporting, the Bernales Commission's figure for deaths in May 1991 was drastically higher. The number of verified political deaths was 526—an average of 17 per day, or twice the rate of killing in 1989. By the end of September, the commission reported 2,261 deaths by political violence during the year. Of these, more than 800 were recognized as civilians, and more than 1,000 came under the somewhat broad heading of presumed subversives.

Americas Watch believes that the Interior and Defense ministries should assume responsibility, in conjunction with the armed forces, to ensure that commission staff and members have protected access to zones of conflict to verify information and collect testimony on-site. It is in the interests of an effective counterinsurgency strategy to keep the public informed—by sources it can trust, like the commission—therefore, in the government's interests to see that credible investigations can be carried out.

DISAPPEARANCES

Forced disappearances began in Peru in 1983, and since then the phenomenon has been closely related to the imposition and maintenance of the state of emergency. Human rights organizations in Peru registered the highest number of cases in 1983 and 1984. In the late 1980s, however, those numbers steadily rose again, and from 1987 to 1990 Peru had the sad distinction of being the nation with the highest number of new disappearances in the world, according to the United Nations' working group on the issue.

Almost all disappearances have been carried out by agents of the military and police, with a handful attributed to unknowns, to rebel groups, or to paramilitary agents believed to be linked to the armed forces. Among the military services, the army is by far the most involved in the practice.

According to the Lima-based Comisión de Derechos Humanos (COMISEDH), 2,405 Peruvians disappeared in the years 1983–89.[31] The figures break down as follows:

1983	696	1987	69
1984	574	1988	293
1985	253	1989	306
1986	214		

Amnesty International figures on disappearances are slightly higher. In an April 1990 report, Amnesty put the figures at more than 3,000 since January 1983.[32]

For 1990, as well, sources differ. The Coordinadora Nacional de Derechos Humanos, which combines Peru's major human rights organizations, reported 204 unresolved disappearances; the official figure was higher, however. The Fiscalía de la Nación received more than 350 cases by the end of the year, some of which were later "resolved," the victims found either at liberty or dead.

In Peru, by contrast with other countries in Latin America, persons who have been detained and disappeared—that is, whose detention is denied by the authorities—do reappear alive with some frequency. From 1983–89, 533 persons reappeared after temporary disappearance. For 1989 alone, according to COMISEDH, this figure was 135, of whom 90 were freed, 5 were found dead, and the remainder were acknowledged as detainees. And in 1990 the Coordinadora Nacional de Derechos Humanos registered 98 clarified cases. COMISEDH and other human rights organizations do not include resolved cases and reappearances in their figures for the disappeared but publish figures on those cases because, like definitive disappearances, they reflect the incidence of a practice that is carried out with complete impunity and whose outcome rests on the whim of the military authorities.[33]

Unlike confirmed deaths, disappearances appeared to have diminished somewhat in 1990, and President Fujimori took note of this publicly with relief. The decline was not so marked, however, as to suggest that the problem was close to solution. An Americas Watch representative was assured by the Defense Ministry's spokesperson on human rights in May 1991 that the army high command would not tolerate disappearances and that instructions had been issued to clarify that stance. Unfortunately this official's credibility was marred by the repeated contention that disappearances were a fabrication of human rights organizations and international supporters of Sendero, that "50 percent of the supposed disappeared are actually at liberty although human rights groups retain them on their lists," and that one should ask, rather, "where they are engaging in tourism."[34]

By contrast, there were two important recognitions of disappearance as a state practice in 1990. One was the inclusion of disappearance as a crime in the penal code produced by Congress. A second was the appellate-level confirmation of a habeas corpus petition filed on behalf of a disappeared detainee—although the Supreme Court reversed the decision. These are small steps under conditions where the law is violated with impunity, but they are an effort to call things by their name, precisely what the perpetrators of disappearances seek to avoid.

In chapter 6, we describe the practice of disappearances in detail. Campesinos are the most often victimized sector. Minors have not been immune, nor have labor unionists, professionals, students, teachers, or human rights monitors. It is, by now, beyond serious dispute that disappearance is one of the instruments the Peruvian military has chosen to use in its war on the insurgency—a war in which, over the past decade, the targets of violence have been overwhelmingly civilian.

2

THE JUDICIARY

PROSECUTION OF TERRORISM

There is ongoing debate in Peru over how to define terrorism and the most effective way to prosecute it. The administration of Fernando Belaúnde Terry relied on broadly worded security legislation that could be used equally against peaceful or violent dissent. Decree 46, adopted in 1981, established penalties of twenty-five years or more in prison for persons convicted of terrorism. To be convicted, a person could be found guilty of so vague a charge as "adversely affecting international relations" or "speaking out in favor of . . . a terrorist." The law's provision for fifteen days of incommunicado detention—still a feature of Peruvian antiterrorist law—invited the commission of abuses against detainees.

Belaúnde did not waver in his pursuit of ever stricter measures against terrorism, advocating the death penalty for certain terrorist crimes in 1984 and repeating that recommendation in later years. President Alan García's approach was less consistent, in this as in many other areas. During García's last year in office, for example, his government's policy for terrorist prosecutions took one step backward, one step sideways, one step forward, and a stumble. That is, the government faced the challenge to promote respect for the basic rights of detainees while increasing the efficiency of prosecutions and, under a variety of pressures, chose to endorse measures that, among themselves, did not constitute a coherent approach. One in particular, the amendment to Law 24,700, represented a substantial regression with regard to safeguards of due process.

Law 24,700, enacted in June 1987, outlined procedures for the investigation, prosecution, and trial of defendants accused of terrorism. Its approach typified the early García. As originally enacted, the law contained safeguards for detainees during the investigative stage: the police investigation was to be overseen by a provincial prosecutor; the right to counsel was not subject to waiver; incommunicado detention could take place only on a judge's order; and human rights organizations were explicitly authorized to inform the provincial prosecutor of an arrest so as to protect the rights of the detainee.

The police objected to the prosecutor's role, arguing that it delayed and even undermined their ability to investigate effectively. They also demanded a broader authority to petition for judicial orders of incommunicado detention. In July 1989, the law was amended. The new legislation, Law 25,031, returned to the police the direction of investigations. It also broadened the basis upon which police may petition a judge for orders of incommunicado detention and required that, before a provincial prosecutor recommends the closing of a case and liberty for the suspect, he or she must first consult with the district *fiscal superior,* or chief prosecutor.

Law 25,031 also removed the provision for an active role by human rights organizations. Although in practice these organizations may still alert prosecutors to arrests, the cancellation of their activist role under the law was a signal of the government's declining interest in their concerns. Similarly, with regard to the provincial prosecutor, under other legislation she or he still may intervene in an investigation to protect the rights of a detainee, but the reduction of their authority under Law 25,031 alerted prosecutors that such zeal in defense of civil rights had gone out of political fashion.

By 1988 there had already been signs that the protections under Law 24,700 might be repealed. In a report that year Americas Watch observed: "There is ample evidence in Peru to show that, when such controls are lifted, a pattern of serious human rights violations emerges."[1] If applied seriously, the safeguards in Law 24,700 would have reduced abuses. Their removal was a sign that García's government, having failed to curb terrorism, now lacked the will to curb abuses against suspected terrorists. In practice, the legal aid group Instituto de Defensa Legal perceived that the modifications made by Law 25,031 led to arbitrary conduct of investigations by police. In 1989 and 1990 the defendant's counsel often was not present, as required by law, at the investigative stage when the defendant's statement is taken.

The new law modified another aspect of its predecessor. Law 24,700 had authorized the judiciary to create special courts, if necessary, to handle terrorism cases. Law 25,031 required the creation of such special courts, a measure strongly supported by the García government over the objections of the National Association of Magistrates, among others. Those opposed to the special courts argued that ordinary courts were capable of handling terrorism cases, that the money to create new courts would be better spent on the underfinanced existing court system (whose personnel and scarce resources would be drained off to staff and operate the special courts) and that the judges presiding over the special courts would be targets of Sendero, which already attacked judges in the emergency zones.

In contemplating the creation of special courts for terrorism cases, Law 24,700 had also considered the danger facing special-court judges by requiring that the judiciary, the Ministerio Público (public defender), and the Interior Ministry "will take pertinent measures to ensure the protection and security of the judges, functionaries, witnesses, and experts involved in the legal case[s]" tried in special courts. This protection has not been forthcoming, for either the judges of the specifically designated special courts or those trying terrorism cases in two of Lima's correctional courts.

As the president of the Superior Court of Lima, Manuel Matos, wrote in the daily *La República* on May 2, 1990, protection against attack "is not given, and never has been given, to any of the eleven judges of the 12th and 13th Correctional Courts that are responsible for cases of terrorism, except for police presence to protect Drs. Quezada Muñante and Contreras Morosini. But not even for those two does there exist protection of their homes 24 hours a day. . . . The Special Courts . . . for me, are a fallacy."

As cases cited throughout this volume make plain, these judges face enormous danger. The state's inability or unwillingness to dedicate resources to protect judges who try suspected terrorists—who have assumed such enormous risk under a plan the García government forced on the judicial system—is symbolic of the incoherence with which that government approached legal solutions to the problem of terrorism.

Seven special courts were constituted. Three have functioned in Lima, including one created especially to combine the various legal cases against Sendero Luminoso's military leader, Osmán Morote Barrionuevo.[2] The four remaining courts were created for Junín, Puno, Huánuco, and Cusco and Madre de Dios.

In October 1989 more antiterrorism legislation, Law 25,103, was promulgated. It modified Law 24,601, which had been in effect since March 1987; the earlier law in turn had modified Belaúnde's Decree 46 and had more narrowly defined and criminalized the act of terrorism. The 1987 law had also contained an innovative provision in Peruvian jurisprudence, incorporating the possibility of plea-bargaining or, as it is translated from the Spanish, repentance. This concept was the basis for the legislation of 1989: Law 25,103, popularly known as the law of repentance, sets forth the conditions under which a plea-bargain with an alleged or convicted terrorist may occur. Reduction of sentence may be offered if the detainee voluntarily renounces his or her association with a terrorist organization and its activities, confessing to prior activities with the organization. Exemption from punishment may be awarded if information is given that leads to the identification and detention of other members and leaders of the organization, and a conviction and sentence may be set aside if a sentenced terrorist approaches the judiciary with information that makes possible the detention of leaders or members of terrorist organizations.

Americas Watch considers this legislation a positive step, as it permits judicial discretion while requiring concrete cooperation from the beneficiaries—provided, of course, that it is applied seriously and judiciously. To date only one prisoner convicted of terrorism is publicly known to have taken advantage of this provision. But in the long run the mechanism may provide important intelligence and serve as an alternative to the cruder forms of inducement traditionally used in investigations of terrorism.

While this positive measure was being considered, however, President García made a proposal in July 1989 that would have taken the prosecution of terrorist offenses in an entirely different direction. Hard on the heels of obtaining approval for the special civilian courts to deal with terrorism cases, and in open contradiction of that measure, for which he had fought hard, García called for the transfer of terrorism prosecutions to military courts. The idea was not new; Belaúnde had proposed it during his presidency, and it had surfaced from time to time since then. In 1989 it drew immediate support from some sectors of the FREDEMO (Frente Democrático) coalition that later presented novelist Mario Vargas Llosa as its presidential candidate and from former president Belaúnde himself. But the attorney general, the dean of the bar association, the president of the Supreme Court, the minister of justice, and the National Association of Magistrates all strongly opposed the suggestion on the grounds that it was unconstitutional. Debate over the next two months included discussion of whether to amend the constitution, whether the military courts could be impartial in cases where their pursuit of suspected terrorists makes them a party, and whether the president's suggestion had been a responsible political proposal or more in the nature of a political distraction.

Fortunately, at some point the proposal sank from sight. There has been no evidence that military courts in Peru are better equipped than the ordinary court system to investigate and prosecute terrorism. On the contrary, the military courts have resoundingly failed to carry out the constitutional mandate they do enjoy, that of prosecuting crimes committed by military personnel in the line of duty. And the delays in their proceedings rival those in civilian courts.

Even more fundamental, as the Lima newspaper *La República* editorialized, the president's proposal was "a setback for the civil power in favor of the military in the name of an undemonstrated rapidity and severity which may lend itself to greater injustices, in depriving many defendants, who may be innocent, of the guarantees due to them under the Constitution."[3]

Americas Watch viewed with consternation the García government's failure to develop a coherent vision of legal reform as regards the prosecution of terrorism. To maintain the safeguards afforded to detainees in Law 24,700, for example, would seem the very least that a democratic government would guarantee its citizens. That the government did not defend those safeguards but rather acceded to police pressure, was disturbing both in terms of due process and in what it implied for future efforts at reform. We urged in 1990 that the incoming Fujimori administration fortify the civilian judicial system—and thereby the public's respect for legal norms—by legislating protections for terrorism suspects as in Law 24,700.

The new penal code, enacted in April 1991, does not resolve these problems. And although it does lower and simplify penalties, it maintains a cumbersome conception of terrorism. Rather than define terrorism as action promoted and planned by an organization, the law classifies it as an individual crime, not permitting the gradation of penalties according to degree of leadership in the terrorist group or other aggravating circumstances related to the group's criminal conduct and motives for action. In part for this reason, human rights lawyers point out, the legislation sanctions the crime of collaboration with terrorism broadly and in some cases so harshly that a convicted accomplice may receive a longer prison sentence than the person who actually commits a terrorist crime.

Peru, therefore, still has not found the formula by which respect for the civil rights of security-related detainees can be combined with efficient prosecution. The urgency with which the public and successive governments have viewed the security situation has promoted legislative tinkering that, at times producing improvements, at others has bent basic principles disturbingly.

ADMINISTRATION OF JUSTICE

The civilian courts' failure to deter terrorism and criminality has engendered deep public frustration. The issue is broader and deeper, however, than the emergency provoked by Sendero Luminoso or even the spread of crime and the enormous caseload this represents. Peru's court system is cumbersome, representation is expensive, and reform efforts have tended to be conceived as stopgap measures rather than systemic changes. A central problem, which predates the current economic crisis, is that the courts are chronically underfinanced. This contributes to delays and encourages corruption, particularly in prosecutions for narcotics trafficking though also in ordinary criminal cases.

Where terrorism is concerned, there is a widespread public perception, not always justified, that the courts are too lenient and release dangerous subversives on technicalities. One impetus for the government's drive to create the special tribunals was precisely to combine various cases against Sendero leader Osmán Morote, whose first trial, in ordinary court, ended with acquittal in July 1988 (although Morote was convicted that October on other charges). In November 1989 the granting of bail for Raúl Américo Cruzzat Cárdenas, another key Sendero leader, reawakened this controversy. Accused of crimes that took place while Decree 46 was in force, Cruzzat argued that he deserved the conditional freedom permitted under that law. His petition was granted to the distress of the special state prosecutor for terrorism, among others. Another key senderista, Laura Zambrano Padilla, a leader of Sendero's command structure for Lima captured in 1984, made similar use of Decree 46 provisions and, having been sentenced to twelve years, obtained early release on good behavior in May 1991. To the surprise of no one, she immediately disappeared into clandestinity.

High-profile defendants may receive such consideration, but the opposite is also true: defendants against whom there is no sound basis for terrorist charges may suffer lengthy detentions without trial because of the court system's inefficiency. The normal delay before trial in terrorism cases is between two and three years. In a typical case, Raul Quispe Palomino of Lima, arrested on March 16, 1987, was charged with having offered his home for "subversive" meetings (a vague charge that is believed to have been based on statements made under torture in police custody), and his case came to court on April 23, 1990—after more than three years' delay. And appealing a conviction can result in delays of eight months to a year.

The courts are also unable to proceed on cases of military abuse, which include mistreatment and torture of detainees as well as forced disappearance. In disappearance cases, the courts are paralyzed by the combination of military denials of detention and the government's lack of will to oversee military actions in the emergency zones. Because the courts cannot guarantee protection, much less effective investigation and prosecution, witnesses in disappearance cases often dare not come forth.

The penal code enacted in April 1991 may assist the civilian courts in disappearance cases, for it defines "forced disappearance" explicitly as a crime, accepting a proposal made by the Coordinadora Nacional de Derechos Humanos. And in fairness it must be noted that judges and prosecutors do not always lack initiative; indeed, several have distinguished themselves in pursuing cases under hostile conditions.[4] These officials show a quiet heroism for which they can expect little political support and even fewer concrete results. Moreover, in areas under a state of emergency, particularly where armed conflict is acute, many judges and prosecutors have been forced to leave because of a lack of security. In the emergency zones generally, and especially in Ayacucho, Apurímac, and the jungle areas, there is virtually no judicial presence; what little there is is confined to the provincial capitals. In Huancayo, the province within Junín that contains the departmental capital, fully half the districts lacked civil and judicial authorities by mid-1990, according to human rights sources in Lima. This fact is all the more striking because Junín has a relatively short history of emergency. The withdrawal of judicial authorities from the zones of conflict is of a piece with the weakening of the civilian state presence there generally and corresponds to the Sendero program of creating a vacuum of authority that the insurgents seek to fill.

In spite of the honorable work of some judges and prosecutors, the judicial system is highly subject to political manipulation. The Supreme Court, which should offer leadership in judicial independence, has instead repeatedly handed down controversial rulings favoring military jurisdiction over civilian in human rights cases where military personnel have been implicated. In such cases the legal argument is that the alleged crimes were committed in the course of military duty. One example of the results, the Lurigancho riot-suppression case, is described below. At the same time, when the Supreme Court does resist political pressure, such is its low standing that undisguised public pressure may be exerted on it. When President García was betting his image on the creation of the special antiterrorism tribunals and the Supreme Court balked, a member of Congress from the governing party (who was also ironically member of a congressional committee on justice) threatened the Supreme Court with a constitutional challenge to move it along.[5] In most countries such disrespect would be undertaken only at risk of a rupture within the state.

FUJIMORI'S MODEST PROPOSALS

The new government of Alberto Fujimori could not be expected to resolve these deep structural problems at a stroke. Still, President Fujimori's comportment on the issue of terrorist prosecutions, and on prosecution of human rights cases, has reflected his close ties with the army and has been a grave disappointment to the human rights movement in Peru. On December 9, 1990, the executive presented a proposed constitutional change that would have permitted terrorism cases to be heard in closed military courts. Less than a year after scandal was provoked by García's military courts proposal, the new government was repeating the error. As before, the solution was not to take terrorism cases away from civilian judges but to offer those judges full-time protection from terrorist reprisals, sufficient resources to carry out investigations, and political support. Fujimori's proposal, barraged with the same arguments used in García's case, was soon abandoned. Nonetheless, having created controversy with the first initiative, Fujimori presented a second, equally worrisome one. On December 23, 1990, the executive promulgated Supreme Decree 171, which protected military personnel from civilian trials for crimes committed on active duty in emergency zones.

The Peruvian constitution defines military jurisdiction as extending only to *delitos de función,* or crimes against military duty, such as disobedience or desertion. Decree 171, asserting that military personnel are effectively on duty twenty-four hours a day in the zones of emergency (that is, most of the national territory), argued that "the activities they carry out are acts of service or occasioned by same" and are thus the proper province of military courts. Further, military personnel accused of grave abuses require protection, according to Decree 171. Article 2 states that "given the nature and characteristics of countersubversive activity and in order to protect personnel of the Forces of Order involved in it, as well as their families, the identities of these personnel remain confidential and may only be revealed by mandate of the jurisdictional organ [that is, the military court]." The decree thus legitimized and protected the military's common use of false names, or *chapas,* as a hedge against the identification of abusive personnel. Cases described later in this volume provide examples of the use of chapas to forestall human rights investigations; false names evidently protect against prosecution for abuses as much as they guard against reprisal by the enemy.

The Supreme Court has consistently passed human rights cases out of their proper civilian jurisdiction and into military courts, where the investigations languish and the accused are set free. Decree 171 would not have invented impunity by any means—the military has enjoyed impunity for abuses since Belaúnde—but it would have enshrined impunity in the nation's highest law.

Fujimori's justification of the decree was unconvincing: "We cannot demand firmness against terrorism if we undermine the work of the Armed and Police Forces by not giving them sufficient guarantees."[6] Decree 171 was criticized relentlessly by members of Congress, judicial representatives, the media, and national human rights organizations until its repeal by Congress in February 1991. The president, loath to listen, delayed promulgation of the law that contained the cancellation of Decree 171, forcing Congress to put the law into effect.[7]

Although human rights had barely surfaced as a campaign theme in the 1990 elections, and Peru could not have expected so hard a line from someone who had advocated development as part of the solution to counterinsurgency, Decree 171 was not without harbingers. Official relations with the human rights community, for example, had soured even before the outcry over the decree. In November, Justice Minister Augusto Antoniolli launched a verbal attack on human rights organizations for alleged bias and damage to the armed forces. Such groups must be kept from "creating obstacles to police and armed forces' intervention in zones affected by subversion," said Antoniolli, citing the Cayara massacre of 1988 and more recent incidents in the Upper Huallaga as examples of the way human rights groups undermine the counterinsurgency effort. Asked by *Sí* magazine to elaborate, the minister stated, misleadingly, that human rights groups that had spoken with him "investigate only" criminal actions by the state.[8] In another commentary, the justice minister added, "Many times the armed forces and police are criticized for excesses, which at times they have committed, but they are never supported when they strike hard at terrorism. When they do that, there appear the eternal defenders of human rights who, instead of supporting the forces of order, limit themselves to denouncing apparent excesses and thus only contribute to a climate of demoralization among them [the military and police.]"[9] It almost appeared that the defense minister's post had been filled twice and the justice minister's left vacant.

THREE CASES OF IMPUNITY

To record the cases in which military and police agents have escaped prosecution for human rights abuses in the past decade would require review of nearly all human rights cases. In isolated instances, under inordinate pressure, a handful of police officials have received judicial punishments, and administrative sanctions have been applied to some military officers, but not one human rights case tried in Peruvian courts has ended with conviction of a member of the military for an abuse of human rights under emergency authority. In the early 1980s civilian courts prosecuted some major human rights cases, such as the Soccos massacre of November 1983, in which thirty-four wedding-party guests were machine-gunned and then dynamited by counterinsurgency police in Ayacucho. But the pressure of the counterinsurgency campaign, which led to more abuses, made it increasingly difficult for the courts to take on the armed forces: the Accomarca massacre of between forty and sixty-nine Ayacucho villagers by an army patrol in August 1985; the Cayara, Ayacucho, massacre of May 1988, in which between twenty-eight and thirty-one peasants were killed and dozens more disappeared in the hands of the army—these are shocking cases in which the military has protected its personnel by obtaining jurisdiction or intimidating the survivors or both.

Bringing human rights cases forward presents risks for witnesses and prosecutors: during the Soccos trial in Ayacucho, the courthouse was bombed three times; the witnesses to Cayara were systematically murdered and the prosecutor was forced to leave Peru for his safety. The court system lacks the resources to protect its staff, much less to protect numerous witnesses who often live in remote areas; the security apparatus is not a disinterested party and cannot be counted upon to see to plaintiffs' security. Witnesses increasingly rely on the assistance of church and human rights activists to find refuge, and their plight is being brought before international bodies.

But in the circumstances, the vast majority of murders committed by state agents receive little or no judicial attention. And in cases of torture victims seldom file complaints, so common is the practice and so taken for granted as a feature of short-term detention.

The cases summarized below have been selected because of their notoriety as examples of the courts' failure to withstand pressure for impunity.

Artaza: Civilian Court

One rather bizarre example of the judiciary's role, as regards human rights, occurred in December 1989, when a judicial resolution declared navy captain Alvaro Artaza officially dead. Artaza, former chief of the naval base in Huanta, Ayacucho, had been accused of involvement in the killings of forty-nine peasants whose bodies were discovered in graves in Pucayacu during the Belaúnde era. He had also been implicated in the killings of six evangelical ministers in Callqui, near Huanta, and the disappearance of journalist Jaime Ayala Sulca, who entered the Huanta base to file a complaint of police abuse in August 1984 and has not been seen since. The Supreme Court awarded jurisdiction to military courts in the Pucayacu and Callqui (ministers) cases, but in the Jaime Ayala disappearance case the civilian courts were given jurisdiction. In April 1985, just days after the Ayala jurisdiction decision, Artaza vanished, supposedly kidnapped by Sendero. The press questioned the military's version of the story. But the armed forces considered him dead without making any serious investigation; nor did his relatives seek an investigation.[10] Yet, oddly, a legal petition was filed on the vanished man's behalf questioning the civilian court's authority to try the case and requesting military jurisdiction. This was not granted. By declaring his death, however, the court has brought the case against Artaza necessarily to an end. This resolution is hardly satisfactory, given the odd circumstances in which Artaza was suddenly unavailable for prosecution. The navy must show publicly that the declaration of death rests on fact, not on convenience.

Artaza would have had reason to prefer trial in military court. The military courts' failure to prosecute violations of human rights committed by armed forces personnel is so consistent that it must be recognized as a policy of impunity and, as such, as a strong contributing factor in the continuation of abuses.

Lurigancho: Military Court

On June 17, 1986, seeking to embarrass President García during a meeting of the Socialist International in Lima, Sendero Luminoso prisoners at three prisons in Lima and Callao set off coordinated riots to protest their conditions of confinement and government policy toward them. President García ordered the military to quell the riots, and in the San Pedro de Lurigancho and San Juan Bautista ("El Frontón") prisons, the outcome was multiple executions of inmates after their surrender.[11] In all, between 200 and 250 prisoners were killed after laying down their weapons. The legal case involving El Frontón, where the prison was bombarded by the navy and only 35 of approximately 130 prisoners survived, was heard in a secret proceeding before the navy's judge-advocate but never opened publicly. The Lurigancho case, which involved the army and prison police, concluded in June 1990.

Grim penal conditions had provoked riots and hostage-taking—and police overreaction—before. In December 1983, when ten inmates of Lurigancho seized several women as hostages and finally left the prison in an ambulance, police opened fire on the vehicle, killing eight prisoners and one hostage; in a March 1984 incident, inmates of the Lima prison El Sexto took fourteen hostages, murdered three of them in front of television cameras, and thereby brought tensions to such a boiling point that after fourteen hours, police opened fire, provoking a riot, and twenty prisoners were killed.[12] Sendero had encouraged inmates to rebel, but they needed little incitement.

In Lurigancho more than 120 inmates died, most after they had surrendered. A government investigation implicated some ninety officers and soldiers of the Republican Guard (the police who guarded the prisons' perimeters) in those executions. When a civilian judge indicted army general Jorge Rabanal, who had commanded the operation, for murder, the military closed ranks and demanded that the trial be conducted in military courts. In a much-disputed ruling, the Supreme Court awarded the military courts jurisdiction.

That decision had several consequences—among them, that none of the political authorities involved in quelling the riots was indicted, although there was evidence that Vice-Minister of the Interior Agustín Mantilla had made tactical decisions directly affecting the outcome and that other civilian officials, including President García, had also played a direct role.[13] Among the accused were, however, General Rabanal and the director of the Republican Guard, Gen. Máximo Martínez Lira, as well as a guard colonel, Rolando Cabezas, who was considered one of those most responsible for the killings.

The case went to trial in August 1989, and on December 11 the court convicted just two of the seventy-eight accused, exonerating the rest on grounds of insufficient evidence. Neither of the two convicted, moreover, was General Rabanal or General Martínez Lira, the highest authorities at the scene of the massacre. Colonel Cabezas was sentenced to fifteen years in prison, and a guard lieutenant received a seven-year sentence. Although the conviction of Cabezas was well-founded, the exculpation of senior officers and nineteen other defendants was the real message of the trial. Senator Rolando Ames, president of the parliamentary commission that had investigated the prison massacres, voiced the opinion of the human rights community when he said that "we are opening up the possibility that in our country the act of murder will be institutionalized."[14]

Pressure to reconsider the verdicts led the military's highest court, the Supreme Council of Military Justice, to review the case. The results, however, are not encouraging. The full text of the sentences has not been made public, but press and police sources indicate that on June 7, 1990, the Supreme Council handed down the same sentence as the lower court for Col. Cabezas (fifteen years) and a somewhat heavier sentence than the lower court (ten years) for Lt. Javier Martínez, as well as two-year sentences for five guard subordinates. Two Republican Guard officers previously acquitted—Col. Narciso Azabache and General Martínez Lira—were sentenced to six months' and thirty days' military confinement, respectively, combined with temporary separation from the service while serving their sentences. Martínez Lira's conviction hardly merits the term, however: his sentence is absurdly light, he is permitted to serve it without actual confinement (in conditional liberty), and the crime of which he was convicted—negligence—in no way corresponds to the responsibility that pertained to him as director of the Republican Guard in June 1986. In addition, the Supreme Council again absolved nineteen guard officers, forty-five of their subordinates, a general of the Republican Guard, as well as army general Ismael Araujo, and, most disturbingly of all, army general Jorge Rabanal, who commanded the operation at Lurigancho.

In October 1990 the Chamber of Deputies took up a proposal to charge former President García, before the Supreme Court, with responsibility for ordering the bloody response to the riots. When it came to a vote, President Fujimori committed his party's support to García, making possible a defeat of the measure by the slim margin of eighty votes to seventy-five. And in another political postscript to the case, Fujimori soon thereafter proposed the promotion of Rabanal from brigade to division general. The Senate opposed the promotion on December 5, 1990, but a new vote taken the following day reversed the decision.

It is perhaps fitting that, along with Rabanal, defeated and then embraced for promotion was Gen. José Valdivia Dueñas, head of the Ayacucho Political Military Command at the time of the Cayara massacre of May 1988. As one newspaper columnist wrote in stupor following the second Senate vote, "It is formally perfect, morally unacceptable, and politically disquieting."[15]

Castillo Páez: The Supreme Court

On the morning of October 21, 1990, police conducted a counterinsurgency sweep through a Lima slum known as Villa El Salvador, where Sendero had just attacked a bank office. Detained on the street around 11:30 A.M. in the presence of numerous witnesses, Ernesto Castillo Páez, a recent graduate in social sciences of the Catholic University, was taken away in a police vehicle; his detention was subsequently denied, and he has disappeared.

A petition of habeas corpus presented by the young man's family on October 25 was accepted on October 31 and demanded immediate release of the detainee based primarily on the testimony of two witnesses. The judge also found serious irregularities in the relevant police records and formed the opinion that these had been falsified. The prosecutor appealed on behalf of the police. On November 27, the Eighth Correctional Court of Lima, the revisory body, confirmed the lower court's opinion that the habeas corpus petition was well-founded.

The decision was extraordinarily significant: it was the first time in Lima—and only the second time in Peru—that a petition of habeas corpus had been confirmed as well-founded in a disappearance case. The confirmation ruling instructed the Chamber of Deputies to begin a constitutional process against Interior Minister Gen. Adolfo Alvarado Fournier. It also instructed the provincial prosecutor to begin proceedings against the director of the General Police and the head of the police antiterrorist unit, DIRCOTE (Dirección Contra el Terrorismo), and to identify the individual police officers involved. In explanation, the correctional court ruling asserted that, "even if it is true that there is not a direct responsibility on the part of the Interior Minister and the Directors of the General Police and DIRCOTE, there is indirect responsibility, since this attack on individual liberty is a police and military practice which has been repeated for some time, as shown by multiple denunciations concerning disappeared detainees." In addition, the judge determined that the case involved not only illegal detention but abuse of authority, inasmuch as the lower court's demand for Castillo's release had gone unheeded.

The law governing habeas corpus stipulates that a petition confirmed at the appellate level is *cosa juzgada*—what in American jurisprudence is called *res judicata,* a completed legal process, not appealable except by the complainant.[16] In that case a *recurso de nulidad* may be presented; but in no case may the authority accused of the abuse of individual rights seek to nullify a second-level confirmation. The state prosecutor, however, presented a petition to the Supreme Court for a *recurso extraordinario de nulidad* and, when that was rejected, a technical complaint against the correctional court ruling, or *recurso de queja,* which was accepted. This unprecedented and frankly illegal procedure ended on February 7, 1991, with the Supreme Court nullifying the ruling of the correctional court and declaring the habeas corpus petition unfounded—even though the text of the Supreme Court decision contains a description of Castillo's arrest by police and the statement that "in the present case there exists the possibility that unidentified police detained Ernesto Rafael Castillo Páez, with the abominable possibility of his disappearance." Rather than rule on the facts, the Court ruled on the basis that "the present action is ineffective in that it does not identify possible authors." It recommended that another process be initiated for kidnapping and that the provincial prosecutor be instructed to identify the culprits.

The ruling was handled so quietly that it was not communicated to the Castillo family's lawyer, Augusto Zúñiga Paz, for nearly a month. A few days after he learned of the decision, Zúñiga received an envelope on government stationery; when he opened it, his left forearm was blown off.

Castillo has never reappeared. His family's lawyer is undergoing medical care in Sweden. The case is being pursued by other, one must say courageous, lawyers, through charges of abuse of authority as formulated by the correctional court, but such charges are minor compared with that of disappearance. If convicted on these charges, DIRCOTE chief Enrique Oblitas Jane and General Police chief Victor Manuel Alba Plascencia could receive a maximum penalty of four years, which could be suspended. During the investigation they are not under arrest. Alvarado has been replaced as interior minister but faces no congressional charges. The policeman suspected of making the arrest, and of the attack on Zúñiga, is an explosives expert who was at the site during the October 21 sweep and who, according to police witnesses interviewed by *Sí* magazine, was seen bringing Castillo into the precinct; his name is Comandante Juan Carlos Mejía León, and he is still on duty. The two witnesses who were earlier willing to testify have taken Zúñiga's plight as a warning.

3

PENAL CONDITIONS

Nowhere in Peru are human rights more systematically and constantly denied than in the nation's prisons, which contain some 18,500 inmates. Overcrowding, miserable physical conditions, disease, and inmate violence are only a few of the conditions that have led in the past to riots and hostage-taking by security-related prisoners and more recently to hunger strikes by prisoners already near starvation.

Trial delays commonly last three to four years, while inmates from the poorest sectors of society, the vast majority of prisoners, can afford neither legal representation nor bribes to speed up the process. The scarcity of state resources has left recent administrations with few options, although early in President García's term there was an effort to accelerate trial schedules, issue pardons, and build new prison facilities to reduce overcrowding. One result of this policy was the new maximum-security prison Miguel Castro Castro (popularly known as Canto Grande), where most accused members of Sendero Luminoso and the MRTA—some 400 prisoners—are currently confined.[1] Canto Grande was built to hold 1,200 prisoners, but even this new facility is overpopulated, holding more than 2,000 in mid-1990. In the country's 116 penal facilities, the inmate population averages 70 percent above capacity, and in Lima and Callao's largest penitentiary, the all-male prison of San Pedro (known as Lurigancho), that figure is doubled to 140 percent. Lurigancho was built to hold 2,400 prisoners and currently holds more than 5,300.[2]

In the latter years of the García administration, the state did not even possess precise figures on the prison population, as no census had been conducted. What was known, and continues to be true, is that suspects are arrested and imprisoned on minor grounds, that within the prisons no differentiation is made between suspects and convicts, and that suspects without economic resources can expect to remain in prison, awaiting trial, for several years.

The 1990 prison census, taken on the impetus of President Fujimori's concern, demonstrated that in Lurigancho nearly four times as many prisoners were awaiting trial or sentencing as had received full legal process (4,144 versus

1,213). In Canto Grande the comparison was even more dramatic: of a population of 2,003, the census showed 1,900 as not convicted of any crime. Meanwhile, these abandoned citizens lived in such squalor and debilitation that according to a recent director of prisons—who resigned in despair—more than 400 Canto Grande inmates were suffering from tuberculosis.[3]

Because there is neither effective control of inmates' movements in the largest facilities nor separation of dangerous inmates, the weak are inevitably preyed upon. Drug gangs within the prisons control inmates' access to narcotic relief and, conversely, provoke tensions and violent conflict over lack of such relief; other gangs manage the sale of extra food, often robbed from the prison kitchen and in practice almost the only food available. In Lurigancho, according to a frequent visitor, the inmates habitually carry knives for self-defense; the security police responsible for internal order do not interfere with this anarchy.

Indeed, the lack of discipline and extraordinary violence of prison life are promoted by corruption among the inmates' "guardians." Not only do police guards steal from the prisoners and mistreat them physically, but the National Penitentiary Institute (Instituto Nacional Penitentiario, INPE), the state agency in charge of prison administration, was accused, not for the first time, in 1990 by its own workers of high-level corruption. Even in a system that allotted only twenty cents' worth of food per prisoner per day, the amount of food that arrived on prisoners' plates was too small. On a surprise visit to Lurigancho in August 1990, a provincial prosecutor verified that inmates were being fed only once every forty-eight hours and blamed INPE.

In 1986 Americas Watch reported that prison conditions combined "neglect and chaos" with the fact that inmates were "very much in control of the inner workings" of the penitentiaries, creating a "formula for disaster."[4] The riots on June 17, 1986, led by members of Sendero Luminoso in three prisons in Lima and Callao, were to some extent a logical outcome of this formula; those riots were also quelled with stunning brutality, as described in chapter 2. The suppression of the prison riots of 1986 was the most massive instance of the violation of human rights during the García administration.

SECURITY-RELATED PRISONERS

The 1986 riots were incited by Sendero partially to embarrass President García and also to highlight Sendero's opposition to the transfer of its members to the new penitentiary Canto Grande. Since then, however, almost all Sendero inmates, male and female, have been moved to Canto Grande. They are permitted regular family visits, and their relatives may bring food and other supplementary supplies. In general, the Sendero and MRTA inmates of Canto Grande are reported to enjoy marginally better conditions than inmates accused of common crimes. According to social workers who visit the prison, the Sendero inmates have re-created there the internal political organization they maintained in other prisons when they were more dispersed, and indeed completely control their wing, enforcing discipline, conducting indoctrination classes, and preventing the access of non-Sendero prisoners and penal personnel. A portion of their food allotment is given to them in raw form so that they may cook it, and in May 1990, according to a prison specialist in Lima, the Interior Ministry was coordinating plans to improve the delivery of water and food to Canto Grande— benefits aimed mainly at Sendero prisoners that would improve conditions somewhat for the inmate population at large.

The International Committee of the Red Cross (ICRC) has had access to Lima prisons and DIRCOTE facilities in recent years, but even under García, who permitted ICRC access to prisons and detention centers in Ayacucho, the organization's ability to work was limited. Americas Watch commented in 1987 that police resistance to ICRC inspections had effectively blocked access to DIRCOTE headquarters. That situation was remedied in 1989, however. The ICRC was guaranteed access to prisons in Lima and the emergency zones, and since October 1989 an ICRC delegate accompanied by a doctor has visited the DIRCOTE center in Lima daily. During 1989 the ICRC visited 1,290 security-related prisoners held in forty-six places of confinement throughout the country.

The wider admission of the ICRC into the prisons and DIRCOTE was an important step. As described later, however, the police during 1991 did not cooperate fully with the ICRC. Equally important, as of August 1991 the ICRC had not been granted access to military posts and police stations in the emergency zones. Americas Watch urges that the ICRC's access to these places be guaranteed, as one of the most effective measures toward preventing mistreatment in detention and disappearances.

One matter of concern reiterated by several sources during Americas Watch visits to Peru in 1990 and 1991 is the practice of imprisoning young people accused of minor, nonviolent Sendero collaboration and others whose links to Sendero are disputed in the same wing of Canto Grande as known Sendero veterans. In these conditions, according to lawyers and social workers with access to Sendero prisoners, minor offenders and innocent persons come under the discipline and influence of Sendero leaders, and those who may be reluctant to join in Sendero's prison culture fear for their security if they disobey. Sendero indoctrination, moreover, often ends by converting the less-converted. "A school for subversion" was one lawyer's description of the Canto Grande conditions, and he among others recommended strongly that the young and those accused of lesser Sendero-related offenses be channeled into another facility or to a different area of Canto Grande.

LURIGANCHO, MAY 1990

Lima's prisons must be described as infernal. The problems of poor administration, corruption, underfinancing, and lack of control of prison life, which Americas Watch noted in 1986, have worsened with the economic crisis, especially since February 1987. At that time, officials of INPE, which had administered the prison system under the Ministry of Justice, were charged with corruption, and as an emergency measure, the Republican Guard (now called the Security Police) was given authority to maintain order inside the prisons— in effect to replace INPE. This emergency measure has become permanent. The ex-Republican Guards who had formerly policed only the perimeter of the prisons became the sole authority there, and conditions have become even more violent and corrupt.

This situation is extremely prejudicial to the rights of all prisoners, but primarily those of the common inmates, who lack the high political profile, organized family support, ICRC oversight, and internal organization that the security-related prisoners use to protect themselves and maintain morale.

In May 1990, a representative of Americas Watch visited Lurigancho to observe conditions for common prisoners there. The prison was wretchedly overcrowded; no exact count of prisoners had been made in recent years. Such was the administrative chaos, moreover, that prisoners were sometimes not notified that they had completed their sentence and remained in prison while the authorities believed them to be at liberty. The prison itself was in a state of severe deterioration: more windows were broken than whole, the interior environment was filthy, and the yard was strewn with garbage through which some prisoners picked in hopes of finding morsels of food. The water shortage then affecting Lima meant that in Lurigancho, according to an INPE official who accompanied the Americas Watch representative, there was water for only a few minutes in the early morning; the prisoners, dirty and bedraggled, had little water to drink and none to wash with.

The overall decay that is one's first impression of Lurigancho is due to a lack of resources, to corruption that siphons off the few resources dedicated to the prison system, and to inmates' vandalism. But in large part it is also due directly to the control of the interior of the prison exercised by the security police. Inmates, the INPE official, and a regular visitor to Lurigancho all told Americas Watch that since 1987 police guards have robbed the facility of everything that can be transported outside the prison and sold. The workshops that used to operate in the industrial wing have been dismantled; the kitchen stoves no longer function because parts have been stolen (prisoners were cooking for the entire inmate population on kerosene stoves constructed with donated materials). One group of prisoners organizing a workshop to produce brooms had managed to build a few makeshift machines for that purpose, yet one of them was required to watch the workshop constantly to ensure that police guards did not break into it and take away the machinery.

The Security Police did nothing to curb violence among prisoners; an inmate human rights committee did, however, try to impede violence. The leader of this committee described the guards' contribution to peaceful prisoner coexistence as confined to the peddling of drugs to keep inmates distracted. Intra-inmate violence stemmed largely from the presence of drug organizations in the population, but the guards made no effort to deter these. One large hall, which used to function as a theater and meeting area, was being used as a dormitory by "floating" inmates, those escaping violence in their cells and cellblock wings. Prisoners lay curled along the walls, sat weaving baskets, or wandered about in this space where they had sought refuge from the uncontrolled brutality of their peers.

Brutality by police guards was also unrestrained. According to the inmate who headed the prisoners' human rights committee, if the Security Police think an inmate has money they may place him in solitary confinement until he bribes them sufficiently. In addition, judges who receive prisoner complaints of brutality turn the investigations over to the Security Police themselves, with predictable results. This inmate told Americas Watch that since 1987 his committee had filed some two hundred complaints in the courts against police guards, and with one exception—a case in which a particularly brutal guard was transferred—he could not think of a single complaint that had been effective.

The treatment of visitors is another of the inmates' complaints. On regular visiting days, relatives are made to wait outside the prison for long periods and often are allowed to enter only after they pass money to the guards. For the extremely poor, these bribes are a substantial sacrifice: reportedly 100,000 intis (about $3.50 in May 1990) for female visitors and up to three times that much for each man who visits. No space is set aside for meetings with visitors— indeed, given the overall condition of the prison, such amenities would seem to belong to a different world—so prisoners take turns leaving each other alone for visits in the cells.

As mentioned, the Security Police rob both the food provided for the prison and supplemental provisions brought by relatives. Inmates subsist on one meal a day, and it is almost invariably rice. On the day Americas Watch visited, there was to be chicken with the rice, but very little meat arrived at the kitchen after passing through the hands of the police guards. Rampant malnutrition contributes to a high incidence of tuberculosis; at the time of the May visit, medical staff in a special isolation area said they were treating 110 active cases and that many inmates could recover only temporarily because of their weakened state. Between the medical and INPE staff and the inmates a certain solidarity was evident, due to their shared opposition to the police guards and a common despair over the lack of basic services.

The prison hospital illustrates clearly the dual problem of abused authority and lack of state funds. In the hospital building, which had no water and no electricity for its X-ray and surgical equipment, an inmate had been stationed on the roof to ensure that security police did not rob the few medicines in the dispensary. Those medicines had been donated; there was no budget to provide the most basic pharmaceuticals, and prison doctors said that this held true for Canto Grande as well.

The hospital building boasts a clean new surgical wing that has never functioned because of a lack of water and electricity. It houses psychiatric patients for whom, when we visited, there was no psychiatrist; these shaven-headed patients wandered about aimlessly in the dark passageways of the hospital basement, along floors wet with leaks from the bathroom. INPE had been on strike for three months when we visited—another victim of the economic crisis—so the hospital staff consisted of one doctor who lacked even minimal resources to treat his seriously ill patients.

FUJIMORI'S RESPONSE

These conditions led relatives of Lurigancho inmates in April 1990 to denounce the lack of food and medicine, the shortage of water, and the resulting potential for a riot. After agreements were made with the prisoners and then not fulfilled, Lurigancho inmates staged a hunger strike in May, demanding that mistreatment and bribe demands from the police guards be stopped and that legal cases be speeded up. The then-incoming (since resigned) head of INPE promised to heed their demands, but the system is not susceptible to one person's goodwill. On May 24, therefore, just days after the Americas Watch inspection, Lurigancho inmates took to the roofs of the prison, setting fires and committing themselves to a hunger strike until food and legal problems, including judicial corruption, were resolved. It was at this point that Fujimori, as candidate for president, visited Lurigancho, was deeply shocked by what he saw, and criticized the prison system as a nightmare.

The candidate's horror seemed genuine, but ironically, one of Fujimori's early decisions as president brought inmates further suffering. The economic "shock" policy hit the prisons hard; on August 9 and 10, inmates received no food, due to the rise in prices and INPE inefficiency, and on August 16, inmates in Lurigancho again took to the roofs to protest the shock measures and demand penal reform.

Fujimori understood the urgency of the situation, however. As García had done before him, the incoming president took steps to relieve overcrowding—by promulgating a decree to facilitate the release of inmates accused of minor crimes who had already served substantial time while awaiting trial. Published on October 1, 1990, Supreme Decree 17 was projected to benefit those inmates who, under judicial investigation (*sumario*), would have completed no fewer than nine months in confinement or who, facing trial, would have been confined eighteen or more months. Rather than wait for the courts to act, Fujimori sought to establish an ad hoc commission to review cases and recommend pardons. The decree was considered by some to be a creative, if partial, response to a long-neglected problem. According to INPE figures, more than three-fourths of the inmate population had not been convicted and were therefore ineligible for pardon under normal procedures. But the judiciary, and ultimately a majority in the Senate, considered the decree unconstitutional, on those same grounds. Only convicted inmates, they argued, were legally eligible for pardon; those awaiting trial must be subject to an amnesty, a congressional measure. So members of Congress proposed amnesty laws while public concern for the prison issue peaked, and those proposals, predictably, have been stalled as public attention has turned to other issues.

The courts' hostile reaction to Decree 17 may have been based, in part, on the way Fujimori pointed the finger at judicial inefficiency and corruption as causes of the inmates' misery. Defending the judicial branch, the Supreme Court instead blamed the legislature for underfunding the courts and other authorities for the internal problems of the prisons. A Supreme Court statement pointed out that "the Judiciary does not administer the penal establishments. The overcrowding, promiscuity, illness, and hunger that affect the inmates, like the illicit drug and alcohol traffic in the prisons, are the responsibility of authorities other than the Judicial Power."[5] This argument was not without reason. At the same time, some critics noted that, if the judiciary would respond so quickly to other issues as it did defensively to this one, the entire debate would have been unnecessary.

Despite Senate opposition, President Fujimori formed the five-member committee of experts contemplated in Decree 17. This Special Technical Commission on Qualification of Pardons began work in October 1990, presided by an official of the Justice Ministry. Its recommendations were reviewed individually by Justice Minister Antoniolli and the president. According to former commission members, however, the work was complicated by lack of cooperation from the courts and the justice minister. Judges blocked the paperwork; the commission was refused access to all case folders in judicial hands and was forced to evaluate cases based on the preliminary material in police records.

Antoniolli questioned the commission's findings and attempted to undermine its decisions, according to former commission members, with the result that commissioners protested to Fujimori directly. After it had secured ninety-six pardons at the end of the year, the commission's work was further challenged in Congress, which in January 1991 passed a law granting not pardon but freedom on bail to persons detained without sentencing for inordinate amounts of time. Considering their job fulfilled, commission members resigned in February and were not replaced.

The commission's usefulness was limited, not only because the number of inmates who benefited was small but also because most applications for pardon came from Lima. Judicial opposition and a lack of effort by prison directors nationwide meant that the opportunity to apply for pardon was not widely known in the provinces, where the greatest proportion of minor offenders is presumably incarcerated. But the debate generated by the commission and Decree 17 served another purpose, awakening congressional concern about prison conditions and leading to the promulgation, in April 1991, of a new penal code. The new law redefines sentencing for a number of lesser crimes in order to discourage imprisonment; in place of confinement for minor crimes, as had been applied almost indiscriminately under the penal code of 1924, the new code substitutes community service, fines, and other formulas.

More could be done, including the decriminalization of minor infractions. Nor is overcrowding the only problem. At a minimum, reforms should be implemented to safeguard inmates' survival. Food allotments remain worse than inadequate, although the new government raised the budget for provisions slightly. The August 1990 economic shock measures resulted in cutoffs of food to some prisons, and nine inmates of Lurigancho died of malnutrition the next month.[6] Even when INPE is not on strike, its activity within the prisons barely matters, because a rapid turnover of INPE directors, under both García and Fujimori, has made it impossible to formulate a coherent policy for prison management. And, as always, there is the problem of corruption.

Some concrete and not necessarily expensive changes would make a difference nonetheless. Experts with whom Americas Watch consulted on the conditions in Lima's prisons said unanimously that before 1987 the prison situation had been critical and that INPE was indeed corrupt but that police supervision of the prisons' interior is far worse. All urged that the Security Police be withdrawn from the interior of the prisons and that both INPE and the Security Police be brought under a single ministry of the government, the Ministry of Justice. The current division of authority, with the Interior Ministry responsible for the police and the Justice Ministry responsible for INPE, is an administrative tangle that promotes inertia and lack of oversight, to say nothing of inmates' suffering.

4

CONGRESSIONAL INVESTIGATIONS
OF HUMAN RIGHTS ABUSES

The multiple strains on the Peruvian court system, as noted in chapter 2, include underfinancing, corruption, a lack of coherent legislative projects from the government, pressure from government on politically sensitive issues, and hostility from the military on human rights cases. These difficulties make the courts an unlikely source of truth about human rights abuses or of critical judgment into the sources of those abuses. Special parliamentary commissions of inquiry have thus played an important role in recent years. In fact, special commissions have become a favored instrument of the human rights movement, and it is now common for inquiries to be underway on several major human rights cases at once.

The history of special commissions on human rights cases is checkered at best. The outstanding example of human rights investigation during the Belaúnde administration was a special commission headed by novelist Mario Vargas Llosa, which produced still-controversial conclusions on the January 1983 murders of eight journalists in Uchuraccay, in northern Ayacucho. The Vargas Llosa commission found that the journalists had been mistaken at a distance for subversives and attacked on that basis, but photographic evidence that became available later established that they had been able to identify themselves. It seemed, rather, that the journalists had been killed because they were strangers, in keeping with a security policy laid down by the military.

Unfortunately, during the García administration, special congressional commissions created to clarify human rights cases were often unable to produce unanimous conclusions, and the divisions of opinion ran along party lines, with members of the ruling APRA party protecting the government's image. Because APRA held a majority in Congress, the choice of party over principle effectively blunted the impact of what was often reliable research. The investigation carried out by the Bernales Commission, whose reports were summarized in chapter 1, does not appear to have fallen victim to these problems. But the praiseworthy research of the Senate's Ames Commission, whose 1987 reports shed light on the June 1986 prison massacres, was undermined by the refusal of commission members of the governing party to publish conclusions critical of government officials.

During 1989, moreover, two parliamentary commissions treating human rights issues produced disappointing results. The government's increasing defensiveness on human rights was reflected in the conduct of the ruling party's members on these commissions. Important opportunities were lost to clarify, in one case, military responsibility for a massacre in Ayacucho and, in the other, suspected links between APRA party members and officials and paramilitary activity. The results of these inquiries constituted a serious evasion of public responsibility, and the fault for this lies with the party of Alan García.

Since APRA's debacle in the 1990 elections, when no party won a congressional majority, the tide has turned; García and five of his ministers were accused of corruption during 1991, and a congressional commission examined telephone tapping under García. The demise of APRA hegemony meant less-partisan work on human rights cases as well, for example, in the investigation of the Chumbivilcas massacre of August 1990.

THE AMES COMMISSION: PRISON MASSACRES

The murder of some 200–250 inmates, on June 18 and 19, 1986, in three of Lima's prisons, was a crime that, in number of victims, has not been equaled since in Peru. A still-popular, still-confident President García vowed that the massacres would be fully exposed and that he would stake his presidency on punishing the culprits: "Either they go, or I go," he said, during a visit to the site of the bloodshed. Still, behind the scenes his attitude differed, and for several months after the massacres little happened apart from the resignation of the minister of justice and some of his staff. This was partly the fault of Congress, which did not press ahead with a special commission, but executive signals were also mixed. García ordered an investigation of the killings at one prison, Lurigancho, but not at the other scene of mass repression, the island prison of El Frontón.[1] Members of the Republican Guard who had been implicated in the Lurigancho killings were arrested but spent little time in prison; of the several dozen accused, only six or seven remained in custody by the end of 1986, and these were confined in more comfortable facilities. Military courts took over jurisdiction of the Lurigancho case as soon as Gen. Jorge Rabanal was implicated (the case was discussed in chapter 2). President García did not oppose these developments.

More than a year later, however, a Senate commission did get underway. And, in a gesture that would not be repeated in García's government, the opposition was asked to chair the commission. Rolando Ames, an independent elected on the United Left ticket, became the commission's chairperson. The commission was granted limited access to previously classified government documents, to the sites themselves, and to surviving witnesses. This information enabled the staff to reconstruct events carefully, including the process by which officials had decided to use such brutal force.

Briefly, the facts were as follows: on June 17, 1986, Sendero prisoners in the El Frontón, Santa Bárbara (women's), and Lurigancho penitentiaries in Lima and Callao set off coordinated riots, taking hostages and making political and practical demands. By 11:00 P.M., the Santa Bárbara riot had been quelled without heavy loss of life. In El Frontón, the political head of operations, Vice-Minister of the Interior Agustín Mantilla, denied access to the prisoners by judicial representatives who were attempting negotiations, declaring the prison to be a militarized zone over the protests of the prison director. A special antisubversive unit of the Republican Guard initiated the attack, and the navy later directed further attacks. Evidence at the site suggested that the inmates possessed no more than a handful of rifles and some handmade weapons. But little attempt was made to convince them to give up. At 2:00 P.M. on June 18, the operation ended; some ninety inmates as well as three members of the armed forces were dead. Some of the approximately thirty-five survivors of El Frontón told a well-known Peruvian journalist that navy troops had dispensed with surrendered inmates by taking them to the yard and executing them.[2] A 1987 Amnesty International report cited testimony of a naval noncommissioned officer who stated that some survivors were held secretly on a navy base;[3] clandestine graves were later found in cemeteries surrounding Lima, their contents presumed to be these victims.

In Lurigancho, members of the Republican Guard placed explosives around the walls of the industrial pavilion at about 11:30 P.M. on June 18. The pavilion was bombarded with these explosives, then attacked with rifles and grenades, in the early morning hours of June 19. By 3:00 A.M., the Sendero prisoners showed signs of willingness to surrender. According to a hostage who survived, these senderista inmates were taken from the pavilion alive. He later saw several face down in the yard, hands behind their heads. There were no survivors among the Sendero inmates when the operation concluded, however: all 124 senderistas were dead, at least 90 having been executed after surrender by a bullet to the back of the neck.

The government immediately sought to contain the political damage. On June 19, President García first responded to the number of casualties and dead in a Cabinet meeting, where he commended the Joint Command.[4] That day, García issued Supreme Decree 6, which declared the prisons to be restricted military zones and blocked civilian judicial access to the site of the events. This decree was unconstitutional, in that it attempted to apply retroactively and thus to determine jurisdiction of the inevitable legal case, whose jurisdiction could be decided only by the Supreme Court.

Well before the Ames Commission began its work, a key witness died in odd circumstances. This was Republican Guard Capt. Justino Campos, who had tried to stop the executions in Lurigancho and who had recognized the principal executioner there as Republican Guard Col. Rolando Cabezas, when Cabezas briefly removed his ski mask. According to the Republican Guard, an explosives training exercise was the cause of Campos's death the following January.

Campos's testimony would have been important in legal proceedings, but it did not touch on the most divisive issue facing the Ames Commission. Though in accord as to the sequence of events, including the involvement of the cabinet and the president in making fateful decisions, the commission could not agree on conclusions, and in the end it produced two reports. The "majority report" was signed by the APRA members. It accused only the military and police personnel who had participated in the attacks, the prosecutor general, and the director of INPE. The "minority report," signed by Ames and opposition members of leftist and rightist parties, recommended that several high government officials be submitted to a congressional vote similar to impeachment, such that they would lose their immunity from prosecution and be subject to charges. The officials accused in the minority report were President García, Vice-Minister of the Interior (later Interior Minister) Mantilla, the director of INPE, and the prosecutor general (fiscal de la nación), along with an army general and some ninety officers and soldiers of the Republican Guard. The minority report also asserted that the riots were generated in part by official neglect of the prisons and that the government had misled public opinion by exaggerating the violence of the riots, in part to justify the use of extreme, unnecessary force in their suppression.

Congress approved the majority report, and the parliamentary debate on it was disappointingly weak. But the minority Ames Report was published and is widely regarded as an honest, thorough investigation that placed the facts beyond dispute.

THE MELGAR COMMISSION: CAYARA

No undisputed picture of events emerged from this investigation, a prime example of the difference between politics in Lima and life—and terror—in most of Peru. Instead, an undetermined number of very poor Peruvians are dead, and the only official to speak effectively on their behalf is in exile. This has not prevented Cayara from being one of the better-known examples of army abuse in the late García years, however.

On May 14, 1988, the day after a Sendero ambush against an army patrol in a nearby village, army soldiers entered Cayara, province of Cangallo, Ayacucho, and, with gunshot, bayonets, and farming tools, killed between twenty-eight and thirty-one of the male residents of the hamlet. On May 18, the army returned and arrested more villagers, dozens of whom disappeared; the bodies of three were found in early August. The government first attempted to deny that the massacre had taken place, but then the Office of the Prosecutor General's special prosecutor for disappearances in Ayacucho, Carlos Escobar Pineda, was authorized to go to the site.

Among the difficulties Escobar faced was that, although soldiers had buried the corpses near the village, by the time Escobar and his team arrived in Cayara these remains had been moved. Nonetheless, in examining the early graves, and the bloodstains and hair he found there, Escobar verified that killings had taken place.

On June 29, 1988, two of the witnesses cooperating with Escobar were arrested by the army in Cayara and "disappeared."

In August, Escobar examined and identified the three additional bodies that had been found. They included a woman, Jovita García Suárez, pregnant at the time of her death, killed by either a shattered cranium or a stab wound to the heart. Escobar and his team could carry back and conduct an autopsy on only her body; the others had to be left behind. Before they could be retrieved, the two remaining bodies were clandestinely removed from the site. But the initial examinations had confirmed that all three had been among those detained and taken away by the army on May 18. Escobar concluded that twenty-nine peasants had been murdered and forty-four had disappeared in the incidents.

Investigative commissions were constituted in both houses of Congress, with members appointed on May 23, 1988. In both houses, members of APRA, the ruling party, were named to preside. Both, and Sen. Carlos Enrique Melgar in particular, deliberately slowed the pace of the inquiries; when Americas Watch published a progress report in October 1988, neither panel had released any findings.

Melgar was consistently hostile toward prosecutor Escobar. When the two bodies of the May 18 detainees disappeared, he accused Escobar of conducting an illegal exhumation. At a meeting with Escobar, Melgar spent most of the time questioning the prosecutor's credentials. Escobar acceded at that meeting to Melgar's request for the names of witnesses, which until then had been kept strictly confidential. Several days later, five persons were arrested by the army in Cayara and then disappeared, one of them a key witness to the massacre. Melgar himself did not interview witnesses because, he said, he was not "an errand boy of theirs to go around running after witnesses."[5] When they finally visited Ayacucho in mid-June, Melgar and his delegation talked mainly to military authorities and avoided witnesses.

By September 1988 Carlos Escobar was receiving such serious threats to his life that he was obliged to be on the move constantly. He received no police protection; nor did the government offer his inquiry public political support. On the contrary, in October 1988 the prosecutor general ordered him to issue a final report and transferred the case to a provincial prosecutor in Cangallo. In November and December 1988 the Melgar Commission summoned Escobar to answer hostile questions about his conduct of the investigation. His final report had recommended that charges be filed against the political-military commander of the zone, Gen. José Valdivia Dueñas, but this had not been done. Rather, the provincial prosecutor who received the case detained and interrogated several witnesses in an army facility; he ordered the case closed when they recanted their previous testimony.

In December 1988 three witnesses to the massacre who had cooperated with Escobar's investigation, including the mayor of Cayara, were shot to death at an army roadblock.

The majority report of the Melgar Commission was issued in May 1989. It was signed by the APRA members of the commission only. The majority concluded "categorically that there was no abuse on the part of military personnel in Cayara." The report proposed that a legal action be initiated against Escobar for alleged misconduct of the investigation. And the majority expressed their congratulations to the Political Military Command of Ayacucho during 1988, "for its efficient work and spirit of struggle in the task of pacifying the area under their responsibility, a mission they fully achieved, respecting the legal order of the nation."[6]

Three minority reports were issued: one by Sen. José Navarro Grau, a political independent, who did not consider it possible to determine whether the army had been responsible for any crime in Cayara, and two by opposition Senators Gustavo Mohme Llona and Javier Diez Canseco. These two reports conclude that the massacre was "indisputably" the responsibility of General Valdivia Dueñas as commander and of the soldiers who carried out the killings. The reports further state that "everything leads to the supposition that facing the public denunciation of the massacre, the Political Military Command of Ayacucho took a decision to make the evidence disappear."[7]

In September 1989 a nurse named Marta Crisóstomo García was taken from her house and shot dead by eight men wearing hoods and army uniforms. She was the ninth witness to the massacre to have been executed or to have disappeared. She had identified her relative, Jovita García Suárez, and had testified to García's arrest by security forces. Marta Crisóstomo had been receiving threats for several months before her assassination but had not been afforded protection; indeed, she had been transferred to a job in a location that made her more vulnerable to attacks. The army began reportedly seeking a tenth witness, in Cayara, who was forced to flee.

The tremendous public outcry over the cover-up of Cayara forced the prosecutor general to reopen the case in late August 1989. No progress was made in the hands of the prosecutor of the province of Victor Fajardo, Ayacucho, and in January 1990 the case was definitively closed. Eleven months later, at President Fujimori's urging and with Senate consent, General Valdivia Dueñas was promoted.

Meanwhile, prosecutor Carlos Escobar, whose work in Ayacucho led to the reappearance of dozens of disappeared persons and whose investigation into Cayara made it possible for the Peruvian public to believe briefly in accountability, was forced to leave Peru in November 1989 because of threats to his life.[8]

THE LIMO COMMISSION: PARAMILITARY VIOLENCE

This commission, created in the Chamber of Deputies in June 1989, grew out of public concern generally about paramilitary violence and in particular about the assassinations of two deputies, Eriberto Arroyo Mío of the United Left and Pablo Li Ormeño of APRA—Arroyo closely identified with his peasant constituents in Piura and Li the owner of a small business in the Lima slum Villa El Salvador. After these deaths, a statement expressing consternation that the violence was not being investigated or controlled was sent to Congress with five hundred citizens' signatures.

The initiative to form the commission came from United Left deputy Manuel Piqueras, but rather than name an opposition figure to head the panel, the APRA majority in the chamber chose a party member, deputy Abdón Vílchez Melo. The commission's mandate was to investigate the killings of the two deputies and the overall activity of "terrorist groups named after martyrs," in particular the Comando Democrático Rodrigo Franco. Deputy Vílchez resigned in August to take another post and was replaced by APRA deputy César Limo Quiñones.

In its preliminary report, in late August, the commission cited 137 documented cases of violence by paramilitary groups, beginning with the July 1988 assassination of the lawyer Manuel Febres Flores, who had defended well-known senderistas.[9] Of the several groups that had proclaimed their existence, the commission believed that just two, the Comando Rodrigo Franco and the

Comando Manuel Santana Chiri, were real. Of the 137 cases noted, 65 were attributed to the Comando Rodrigo Franco, 5 to other groupings, 6 to presumed political kidnappings, and 10 to agents of the National Police or armed forces. The remainder were determined to be cases of arms possession or attacks. Paramilitary activity had been evident in several departments, but Lima, followed by Ayacucho, presented the most cases. The commission had also uncovered 15 cases of paramilitary group activity between 1985 and 1987.

Concerning the absence of police investigations into the violence, the report stated: "Everything indicates that there exists either an intentional attitude to not investigate these events or a dangerous operative inefficiency on the part of the entities responsible to confront this terrorist activity."[10]

Political pressures now became acute. Interior Minister Mantilla protested in a letter to the commission that "the campaign of calumny . . . of which I am the object is being generated from within the Commission" and sought the disqualification of United Left deputy Gustavo Espinoza as a member of the commission.[11] Mantilla's name had indeed frequently been associated with the Comando Rodrigo Franco. Commission chair Limo then publicly expressed his opinion that the existence of the Comando Rodrigo Franco had not been proven but that he suspected the existence of a paramilitary group linked to the left.

During the course of the commission's investigations, members received threats, and the daughter of Manuel Piqueras, the deputy whose initiative had led to the creation of the commission, was kidnapped briefly by unknowns who threatened her father.

As the commission continued its work, in September 1989 the testimony of a supposed deserter from the Comando Rodrigo Franco was published in the magazine *Oiga,* which frequently represents the views of hard-liners within the armed forces. According to this account, the Comando Rodrigo Franco began recruitment as early as 1983 and was completely identified with the APRA, while Agustín Mantilla, in close coordination with the National Police, had been one of its founders and principal figures.

The investigation took a turn late that month with the arrest of Jesús Miguel Ríos Sáenz, the sole survivor of an October 1987 bombing attack on the senderista newspaper *El Diario.* In that incident, the two other perpetrators had been killed and Ríos had been wounded; all were members of APRA. The commission had sought Ríos's arrest for months. But he was brought before the commission members without warning, right after his surprise arrest, and immediately after his appearance he was set free. Ríos denied knowing Mantilla or even being a member of APRA—a statement Mantilla himself contradicted. Although Ríos's testimony contained such basic contradictions and he refused to speak about certain known facts, Limo announced that he considered Ríos honest and believed Ríos to have been a victim, not a perpetrator, of the bombing of *El Diario.*

The Ríos case suggests the complexity of the paramilitary phenomenon in the context of Peruvian democracy. After the *El Diario* bombing Ríos, gravely wounded, was treated in the police hospital, but his medical record—for which he used a false name—later disappeared. Ríos had been photographed with Alan García while the APRA candidate was campaigning for president. The car driven by the *El Diario* attackers had been traced to Augusto Callejas, chief of logistics in the Interior Ministry.

Before opposition members of the commission could call Ríos for another appearance or seek testimony from Callejas, Limo ended the investigation. He did not produce a majority report until much later. He did, however, suggest that the opposition deputies Manuel Piqueras, Gustavo Espinoza, and Celso Sotomarino, who presented a minority report, were echoing assertions of the MRTA guerrilla organ *Cambio*. This innuendo, like Limo's earlier statements about possible leftist paramilitary activity, was an attempt to distract public attention from criticism of the APRA, and its tone was reproduced in the majority report, which played down evidence on the Comando Rodrigo Franco.

The minority report accused Interior Minister Mantilla, as well as two active-duty generals and one retired general, of being the key figures in the Comando Rodrigo Franco. It also urged that the APRA distance itself from the "individual practices of some of its militants" as a means to diminish violence in the country.

Because of the government's failure to cooperate, the special commission was a lost opportunity to investigate a troubling and apparently uncontrolled source of violence. Although the commission focused attention on the paramilitary groups, particularly the Comando Rodrigo Franco, a thorough inquiry, backed by the government's political will to halt paramilitary activity, remains to be done. Though not apparently coordinated, death-squad activity is still a serious problem in Peru, and although the Comando Rodrigo Franco as such appears to have reduced its activity, this may be less a sign of greater police efficiency than a happy coincidence, a reflection of the decline from power of the civilian elements—Mantilla in particular—that allegedly gave the group its political protection.

THE MOHME COMMISSION: CHUMBIVILCAS

Chumbivilcas is a province in the department of Cusco, an area that until recently had not been placed under state of emergency. Cusco department has a tradition of strong social organization, which made the difference in drawing congressional attention to the events that occurred between April 20 and 28, 1990, in Quiñota district. After the massacre occurred, a united campaign by peasant organizations, the education workers union, the mothers' club, and municipal and church authorities alerted Congress and human rights organizations, and the Chumbivilcas massacre became, like Cayara before it, a symbol to the nation as a whole.

A Senate commission was constituted on October 24, 1990, presided by Sen. Gustavo Mohme Llona of the Acción Política Socialista party and including two other well-known advocates of human rights, Sen. Raúl Ferrero Costa, whose Libertad party is associated with the political right, and Javier Diez Canseco, one of the more visible representatives of the legal left. The commission was initially empowered to investigate both Chumbivilcas and another set of events; more cases were later added to its mandate. The discussion here is limited to the first part of the inquiry; the September 22, 1990, massacre in San Pedro de Cachi, Huanta, Ayacucho, is covered in chapter 7, as it involves village self-defense patrols.

The communities affected in Chumbivilcas are particularly isolated and high, at more than thirteen thousand feet above sea level. In this area, hamlets lie some distance apart, with neither large road nor telegraph to unite them with the nearest cities. At the time of the events, neighboring provinces were under state of emergency (Antabamba and Cotabambas, in Apurímac, since 1987 and 1988, respectively; La Unión, in Arequipa, since March 1990), but the high provinces of Cusco, including Chumbivilcas, were not. The police held the responsibility for security, and the inhabitants theoretically enjoyed the exercise of all their constitutional rights.

The commission began its investigation in November 1990, and at the end of January 1991 traveled to the city of Cusco to interview witnesses. Its plan to follow the path of the guilty army patrol was frustrated by the Defense Ministry's failure to provide a requested helicopter. On May 28, 1991, the commission submitted its report to the Senate presidency. Its findings included not only murder but a catalog of other unprovoked acts of cruelty against civilians.

Between April 20 and 28, 1990, the Mohme commission found, twelve peasants had been executed and eight more had disappeared in the environs of Nanrapata and Ccasahui, district of Quiñota, Chumbivilcas. The assassins were a group of approximately twenty armed men in civilian clothing. Ballistics evidence revealed the use of light machine guns to kill most of the victims and grenades to kill two of them. Area residents testified that soldiers from the army base in Haquira, Apurímac, frequently patrolled Chumbivilcas, although it lay outside their area of authority. A patrol had passed through these communities no more than a month before the massacre, and during April 1990, the Buitre patrol from the Haquira base was carrying out operations in the nearby region of Inka, also part of Cusco. The commission found proof that the army base in Haquira knew that a patrol, dressed in civilian clothes, had been active in Chumbivilcas between April 21 and 30—clarifying that the patrol was not a rogue operation. Although the troops attempted to hide their equipment by wearing ponchos, witnesses stated that they performed in disciplined fashion, under orders from an officer believed to be a lieutenant, and that they used military terms and forms of address.[12]

The army later denied that its personnel had been in the area, but the various versions of its denial were contradictory. The minister of defense (a retired army general) suggested to the commission that subversives had committed the atrocity, and high army officials contended that radio transmissions indicating the presence of the patrol at the site of the massacre had been fabricated by those subversives; in this version of events, witnesses' testimony was described as coerced by Sendero Luminoso. The commission was unconvinced by this account, in part because the contention that armed opposition groups used grenades to blow up their victims had no precedent and in part because the radio transmissions were confirmed as authentic. Sendero does execute peasants, often brutally, but as the commission's report notes, it rarely does so without a so-called popular trial, which did not take place here.

The report establishes a probable sequence of events, based on forty-five sworn statements and the investigations of judicial and police authorities from the zone. The language it uses is unadorned: the words *torture, rape,* and *massacre* are all appropriately used. The reconstruction of more than a week of abusive activity is worth summarizing here in detail, as it reveals one way the "war" is being fought. The Mohme Commission's care in reconstructing the events also stands in salutary contrast to the Melgar Commission's majority report on Cayara. The Mohme Commission did, however, have the benefit of two factors lacking in the Cayara investigation: a well-organized, outraged population in the affected area, which translated into a wealth of testimony from survivors who refused to be intimidated, and the fact that the police, always in institutional competition with the army, supported a thorough investigation. Because Cusco remains something of an exception in Peru—it is an area where Sendero has had difficulty penetrating, where local organizations command authentic support, and where the church in particular has distinguished itself by its defense of both political and economic rights—so this investigation enjoyed exceptional advantages.

The Mohme Commission established that an army patrol composed of twenty-one soldiers on horseback, wearing civilian outer clothing but boots and undershirts of military issue and carrying identical weapons, began its operation on April 20 in a hamlet called Qochopata, in Totora Oropeza, Antabamba district, Apurímac. There they arrested a four-member family and, taking them to nearby Huanchullo, ordered the community to watch their interrogation; witnesses noted a total of five detainees—the family and an eight-year-old girl. Seven members of the community were arrested on the word of an informer brought along by the troops, and the soldiers interrogated villagers until about 3:00 A.M. on April 21, when they mounted their horses and had one of the detainees guide them to another hamlet, this one in Chumbivilcas province, Cusco. The detainees and the informer were taken along.

That day the commanding officer took half the patrol out with him, leaving instructions on how to interrogate the Huanchullo detainees. Those detainees were tortured by immersion in the near-freezing water of a river close by. The first detainee to be tortured in this way, a young man named Victor Huachaca, did not return; soldiers said he had paid them to be released. Around 7:00 P.M., however, when this portion of the patrol moved on, the remaining detainees saw soldiers bring something from the river bank and load it on a horse; later, in the hamlet of Puchungo, where the two halves of the patrol reunited around 11:00 P.M., soldiers could be heard with picks and shovels, evidently digging a grave. The victim's body was later recovered, bearing no bullet or knife wounds, which led the commission to presume that he had been drowned during interrogation.

In the hamlet of Puchungo on April 21, the half of the patrol led by the commanding officer detained, stripped, and tied members of two families and two visitors from a nearby town to interrogate them and later took their detainees down to the river, submerged them until they lost consciousness, and left them. When asked to identify one detainee as Sendero, however, the informer did not know him. That afternoon there was further punishment of the detainees, with the use of what the report calls "various methods of torture" and threats of death. While the women were forced to cook for the soldiers, the men were imprisoned in a room. Later, the head of the operative group raped one of the women, who was held overnight and raped by the other soldiers as well. A second woman detainee, raped by the commanding officer that evening, was raped by two other soldiers later that night.

On April 22 a campesino picked up by soldiers as he walked toward Puchungo was found wounded and dying on the ground; other peasants were detained, beaten, and held in the icy water. On April 23 in the Collama community in Quiñota district, a family was detained, beaten, and held with the others, and a woman who happened to cross paths with the patrol in the countryside was raped by the operative head of the patrol, called Negrón, and was later raped by the other soldiers until she lost consciousness. That day the patrol moved to the adjacent area of Tirani, taking seven prisoners and the eight-year-old girl, who, it seemed, was being held hostage until her father could be found. The soldiers entered the Chuchumake sector of the Tirani community, greeting villagers with a "good evening, compañeros," and when the campesinos politely responded in the same terms, the soldiers took their use of the word *compañero*—a term of kinship associated with the left—as proof of their adherence to Sendero. For having used that word five villagers and a visitor were tied and repeatedly submerged in icy river water for a period of about three hours under interrogation.

Elsewhere in the hamlet more people were detained and mistreated until the next day, when the patrol moved on; an elderly man, whose name is not known, died as a result of torture. On April 24 the woman arrested in the countryside and already the victim of multiple rape, was again raped repeatedly before being released.

Also on April 24, on the way to Nanrapata, part of the Collama community, the patrol arrested nine campesinos and tortured them to secure confessions that they were "terrorists." The following day, torture of other detainees included, aside from beatings and death threats, being forced to drink alcohol and, in one case, drinking alcohol with a sugar-like substance that made the victim lose consciousness. The wives of two detainees and the mother of a third, who walked to the community early on April 25 to show the patrol their relatives' documents and plead for their release, were tied by the neck and arms to large boulders and raped, and then held several hours before being released. In nearby Ccasahui that day, a portion of the patrol arrested others and spent the night there.

The massacre occurred on April 26 at about 9:00 A.M. The sixteen detainees (apart from the eight-year-old girl) were taken from their place of confinement in a house; four were separated from the others. One of the twelve who remained, an old man, was given liquor to which had been added a strange substance; he died that night in his sleep. The eleven remaining men were taken to a hilltop, where they were killed by explosives and machine gun fire. The patrol left Ccasahui at 11:00 A.M., passed through the community of Moscco in early evening and, around 7:00 p.m., arrived to spend the night in Accacco, in the sector of Palcca, bringing the four remaining detainees and the little girl hostage. Along the way they picked up another detainee, who promised to show them where arms were kept; in the house he indicated, there were no arms, but there were two women, whom the soldiers raped.

The next morning these women were stripped and taken to the river, where the soldiers beat and submerged them, demanding to know where their husbands kept the terrorist arms. When one of the women admitted that her father-in-law had a licensed pistol and showed the soldiers the gun and license, they let her free. Later that day the patrol arrived in Qochani, where the community had assembled to discuss the construction of a school. During this encounter the commanding officer wore a ski mask. One of the five detainees was questioned and ordered to point out a terrorist among the villagers; when he pointed out one man, the patrol took him prisoner. At 2:00 P.M. they arrived at the sector of Mosccopata, community of Moscco.

On this night, April 27, the patrol began to retrace its steps through Ccasahui and neighboring hamlets. Residents could see the flashlights of the soldiers and fled ahead of them. Entering the home of one of the women raped on April 25, the soldiers ate what food was available, occasionally going to the door to call out to the hiding villagers, "Come back, we are calm, nothing will happen to you." No one reappeared. On April 28, passing through Nanrapata, the patrol found it empty, killed a lamb, and slept in the abandoned place with their four detainees and the little girl. On the way to Tirani next day, the soldiers stripped and beat a peasant who was leading three horses loaded with wool, then took him prisoner as an accused terrorist. In Puchungo by early afternoon, they arrested another two men. The final day, April 30, two more arrests were reported as the patrol withdrew toward Antabamba.

The Mohme Commission concluded that the army base in Haquira maintained effective control of the area in which the abuses occurred, as evidenced from the irregular but frequent patrols and radio communications with the police base in Santo Tomás, the provincial capital. Although unable to identify the abusers by name, the commission could establish that the Buitre patrol from the Haquira base had been in the area around the crucial dates.

Pointing out that the crime had been compounded by authorities' attempts to cover it up, the commission laid political responsibility at the door of the Defense Ministry, naming Gen. Julio Velásquez Giacarini (minister at the time of the massacre) and retired Gen. Jorge Torres Aciego (minister at the time of the investigation) as having acquiesced in a grave violation of human rights. Facing the probability that the case would eventually go to military courts, the commission noted that "impunity constitutes an indispensable component" of the crimes and that active interference in legal investigations—like the attempted cover-up—is punishable as harshly as the original crime. To that "primary complicity," said the report, should be added charges of obstruction of justice.[13] The commission demanded legal action against the commanding officer of the Haquira base, against Gen. Petronio Fernández Dávila Carnero, then chief of the Political Military Command of Ayacucho, and against Colonel Calle, the military commander in Apurímac. As for the defense minister, General Torres Aciego, the report recommended that the Chamber of Deputies consider stripping him of his immunity from prosecution.

The report on Chumbivilcas was the first major investigation of a human rights case to be instituted after President Fujimori took office, and it did not concern abuses carried out during his administration. It was, however, his defense minister who had attempted the cover-up, a controversial precedent. And in May 1991, as the report on Chumbivilcas was being completed, the Senate determined that the senators comprising the Mohme commission should investigate a group of four disappearances that had indeed occurred under Fujimori only two months earlier (the Chuschi disappearances are described in chapter 6).

Four of every five houses in Peru lack running water, sewage disposal, and electricity, as this slum outside Lima in 1989 illustrates. Photo © Vera Lentz/Black Star.

People from the slums march to the palace in Lima to protest their lack of water, 1989. Photo © Vera Lentz/Black Star.

Armed guards protect participants in a rally preceding the 1990 presidential election. Photo © Vera Lentz/Black Star.

Peruvians enter the polls to vote in the 1990 presidential election. Photo © Vera Lentz/Black Star.

Ayacucho, 1991. Photo © Marcelo Montecino.

Girls from Seches Lambra, Ayacucho, drilling for civil defense in 1989. Photo ©
Vera Lentz/Black Star.

A civil defense patrol in Ayacucho, 1989. Photo © Vera Lentz/Black Star.

Villagers from Urpay, Ayacucho, watch as a campesino's body is examined, 1990.
Photo © Vera Lentz/Black Star.

Campesino killed by Sendero Luminoso while serving in a civil defense patrol in
Urpay, Ayacucho, 1990. Photo © Vera Lentz/Black Star.

Lurigancho Prison, where in 1986 Sendero Luminoso inmates staged a riot that was brutally quelled, resulting in the massacre of more than two hundred inmates, many of them killed after laying down their weapons. Photo © Vera Lentz/Black Star.

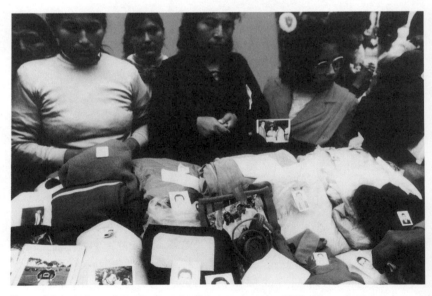

Funeral for victims of the Lurigancho Prison massacre, 1986. Photo © Vera Lentz/Black Star.

MRTA political prisoners in the maximum security prison of Canto Grande in 1989. Forty-eight members of the MRTA escaped from Canto Grande in 1990. Photo © Vera Lentz/Black Star.

Uchiza police post after a five-hour battle with Sendero Luminoso in 1989 that resulted in Sendero's capture and execution of ten police officers. Photo © Vera Lentz/Black Star.

Eradicating coca plants in the Upper Huallaga River valley, 1989. Photo © Vera Lentz/Black Star.

Family picking coca in the Upper Huallaga River valley, 1985. Photo © Vera Lentz/Black Star.

5

VIOLATIONS OF THE LAWS
OF WAR BY INSURGENTS

The standards set forth in Common Article 3 of the four Geneva Conventions of 1949 explicitly address conflicts that are not of an international character. Americas Watch applies these standards where insurgent forces do not exercise formal, consistent control over population or territory, as is the case in Peru.[1] We do not discount the possibility that, if current trends continue, Sendero may function as a quasi-government in some part of Peru in the relatively near future, but available data indicate that this situation had not been achieved by late 1991.

The minimum rules contained in Common Article 3 stipulate that persons taking no active part in the hostilities, including members of the armed forces who have laid down their arms or have been placed hors de combat for any reason, shall be treated humanely in all circumstances. Common Article 3 therefore prohibits, in the treatment of such persons: violence to life and person, in particular murder of all kinds, mutilation, cruel treatment, or torture; taking of hostages; outrages upon personal dignity, in particular humiliating and degrading treatment; and the passing of sentences and the carrying out of executions without previous judgment pronounced by a regularly constituted court, affording all the judicial guarantees that are recognized as indispensable by civilized peoples.

The text of Common Article 3 explains that application of the article does not affect the legal status of the parties to a conflict, and Americas Watch, in applying this standard, confers no special status on the insurgent forces in Peru.

Both Sendero Luminoso and the Movimiento Revolucionario Túpac Amaru MRTA have violated Common Article 3; Sendero in fact kills many more unarmed persons than it does soldiers in combat. Americas Watch condemns these acts in the strongest possible terms.

INSURGENT IDEOLOGY AND MILITARY PROGRESS

By the middle of 1991, close observers of the Sendero phenomenon were estimating that the insurgents held a shifting, relative control over at least 10 percent of the national territory, in areas where the absence of legal authorities or other government presence left Sendero without competition. As expert Gustavo Gorriti describes Sendero "control" of an area, it means that Sendero directs communal affairs, including education, security, and taxes. The military may be able to recover control of the area—in fact, there are few areas where Sendero's control is not superficial and to some degree enforced by terror—but the state does not have continuity.[2] Obviously, when territorial control is so fluid it is extremely difficult to estimate the number of people under Sendero "control." Sendero's military organization includes three levels of involvement and skill: the base or local level is composed of persons who drill irregularly with such crude weapons as knives or sticks and who, in combat, are most likely to be used as cannon fodder; the regional level includes militants with somewhat more sophisticated training; and the principal level, which is well trained, consists of the armed combatants, the nearest Sendero approximation of an army. As Gorriti points out, the margin for error in estimates of Sendero armed strength is enormous, and estimates of 3,000–5,000 fighters at the principal level—the figures most often cited in recent years—should be seen in that light.[3] The insurgents' semiclandestine front organizations, described below, also blur the line between military control and political influence.

As noted in chapter 1, Sendero Luminoso began among university students, principally in Huamanga, the capital of Ayacucho, and built on a thirst for autonomy and empowerment among the indigenous people of the sierra, who are among the poorest in Peru and the most abandoned by white-Lima cultural values and government. Sendero gathered support among the campesinos of Ayacucho, Huancavelica, and Apurímac, although its political discourse is not sensitive to traditional indigenous demands or culture and although, as C. I. Degregori points out, the Sendero concept of revolutionary authority is pyramidal, with the educated—the owners of the absolute truth—on the top and the poor majority on the bottom.[4] The cult of knowledge, the equation of education with virtue and progress, were aspects of the highland peoples' attitudes on which Sendero's elitism could build. Originating in a 1964 split in the Partido Comunista del Perú, the ideology of Sendero is not traditionally Marxist-Leninist but is rather more Maoist; it combines fundamentalism at the administrative level—as witness its program of enforcing strictly self-sufficient local agriculture to maintain its bases separate from the corrupted urban centers and bourgeois economy—with a generally Maoist military strategy of progress from the countryside to the cities through prolonged popular war. Though highly pragmatic in politico-military tactics, Sendero is absolutist in its definition of its mission. The movement's favorite words are *destroy, eradicate, erase,* and *dismantle.* What is to replace the dismantled system is not clearly defined; the party's newspaper, *El Diario,* which circulates clandestinely since it was closed by the government in 1989, published the Sendero platform of government in early 1991, and apart from a commitment to promote the rights of women, the platform referred overwhelmingly to what would be wiped out rather than what would be built. But as ignorance is associated with vice, Sendero has a moralistic streak that reinforces values of discipline and anti-individualism (adherence to absolute values). In a society where the state is, and has long been, perceived by the highland peoples as dispensing a corrupted, racist justice—or where the state's justice system does not even effectively reach—Sendero has offered justice of a moralistic kind, such as its punishments of drunkards and adulterers (and traitors and enemies) and its insistence that the public witness its "people's trials." There is about its taste for killing a strain of zealous, ritual purification as well as the pragmatic assertion of power over life and death.

Sendero announced the beginning of its prolonged popular war on May 18, 1980. That was the day of the elections to return Peru to civilian rule, and Sendero proclaimed the outset of its struggle by stealing ballot boxes in Chuschi, Ayacucho, and declaring an election boycott. Typical of its taste for ritual, the insurgency celebrates that anniversary every year with a spate of violence.

Having formed a base in the 1970s—while the military's so-called vigilance failed entirely to foresee or control its growth—Sendero faced and withstood the repression of Fernando Belaúnde's government, which peaked in 1983 and 1984. When Alan García criticized human rights abuses in 1985, attempting to curb those assaults on the populace, Sendero took full advantage of this political space and the army's unpopularity to expand. Wherever the state has attempted to exercise a civic-action strategy—less repression and more political contact with the people, more sensitivity to their economic and social needs—Sendero has sought to eliminate that space of dialogue and, through military actions and the calling of armed strikes (*paros armados,* or enforced work stoppages), to create chaos that will force the state to harden its line. This exacerbation of antagonism between citizens and state has been combined with a campaign to eliminate representatives of the state and leaders of independent popular organizations—possible bridges between state authority and the masses. That Sendero did not need to invent the antagonism and that these bridges already lacked cohesive state support, should be evident from previous examples provided in this book.

In 1988 Sendero forced the state to extend emergency authority into part or all of Huánuco, Pasco, San Martín, Callao, metropolitan Lima, and, toward the end of the year, Junín. The García government recognized its failure to woo the population away from Sendero. This failure was due not just to the state's limited resources and vision but to Sendero's strengths: on the positive side, the genuine support it retained, especially in the highlands, and the mutually beneficial arrangement it offered the coca-growing peasants of the Upper Huallaga Valley; on the negative side, its considerable use of terror to establish and maintain control. Like the army, Sendero does not recognize the right to neutrality.

Sendero determined in 1988 to increase the pressure and to advance, in its terms, toward "strategic equilibrium," a condition it describes as the prelude to the final offensive. *El Diario* asserted in May 1991 that strategic equilibrium had been achieved, based on military and political progress made in the previous two years. Although the claim appears exaggerated, the guerrillas' progress has indeed been significant.

During 1989 the conflict spread to new areas of Peru, becoming particularly intense in the eastern and central departments of Ucayali and Junín as well as in the north-central departments of San Martín and Huánuco, which contain the Upper Huallaga Valley (the history of coca cultivation and the insurgency in the Upper Huallaga is discussed in chapter 8). Eight of the nation's twenty-four departments experienced persistent conflict, and in parts of four political violence had increased perceptibly. The coastal department of Ancash and the southeastern department of Puno, for example, were both areas that, though not under state of emergency, saw a significant rise in insurgent actions; parts of Puno were placed under emergency authority the following year. And Lima was the target of about one-third of the violent actions by insurgent groups during 1989, primarily acts of sabotage or political actions accompanied by intimidation.

By the end of that year, Sendero Luminoso was active in twenty-one of Peru's twenty-four departments; its armed strength was most frequently estimated at three thousand fighters. The MRTA and Sendero confronted one another in Junín, and the MRTA was also responsible for actions on the coast, in Huánuco, and elsewhere. It is important to note, however, that although the insurgent presence spread over more territory, neither Sendero nor even less the MRTA, had the military capacity to engage directly with the armed forces except through lightning attacks or ambushes; their reliance on terror was a compensation for this relative weakness. The exception to this rule was Sendero's activity in the Upper Huallaga Valley during early 1989, the first time Sendero deployed regular combat columns and engaged in prolonged battles with the army. The army's all-out retaliation in July, however, held back the Sendero expansion for the rest of the year. In general, during 1989 Sendero engaged in fewer direct confrontations with the military and increased its attacks on the campesino population in areas where villagers resisted Sendero's presence. As civil-defense patrols expanded during 1990, Sendero concentrated attacks on their members as representatives of the state's military policies.

Important regional differences presented the insurgent groups with varying degrees of popular support and resistance. Sendero's continuing attempts to penetrate Puno, for example, were strongly resisted by the well-organized campesino movement and the regional church, which supported campesino demands. Although the insurgency made progress here during 1990 and most of the department was militarized by mid-1991, Sendero progress was slower than elsewhere. Sendero had more success in Junín, a crucial area; Lima's food supplies and principal source of electricity, as well as the major mines of Peru, are concentrated there. Junín has a complex social fabric, including not only such developed sectors as mines and industry but also campesinos. It had been considered relatively immune to Sendero because of its level of commercial and social development, so different from the extreme isolation of Ayacucho and the other departments of long-standing Sendero activity.

The penetration of Junín's central rain forest became even more decisive a political and military factor in 1990 and 1991, for Junín has been and is expected to become again the scene of conflict between the army and Sendero, between Sendero and the MRTA, between the armed forces and the MRTA, between newly created civil defense patrols and the two insurgent groups— with all these forces preying on, exhorting, and seeking to control the civilian population. The elements at work in Junín also include the cultivation of coca along a central corridor and into the Ene River valley in the southeastern section of the department. This eastward-facing section of Junín borders Pasco department to the east and, to the south, Ayacucho's provinces of Huanta and Huamanga, where Sendero began. Control of the Ene, for which Sendero fought in 1990, currently permits the insurgents to travel by water into Ayacucho. And for several months in 1990 Sendero administered in the Ene River area its first clearly defined zone of control, an area that Gustavo Gorriti has estimated at 7,000–7,700 square miles, approximately the size of Kuwait. Two places in this general area where Sendero has maintained an especially strong and fortified presence are a stretch of caves at the mouth of the Anapata River in Satipo province and the environs of Puerto Prado, where the Ene and Apurímac rivers meet.[5]

In Ayacucho, Sendero's original stronghold, there have been recent signs that the population has become sufficiently organized against the insurgency to present it with difficulties and that at least part of the population has become exhausted by Sendero. Sendero's paros armados during 1989 and 1990, for example, were not completely successful; those in opposition to the second-round vote in the presidential elections of June 10, 1990, were a signal failure, as the population voted massively for Fujimori rather than support the Sendero boycott. When Sendero called a paro armado in response to the Fujimori economic shock measures of August 1990, this, too, was unsuccessful, in spite of crippling price increases and the betrayal of promises that the measures represented. And villages in some parts of Ayacucho voluntarily formed self-defense patrols (*rondas campesinas* or *montoneras*) in opposition to Sendero during 1990. Nonetheless, Sendero presence in Ayacucho, as in neighboring Apurímac and Huancavelica, has remained strong.

In early 1990 there were some signs of internal tensions within Sendero, reportedly due to a difference over whether to pursue a purely military strategy or one combining military and political tactics. Observers in Peru were uncertain as to how seriously these signs—such as a reported division among the Sendero prisoners in Canto Grande—should be taken. Whatever the extent of these problems, they seemed to have been resolved by the end of the year.

Sendero is, in fact, omnipresent in Peru. It has created a political presence in urban settings with organizations that speak for it and call for specific mass actions. These front organizations, which have been part of the Sendero strategy since its beginnings, seek alliances with legal and representative organizations of the dispossessed—unions, women's groups, neighborhood associations in the slums—and infiltrate those organizations with an aim to provoking conflicts between the established leadership and the members. The front organizations are on the social plane what Sendero's military tactics are in the field of military and political authority: they polarize, they eliminate dialogue. These expressions of *senderismo,* whose names tend to call attention to their "class," "popular," and "resistance" character, also spread the word and practice of Sendero with the aim of creating a cohesive popular movement, critical in the plan to take over the cities. Like Sendero's Comités Populares Abiertos, where members must produce in communal fashion, eat at the same time, and share tasks, the political fronts are a training ground, often organized by work sector, to shape the "new" culture or "new" economy. At the critical moment, these adherents are to join with seasoned Sendero fighters to deliver the final blow. When a sector resists Sendero penetration in this manner—as many labor unions have—its leaders are killed.

In the countryside, Sendero support committees operate openly in some towns, their authority derived either from genuine support for Sendero or from fear of it. Another mechanism of control is Sendero's selection of "delegates" responsible for reporting on village events, residents' movements, and the like. Delegates do not always volunteer, in which case they are drafted, and if they do not comply with the requirements of their position, they are killed. A common scenario for such executions is the constitution of a "popular court" by invading

Sendero fighters; the victim is found guilty before the population and executed, in precisely the type of exercise that Common Article 3 condemns.

The MRTA is a more traditionally leftist insurgent group that began as an urban guerrilla movement in the 1960s. It has a certain base of support among the poor in Lima but lags well behind Sendero in its presence in rural Peru. A statement by the Interior Ministry in June 1989 indicated that the MRTA was active in the northern part of San Martín department and nearby provinces in Loreto, as well as the rain forest areas of Huánuco, Pasco, and Junín and the area around Pucallpa in Ucayali department. By the end of 1990 the MRTA had established itself as the clearly dominant of the two insurgent groups in the Central Huallaga valley, which stretches north from Juanjuí, in San Martín, and is thus north of the Upper Huallaga; this became its principal base. It had suffered reverses in the central sierra during 1989;[6] during 1990 its presence in the central region of the country was expressed through activities more urban and political than rural or military.

Like Sendero, the MRTA has increasingly focused its energy on Lima and its environs and suffered a setback when the 1990 elections drew greater than usual participation. But the insurgent groups, often violent competitors, have strong differences. The first is ideological and programmatic: the MRTA's ideology is closer to that of Peru's legal left than to Sendero, and its objectives are less clear than Sendero's, a problem exacerbated both by the post–Cold War crisis of the left throughout Latin America and specifically by the splits and quarrels of Peruvian leftist parties. The second is a difference of self-image: while Sendero emerged from a Maoist tradition and attempts to extend its almost cultish influence beyond Peru, it is largely sui generis; the MRTA, by contrast, locates itself within a long and international—if currently confused—leftist tradition. The third is a matter of style: whereas Sendero has the uncanny mystique of the unstoppable, the juggernaut, the MRTA is a much more familiar phenomenon and compensates for its smaller numbers by staging actions with flair—such as the July 1990 escape from Canto Grande prison of forty-eight top fighters, the video released later that was purportedly filmed during the escape, the March 1991 escape by veteran fighter Lucero Cumpa (her second in nine months), and the May 1991 capture of and negotiations over nine police officers in Rioja, San Martín. If by such actions the MRTA seeks to create a romantic public image, the flip side is high-profile assassinations, kidnappings, and indiscriminate bombings that endanger civilian life. The MRTA acts to some extent by reacting—to momentary political conditions, to Sendero initiatives. But like Sendero, the MRTA has tended, on a far smaller scale and more selectively, to commit ruthless acts of violence.

There is a moralistic streak in the MRTA, as in Sendero; the group has murdered homosexuals, for example, to "clean up" society in Tarapoto, San Martín, and this alienated some of its political base. And both groups deal ambiguously with the narcotraffickers in their zones of activity. Sendero, in the Upper Huallaga, collects a tithe from those who wish to use landing strips and otherwise operate unmolested, although it does not appear to be directly involved in the drug trade. During 1988 and 1989, Sendero also served as negotiating agent for the peasant *cocaleros,* the growers of coca; it wanted to tie the peasants to its program in the region, and the peasants needed a go-between and protector with the traffickers, representatives of the Colombian drug cartel. The MRTA's relations with the traffickers, in San Martín, are also a mixture of principle and opportunism; in 1988 the policy was to confront traffickers and drive them out, but there are now many signs that the MRTA tolerates the drug traffic—for example, by collecting "taxes" on the use of airstrips. Social workers with experience in the Central Huallaga told Americas Watch in May 1991 of incidents in which residents of towns in San Martín had met with the MRTA representatives to demand the MRTA stop protecting the "narcos," who bring violence and corruption with them and destroy the social fabric of an area as surely as the armed conflict.

Both the MRTA and Sendero Luminoso operate in San Martín and Ucayali, and in 1990 and early 1991 there were bloody battles between the two. Conflict between the groups was also reported in Puno in early 1991. The rain forests of Junín, where the MRTA was routed in 1990 and is trying to reinsert itself militarily, are a third theater of confrontation. As this study is completed, Peruvian observers expect an escalation of violence between insurgent groups in the central rain forest, and Huancayo, the capital of Junín, has become the leading city for assassinations, where the military, Sendero, and the MRTA are all active and in competition.

VIOLATIONS BY SENDERO LUMINOSO

Sendero has been responsible for selective assassinations, group killings, kidnappings, and an indeterminable number of threats of death and other acts of intimidation against unarmed civilians and peasants organized for self-defense. Its principal targets since 1988 have been representatives of the state, leaders of campesino and labor organizations, and peasant communities in areas where it has sought to establish or maintain control. These practices are consistent with Sendero's tactics in previous years. There can be no question that murder of the defenseless, often in grotesque fashion, is Sendero policy.

Sendero Luminoso systematically undermines the presence of the state in its areas of action, targeting especially mayors, governors, and the personnel of development programs. A study done by the human rights group Comisión de Derechos Humanos (COMISEDH) on the first seven months of 1989 details the assassinations of twenty-five mayors by Sendero in the departments of Lima, Junín, San Martín, Pasco, Cajamarca, Puno, La Libertad, Huánuco, Ancash, Ucayali, and Huancavelica. During the same period, Sendero assassinated ten governors and lieutenant-governors, six engineers and officials of development projects, seven judicial officials, and nineteen other public officials, according to the COMISEDH study.[7] From January through October, 46 mayors were killed by Sendero, and a further 263, facing death threats, resigned.[8] By year's end, 52 mayors had been assassinated by Sendero. The magnitude of this campaign, and subsequent attacks on public officials, have had the desired effect: in the municipal elections of August 18, 1991, for example, such was Sendero violence against political candidates and so great was the fear of Sendero reprisals that, as of a week before the vote, 123 districts—more than a fourth of the 435 districts nationwide—had not registered any candidates.[9]

Persons not holding public office but known to be active in their political party are also victimized. While professor Marcial Capelletti Cisneroshe of the San Cristóbal University of Huamanga, Ayacucho, was giving an examination to forty students on May 29, 1989, his classroom was invaded by three armed members of Sendero, who shot him twice. Capelletti was the brother of an APRA deputy and worked closely with the party, but he was a full-time teacher at the university. Operating on similar logic, senderistas took over a day care center in Chimbote, Ancash, on October 10 and, rounding up the teachers, threatened to kill the children of local APRA members and politicians.

The Sendero campaign against representatives of the state in 1989 reached its peak in the period leading up to the November 12 municipal elections. In areas where it was active, Sendero assassinated mayors, mayoral candidates and their immediate relatives, and local electoral officials. Although candidates of all major parties were victimized, Sendero appeared to concentrate on representatives of the United Left coalition, which it considers a rival for the loyalties of organized labor and campesinos.

Among the most notorious acts of terror was the September 19, 1989, assassination of Fermín Azparrent Taype, mayor of Huamanga, the capital of Ayacucho. Azparrent, representing the United Left, had organized neighborhoods in Huamanga to resist the paros armados promoted by Sendero in 1988; he also outspokenly denounced abuses of human rights by the military. As a result, he told the press a few weeks before his murder, he had already suffered seven attempts on his life: four by Sendero and three by the Comando Democrático Rodrigo Franco. Sendero took credit for the assassination—something it rarely does—through a communiqué that called Azparrent an "agent of Russian social imperialism and servant of the APRA government whose execution is a severe warning to those who wish to be candidates in the electoral farce."[10]

The funeral for Azparrent, attended by more than five thousand residents of Huamanga, transformed itself into a march for peace. Nevertheless, all candidates for mayor but one resigned because of threats by Sendero; the remaining candidate was attacked by Sendero on October 25 but survived. After the elections, there were Sendero reprisals against the newly elected authorities. Some were killed, while others resigned under threat of death. Sendero also took revenge, especially in rural areas, against those who had voted. A typical case occurred on December 21, 1989, in the village of Pallqa, district of Sacsamarca, within Ayacucho department. Some seventy senderistas entered the village and murdered eleven campesinos for having voted, first wounding them with machetes and then shooting them in front of their families.

Sendero's expansion into new areas and its control of old ones is often contested by peasants. Where it has found resistance among campesino organizations, Sendero executes leaders of those organizations. In the first seven months of 1989, senderistas assassinated forty-seven local leaders, most of them from peasant communities.[11] Where the villages resisted with community self-defense patrols, Sendero targeted these patrols.[12]

Some or all of these elements are present in the following examples of Sendero executions:

- On April 12, 1989, in the province of Chongos Alto, Junín, a column of fifty to sixty senderistas split into two groups for a coordinated action. One group attacked a bus on its way to Huancayo, the departmental capital, and detained some twenty passengers, whose documents they examined and compared with a list they carried; the other group took the town of Chongos Alto, the provincial seat, and rounded up a number of people who lived in nearby towns. The two Sendero groups reunited in Chongos Alto to hold trial. Accusing their more than twenty detainees of wanting to organize self-defense patrols and of being representatives of "the old state," they separated twelve persons on their list who were former or current local authorities, "sentenced" them, and shot them in the head or back. Those who had not been killed were forced to set the town meeting center and local clinic afire.
- A series of coordinated attacks on December 11, 1989, in response to the formation of civil defense patrols in the provinces of La Mar and Huamanga left fifty Ayacucho peasants dead. In the district of Vinchos in Huamanga Sendero simultaneously took three communities and assassinated dozens of peasants before their neighbors and relatives. One account put the dead in the communities of Paccha, Andabamba, and Chaquispampa at thirty-nine and described the

weapons used as firearms, sticks, and stones. Other sources concur on the number of deaths but suggest that in at least sixteen cases, and possibly all, the victims' throats were slit. In La Mar, another Sendero contingent attacked the communities of Vicus and Tanyac, in Tambo district, searching from house to house for members of the self-defense patrols and rounding these up in the central square. Eleven people were executed, including the area president of the rondas.

- On April 12, 1990, Sendero attacked the village of Naylamp de Sonomoro, a hamlet in the district of Mazamari, Satipo province, Junín. (The background of this incident is described below, in the section on self-defense patrols.) According to agricultural specialists who visit the zone, Sendero entered the village in a column composed of men, women, and children. The men sought out specific people and executed them; then the women and children killed others. Finally, they burned the houses and the bodies. Some thirty-five residents of Naylamp were murdered and twenty-six were wounded, according to these sources; some bodies were burned beyond recognition.

Sendero has also murdered members of the police force whom they had captured and disarmed. One incident that outraged public opinion occurred on March 27, 1989, at the police post in Uchiza, Mariscal Cáceres province, San Martín. The post had been established less than a month earlier and was garrisoned by fifty-seven police led by Maj. Carlos Farfán Cárdenas. Sendero attacked with mortars and set fire to the post, and a five-hour battle ensued, during which Maj. Farfán requested help from the U.S. constructed antidrug base in Santa Lucía nearby. Although the Ministry of Defense attempted to send reinforcements, a combination of factors prevented help from being sent, and Sendero captured the post. The police surrendered. The insurgents identified the officers and separated them from their subordinates, then called the population of Uchiza into the main square, held a "popular trial," and executed the officers. In all, ten law officers were killed and fourteen were wounded. Major Farfán was forced to raise the flag of the hammer and sickle over the town square and then was murdered. According to *El Diario*, Farfán "was executed . . . by a child combatant nine years old, who shot him in the head."[13] This claim is not inconceivable, as Sendero is known to kidnap and forcibly indoctrinate young boys. *El Diario* also stated, however, that the major's throat was slit.[14]

The conflict in the Upper Huallaga—the coca-growing region where the police post was located—put that area virtually off limits to journalists because of the conflict, but on November 17, 1989, an American freelance reporter, Todd Smith, traveled from the U.S. antidrug base in Santa Lucía to Uchiza without army protection. His body was found on November 21 near Uchiza's main square; he had been strangled, and a note signed by Sendero Luminoso had been left on his body. The sequence of events that led to his death was in doubt, as it was suspected that drug traffickers may also have played a role; Sendero is believed to have been involved at least in kidnapping Smith and perhaps in executing him. And this was not the first time Sendero had been implicated in killing a journalist. The previous January, Luis Piccone, a Peruvian journalist working with Radio Independencia, was shot in Ica, south of Lima, by a gunman believed to be a member of Sendero. On April 16, 1989, presumed senderistas killed Austrian journalist Josef Peischer, press director for a development project in Ucayali, accusing him of being a CIA agent. And on May 31 in Huancavelica, Sendero beat to death Peru's foremost environmental journalist, Barbara D'Achille, who had been working for the Lima daily *El Comercio*. One of her traveling companions, engineer Esteban Bohórquez, was shot and killed.

In 1990, for the presidential and parliamentary elections of April 8, Sendero again threatened the lives of candidates and voters. On March 17, Interior Minister Agustín Mantilla revealed intelligence of a Sendero plan to assassinate candidates of all political tendencies. As of March 28, police and military protection had been given to the nearly 3,500 candidates, and life insurance was given to voting officials. The elections commission decided not to require the inking of voters' fingers after they voted in emergency zones to prevent reprisals by Sendero.

Sendero nevertheless launched a campaign of executions. The day before the elections, for example, Sendero attacked the village of Pampachacra, in Ayacucho, and executed seventeen people, most of them old men, women, and children who remained at home while others had left to vote. Sendero caused a blackout in Lima on April 11, 1990, and took advantage of the darkness to assassinate a police officer and a labor leader. On April 17 the former mayor of Chiquián, in Ancash department, was executed by presumed senderistas. A "liquidation squad" of Sendero assassinated two police officers in Lima on April 26. The weeks before and following the April 8, 1990, elections, according to Senator Bernales of the Senate's commission on violence in Peru, were "the most violent of the decade" because of such actions as these.[15]

In keeping with its effort to penetrate the areas just north and south of Lima, and thus progress toward its goal of strangling the capital, Sendero was active during 1990 in such coastal provinces as Huaral, Barranca, and Huaura, in Lima department, striking at agricultural businesses and their owners. In Huaura, the agricultural businesspeople now pay Sendero for their security; and there Sendero assassinated conservative political figure Javier Puiggrós Planas on November 23, 1990. This execution was one of the most vehemently condemned of Sendero's crimes that year.

Javier Puiggrós Planas, an engineer and national secretary for Campesino Affairs of the conservative Partido Popular Cristiano (PPC, a member of the FREDEMO electoral coalition), was also owner of a plantation in Vilcahuara, province of Huaura. On November 23, around 7:00 A.M., Puiggrós arrived at the farm to pay workers' salaries, and a column of more than twenty Sendero fighters entered the farm in a truck shortly thereafter. Among the senderistas was a woman who called herself Chata. Having located Puiggrós, the senderistas brought him before the workers and berated him for mistreating them. The workers protested that Puiggrós was a decent man and asked the guerrillas not to kill him.

While under interrogation, Puiggrós was tied hand and foot and mistreated physically, but when workers attempted to help him they were threatened with harm. According to a witness, the helpless captive was executed with four shots to the chest. Other senderistas, meanwhile, sabotaged farm equipment and buildings. The administrator of the plantation, Manuel Salazar, was kidnapped and executed, his body left for police to find.

Similarly, on September 21, some two hundred Sendero combatants entered five farms on the outskirts of Pisco, destroying property and submitting one farm owner, Luis de Bernardi Crovetto, to a "popular trial" and executing him. Two days later, in Lima, former APRA senator and labor minister Orestes Rodríguez was assassinated with his son Oscar as they returned from a sports activity. A parliamentarian of the current governing party Cambio 90, Alejandro Vicoria Mendoza, was murdered by Sendero on December 16.

Police work in Lima that led to the arrests of seventeen alleged Sendero members in January 1991 did not slow the pace of the group's violence. A week after the widely publicized arrests, Sendero struck back in Lima with a series of almost sixty violent attacks. On February 23, a Sendero column invaded the hamlet of Ccano, Ayacucho, and killed twenty-three campesinos before robbing and burning their huts. A week later, on March 1, another column entered Pago Mantaro, La Mar province, Ayacucho; among its thirteen victims there were old people and children.

A single month's recent reporting by a human rights organization provides the following examples of Sendero brutality:[16]

- On June 24, 1991, a Sendero column entered Huatasani, Huancané province, Puno department, burning a handicrafts workshop supported by the local church and murdering three recently arrived policemen and a former local official.

- On July 2, again in Huancané province, Puno—this time in Moho district—some thirty senderistas took over a hamlet for four hours and left six dead, among them an agricultural engineer and a veterinarian working with an aid project, as well as the president of a federation of agricultural cooperatives and two peasants from the community of Caluyo, whom they had kidnapped shortly before.
- On July 9, the mayor of Huacrapuquio district, Huancayo, Junín, was assassinated by Sendero members outside his house. The thirty-two-year-old mayor, Tito Quispe Yupanqui, had received several death threats for refusing to resign.
- On July 12, economics professor Iván Pérez Ruibal, a Cusco city official and leader of the regional branch of the leftist PCP Unidad party, was shot to death by Sendero while preparing for classes in the university. Sendero warned "revisionists and collaborators of the government" that they could expect similar reprisals.
- On July 13, the leader of the civil defense patrollers of Alto and Bajo Tulumayo, Concepción, Junín, was executed by Sendero. Just two weeks before, the victim, Leoncio Enrique de la Cruz, had received arms personally from President Fujimori for the civil defense campaign.
- On July 16, Sendero kidnapped the mayor of the province of San Antonio de Putina, Puno, along with several other officials. The mayor's body appeared on July 25 in another province; the remaining captives were freed.
- On July 17, four workers with World Vision, an evangelist development agency, went missing between Lima and Andahuaylas, Apurímac. On July 23 their dynamited truck reappeared; those dead on board included the four missing workers and the Andahuaylas provincial general secretary of Cambio 90, the governing party.
- On July 19, Adalberto Campos Otiniano, chief of security for the University of San Marcos in Lima, was assassinated by senderistas while returning home in his car. Campos had cooperated with the army when soldiers had searched the university for subversives.
- On July 26, six peasants were shot to death by presumed senderistas in two hamlets near the airport of Huancabamba, Andahuaylas.
- Also on July 26, in an attempt to enforce a stoppage of economic activity in Cerro de Pasco, department of Pasco, senderistas killed an entire family and set fire to two interprovincial buses. This action was part of a campaign to intimidate the population in Junín, Pasco, Huancavelica, Ayacucho, and Puno departments and permit a show

of Sendero strength in those areas during the festivities surrounding the national independence day.

The month of August was, if possible, even more bloody: on August 2, for example, senderistas killed four engineers and thirteen members of civil defense patrols in Huancavelica, and on August 15, fifty miners in Huancavelica were killed, presumably by Sendero.[17]

In the latter months of 1991 Sendero was directing some of its hostility at foreigners and church workers. Sendero executed a Soviet technician in Lima on June 5, and Japanese have become particular targets, no doubt because of President Fujimori's extraction. Three Japanese with a development project were assassinated on July 12, and a Peruvian of Japanese descent, businessman Manuel Inamine Shimabukuro, was murdered by Sendero on July 24. Two Polish priests of the Franciscan order were executed on August 10 on the outskirts of Pariacoto, Huaraz province, Ancash; the two had been working with base communities for a year and a half and were much admired. Earlier, on May 21, Sister Irene McCormick, an Australian nun, was assassinated in Huasa-huasi, in Tarma province, Junín, along with four town officials. This campaign continued into September, when senderistas held an Italian priest hostage in Apurímac and a Peruvian priest in Chimbote was forced to flee senderistas seeking him out for execution.

It is important to note that Sendero not only takes vengeance on the civilian population; it also uses people as shields for its fighting units. Forcible recruitment of civilians, including women and children, pads its attack force, so that the most valuable, best-trained combatants are protected by the bodies of the "expendable." As the Bernales Commission's report on 1990 commented, a portion of the dead officially counted as subversives are likely to be "people forced to join and to participate in military incursions."[18] Women and children are often drafted into the military-imposed civil defense patrols (see chapter 7); Sendero's forced recruitment is the other face of this coin.

VIOLATIONS BY THE MOVIMIENTO REVOLUCIONARIO TÚPAC AMARU

During 1989 and 1990 the MRTA carried out one sensational and prolonged kidnapping, assassinated a former minister of the government, and engaged in other selective executions. Although the scope of its actions is not to be compared to Sendero's, the actions themselves are equally condemnable. The MRTA was having difficulty presenting itself as the armed front of the social movements of the poor, which rejected this association; it also suffered military setbacks at the hands of the army and police. These two factors may have contributed to its engaging in terrorist acts that it had avoided in earlier years. Examples of the MRTA's actions during this period follow:

- On March 3, 1989, members of the MRTA assassinated the mayor of Pillhuana, near Tarapoto, San Martín, as well as the area governor and judge.
- In Tarapoto and in Pucallpa, Ucayali, the MRTA targeted people whom they considered to be bad social influences. MRTA flyers circulated in poor urban neighborhoods condemning to death all homosexuals, drug addicts, and prostitutes, and in May 1989, eight such presumed delinquents were murdered in Tarapoto. The MRTA took credit for the killings and justified the murders as a measure against crime.
- The group threatened popular leaders in San Martín, ultimately executing Julio César Sánchez Vela, general secretary of the Educational Workers Union and president of a broad front of popular organizations in Shapaja, on November 4, 1989.
- The MRTA kidnapped Héctor Delgado Parker, a powerful businessman and close personal friend of Alan García, on October 4, 1989, and did not release him until seven months later. During the kidnapping Delgado's chauffeur was shot to death and his bodyguards were wounded.
- On December 8, 1989, the MRTA assassinated Alejandro Calderón Espinoza, president of the Asociación de Nativos del Pichis (ANAP), which represents Ashaninka indigenous communities around the Pichis River in Pasco. In the same incident, two Ashaninka villagers were kidnapped and later executed. The MRTA accused Calderón and the others of having twenty-five years earlier turned over to the army a guerrilla leader, Máximo Velando of MIR (Movimiento de Izquierda Revolucionaria), which was then active in the area. In addition, the MRTA charged Calderón with being a key to the military's plans to form local paramilitary groups. The killing of Calderón set off a chain of violent events and backfired on the MRTA both politically and militarily—a portion of the Ashaninka population went on a rampage, apparently with army and navy support, in search of MRTA suspects—and the MRTA later regretted the action in public (see also chapter 7).
- The MRTA assassinated retired army general Enrique López Albújar Trint on January 9, 1990, in Lima's San Isidro district, accusing him of involvement in an April 1989 confrontation in Jauja, Junín, in

which sixty-two MRTA members and others died, allegedly in "combat" with the armed forces, without leaving any wounded or survivors (see chapter 6). General López Albújar was the defense minister at the time of those killings. His assassination was not only a clear violation of the laws of war, as retired military officers no longer take part in a conflict, but it was also an act of extreme military provocation, one that could have resulted in a reaction against democratic institutions.

- On November 16, 1990, the MRTA assassinated a Lima judge, César Ruiz Trigoso, who was linked with the forcible removal of squatters from private land. Specifically, Judge Ruiz had ordered the eviction of families occupying El Naranjal farm, in Los Olivos, Lima, in April.[19] A few days before his death, Ruiz had also ordered the eviction of workers who had occupied a factory in support of salary demands; in that operation a minor died and ten workers were wounded. Nonetheless, the affected union condemned the assassination.

In early 1991 the MRTA placed bombs in places with heavy civilian traffic, like the environs of government buildings and police barracks; fortunately, these seldom exploded. It also targeted certain foreign entities. During January and February, protesting the war in the Persian Gulf, the MRTA dynamited the Lima Pizza Hut and Kentucky Fried Chicken, several Mormon churches, the Italian embassy, and the U.S.-Peruvian Institute, among other targets, and twice shot rocket-propelled grenades—antitank weapons—at the U.S. embassy, on one occasion spraying the front of the building with bullets at midday. By sheer chance, the missiles had been aimed too high to severely damage the U.S. embassy, and there, as well as at the other targets, there were no casualties.

GOVERNMENT POLICY AND THE LAW OF WAR

International humanitarian law, or the law of war, is little known in Peru on either side. In November 1991, after Americas Watch released an open letter to Sendero leader Abimael Guzmán holding him responsible for a war crime committed by his followers, President Fujimori issued an official communiqué charging Americas Watch with legitimating the insurgents. Not only did this accusation contradict the president's other critique of Americas Watch— namely, that the organization allegedly does not denounce rebel abuses—but it displayed a lamentable, possibly willful, ignorance of Common Article 3, whose application does not confer legitimacy.

MRTA leaders appear to understand the relevant law, while respecting it mainly under circumstances of their choosing. A notable example is the MRTA's post-battle capture of nine police officers in Rioja, San Martín, in May 1991. The rebels cited humanitarian law for political advantage in this case. But the government mishandled the incident, revealing how far behind events is its appreciation of its circumstances. The government's ignorance of the law of war and of the mandate of the International Committee of the Red Cross (ICRC) as a humanitarian agency operating under law-of-war guidelines were painfully apparent.

On the night of May 10, 1991, an MRTA force entered the town of Rioja and attacked the police post there after having blacked out the town. Police resisted for about two hours, making radio calls for help as far away as Tarapoto and even Lima. The nearest potential reinforcements, in Moyabamba, fifteen miles away, were blocked at the road out of that town by two trucks evidently occupied by MRTA fighters, who engaged them in gunfire. In Rioja, the two senior police officers proved incompetent and left the defense to nine subordinates, who were taken prisoner. The MRTA communicated to the International Committee of the Red Cross its willingness to turn over captives; immediately on receiving the message on May 13, the ICRC representative in Lima informed the government and made clear the organization's willingness to receive the prisoners as a humanitarian gesture. This is the sort of handover for which the ICRC was constituted, and it has nothing to do with political negotiations or with defining the guerrilla group in question as a belligerent in the conflict.[20]

Normally, the ICRC keeps such communications secret, but in this case the government so misrepresented the ICRC's prospective role that the organization was forced to clarify its position publicly. First, on May 14, the newspapers carried declarations by the defense minister that the government had rejected ICRC intervention, before that position had been communicated privately to the ICRC. Second, the defense minister's statements referred to negotiation, which had been mentioned by neither the MRTA nor the ICRC. An additional incongruency was that, having signed an antidrug agreement with the United States that very day in which it is stipulated that the ICRC shall be given unrestricted access to carry out its humanitarian work, the government was now refusing the ICRC such access. The contradiction was neither explained nor, perhaps, understood by the government.

The police officers were released within a month and had not been mistreated; the incident ended without major mishap. Because the capture of the police was legitimate wartime conduct, Americas Watch is disturbed that the government did not manage this situation with greater sophistication. In a conflict where so few are wounded and captured, humanitarian considerations dictate efficient, informed responses to any situation in which prisoners have been taken and may be spared. Furthermore, although the government's reluctance to give publicity or any shred of legitimation to the MRTA is understandable, the rebels received more attention from official delays and public anxiety over this case than they would have received had the ICRC performed its customary quick, discreet work.

The MRTA is often guilty of violating the laws of war, and Americas Watch urges that it perform in future cases as it did in this one, such that captives, whether military or civilian, may enjoy the protections to which they are entitled.

6

HUMAN RIGHTS VIOLATIONS

As the U.S. Department of State summarized the situation during 1989, "There is little oversight of military activities in the emergency zones by civilian judges or prosecutors, and the constitutional rights of persons detained by the military are routinely ignored."[1] By the end of that year, nine of Peru's twenty-four departments, and part of a tenth, were being governed under state of emergency. The rights to free assembly, free movement, and inviolability of the home were suspended for 47 percent of the Peruvian population. During 1990, areas not formerly affected, like part or all of the departments of Ancash, Cusco, La Libertad, Piura, and Puno, came under state of emergency authority for part or all of the year.[2] Reporting on 1990, the State Department noted that the "number of provinces declared in emergency for at least part of the year [rose] by seven . . . , the ninth straight annual increase" and that "[s]ecurity forces personnel were responsible for widespread and egregious human rights violations."[3] By April 1991, the portion of the population living under effective military control had increased to 55 percent and the national territory affected had spread to nearly 40 percent.[4]

The Fujimori government occasionally has used emergency procedures in an original fashion. When imposing economic shock measures in August 1990, for example, the government applied the state of emergency to Lima and ten other important cities. In Lima this was the first time the military rather than the Interior Ministry had been given ultimate power to enforce the emergency measures, in effect temporarily suspending civilian government control. In October the city of Huamanga, Ayacucho, was relieved of its state of emergency, but the symbol and locus of authority for the state of emergency—the Political Military Command, or PMC, which supposedly exists only in state of emergency—remained in place.[5] The lines between peace and war, between civilian control and military authority, have become steadily harder to draw.

The model for emergency authority in Peru is the PMC first established in Ayacucho. The PMC for each emergency zone, which may comprise more than one department, is commanded by an army general who holds the post for a

year. The police come under the PMC's overall authority, as do civilian government personnel. Proposals to strengthen civilian authority in the emergency
zones are frequently made in Peru, but no progress has been noticeable during
the past several years. If anything, the intensification of terror and the spread of
the conflict have thinned the ranks of elected officials, judges, prosecutors, and
other civilians who might counterbalance the army's overbearing and abusive
practices. Manuel Espinoza, the provincial mayor for Leoncio Prado, department of Huánuco, for example, was the last mayor active in the entire province
until he was assassinated by Sendero Luminoso on June 15, 1989. Nor do
conditions permit journalists to report systematically from emergency zones;
the work is too dangerous in many places, and the PMC does not generally
welcome reporters. The press must rely on military accounts of confrontations
with the insurgency and on the military's definition of the dead.

The Peruvian military and police have varied their counterinsurgency tactics
during the past decade, but at no time has the civilian population not been
victimized in the campaign. The navy and the Sinchis—counterinsurgency
units of what was then the Civil Guard—were initially as active, and as harsh,
as the army is now. A counterinsurgency expert in Ayacucho told the *New York
Times* in 1984: "The idea is to reduce the terrorists to their hard core by using
greater terror."[6] In this campaign, the Peruvian government profited by the
experience of Argentina, where in the 1970s the military had fought an urban
guerrilla movement with disappearances and murder, in the process killing
thousands of peaceful opponents to authoritarian rule. The *New York Times*
cited Peruvian intelligence sources who said that Argentine experts in interrogation and intelligence were training Peruvian military officers in both Peru
and Argentina.[7] Thus were the basic methods established under Belaúnde, and
1984 was a peak year for repression. The rate of disappearances and political
killings decreased somewhat with the advent of Alan García's government, but
abuses did not end, and by 1988 their numbers were rising quickly once more.
As was noted in chapter 1, in 1989 and 1990 killings were more numerous than
in any year since 1984, and, not surprisingly, most of the dead were in two
categories—civilians killed by Sendero, and supposed subversives (some of
whom are believed to be civilians) killed by the forces of order, paramilitary
groups, and civil defense patrols.

At the same time, since the beginning of the counterinsurgency campaign
some within the military have urged that military force not be substituted for an
integrated approach to the social and economic causes of the conflict. General
Adrián Huamán Centeno, commander of the PMC in Ayacucho for a brief seven
months in 1984, blamed government corruption and disinterest in the region for
the rise of Sendero. His opinion was echoed in the late 1980s by retired Gen.
Sinesio Jarama and Gen. Alberto Arciniega, among others. The argument is

somewhat self-serving: the military ruled for twelve years while Sendero was in gestation and appears not to have understood the phenomenon. But civilian governments have been equally—and, since 1980, in the face of all reason—neglectful. These military men argue that the armed forces have been forced to assume the debts incurred by a profligate civilian political structure, and they wish to win the battle they confront. Considerations of practicality lead them to seek allies in the population. Theirs has not, unfortunately, been the dominant view for any appreciable period during the past decade.

Americas Watch has frequently denounced the Peruvian army's abusive treatment of the population in the emergency zone. The army's aggressiveness toward rural civilians goes along with a general failure to protect that population from Sendero terror. As evidence of this grotesque dual pressure, peasant communities frequently call for more army and police presence, even while complaining of mistreatment by official forces.

Each PMC commander enjoys substantial autonomy, and if one thing is clear, it is the inconsistency of counterinsurgency tactics both among different areas of the country and over time within an area.[8] But as a general matter, the army in rural emergency zones has little interaction with civilian communities except as an occupying force, because army patrols tend to be rapid operations; soldiers are reluctant to risk a Sendero ambush. After these operations, the military retire to their barracks and leave the population to Sendero reprisals. Another factor that affects the distance between the military and population in the emergency zones is that most soldiers historically come from the coastal areas and lack either knowledge of or sympathy for the racially, linguistically, and culturally different people of the interior. The Defense Ministry promised in 1991 to correct this practice by assigning soldiers to their home areas, but whether this was part of the government's overall public-relations effort to humanize the military's image or whether it will be put into practice remains to be seen.[9]

During the past several years the bulk of human rights violations by official and officially tolerated forces have occurred in the emergency zones, but there have also been serious abuses in other areas—parts of Cusco and Puno, for example, before they were placed under military authority—and the victims, though still predominantly campesinos, included labor leaders, students, and professionals. Apart from abuses associated with the rural counterinsurgency campaign, a notable development since the late 1980s has been the wider use of force by police who, sometimes in conjunction with the military, have suppressed peaceful protest gatherings, conducted wholesale arrests in poor Lima neighborhoods in the wake of Sendero actions, and invaded universities in search of Sendero sympathizers.

According to the police official responsible for metropolitan Lima, Col. Victor Torres Sarmiento, from January 1988 through October 1990 the police carried out nearly fifty thousand countersubversive operations in the capital with 2.5 million "interventions" (detentions short of arrest) resulting. This extraordinary figure represents nearly four in every ten Lima residents.[10]

Those arrested in sweeps were generally held no longer than the fifteen days allowed by law in cases of suspected terrorism, according to Peruvian human rights monitors; many were held for less. This is an improvement over past practices of holding detainees for long periods on manifestly unfounded charges of terrorism, as occurred under Belaúnde. But the scope of these arrests is cause for concern. Mistreatment during and after arrest in such cases is routine, and according to these same sources, there are cases in which detainees have been freed only after paying the necessary bribe.

Police forces were reorganized during 1989 and united under a joint National Police command. The police service in charge of investigating crimes and preparing sworn statements of the accused before they are tried—formerly called the Policía de Investigaciones (PIP)—was renamed the Policía Técnica. The police patrolling in the countryside, formerly the infamous Guardia Civil of brutal practices in the early eighties, was renamed Policía General.

Alan García defined 1989 as the year of all-out effort against Sendero. He called on the population to identify itself with the effort to combat subversion and terrorism by supporting the army and police and, in rural zones of emergency, by forming community self-defense patrols. At the same time, the government's defense of the military and police translated into a policy of impunity that seriously undermined public confidence. This contradiction was not resolved by the time García left office. Paramilitary groups murdered labor leaders and politicians while the police were notoriously unable to discover the culprits. In rural areas the self-defense patrols proliferated with complex and often bloody results, increasing the problem of analyzing whether campesino dead should be considered combat casualties or victims of extrajudicial execution.

In the first year of the Fujimori government, there has been no evident new coherence in counterinsurgency thinking or protection for the population. Through the last months of 1990, after his inauguration, Peruvians expected their new president to offer a fresh approach to counterinsurgency, but he did not. In the meantime the army distinguished itself by ineptitude in some cases, like the failure to stop Sendero from attacking the Mobil Oil subsidiary in the Upper Huallaga valley—an incident which, as a congressional commission determined, involved army negligence and passivity (see chapter 9). The emphasis on self-defense patrols, explored in chapter 7, has been accompanied by a forceful campaign to improve the military's image. But the results are mixed in different parts of the country; in Junín, for example, where conflict has intensified since early 1990, there is active confrontation with Sendero in particular but also heavy loss of civilian life. Junín, which was placed under emergency authority only in late 1988, led the country in political deaths in 1990, with a total of 719 for the year.[11] Human rights groups note that during 1990, press accounts and other evidence showed that the greatest number of confrontations with guerrillas was carried out by self-defense patrols rather than the military, a development that is also evident in the relatively modest figures for military dead during the year. The rate of reported disappearances nationwide has declined somewhat since 1989, but authoritative sources are divided as to whether that change is real, and in any event the practice is unacceptable (see chapter 1). During Fujimori's first year in office, Peruvian human rights organizations registered more than 230 unresolved disappearance cases. During 1991, meanwhile, the rate of political deaths began to accelerate again, threatening to rival 1989 or even 1984.[12] In sum, the situation remains bleak.

SUPPRESSION OF PEACEFUL PROTEST

The economic crisis has led to organized protests by campesino and labor movements throughout the 1980s. These legal and peaceful manifestations of discontent, including those involving the right to strike, are frequently suppressed.

On February 1, 1989, for example, hundreds of workers from various unions demonstrated in Lima to protest a package of price increases announced the day before. About fifty were arrested. Six days later, state employees demonstrated in Lima over economic demands; this sector has been one of the most affected by the collapse of real wages, with a fall for 1989 of almost 50 percent.[13] Police officers violently suppressed the demonstration, leaving five wounded and thirty-five detained.

Similar tactics resulted in 8 dead, dozens wounded, and some 350 persons detained in Pucallpa, Ucayali, on February 9, 1989. A peasant gathering called in support of an ongoing general strike by campesinos in the eastern departments of Peru was attacked by police, who shot into the crowd. Among those detained was the secretary general of the departmental federation of campesinos. Many of the detainees were forcibly removed from places where they had taken refuge from police gunfire. The Interior Ministry, in a communiqué issued the same day, stated that the gathering had been the work of agitators and that police had been forced to fire after those agitators had overturned a police car and attacked its occupants. A videotape of the events showed clearly that this version was untrue, that the gathering was proceeding peacefully when police opened fire.

Civil construction workers in Lima demanding wage increases mounted a demonstration on July 6, 1989, to protest the latest resolution of the Labor Ministry, and after the protest, as they returned to their headquarters for a meeting, police officers approached five with the intention of detaining them. When their companions called for help, police fired on the workers, killing one and wounding another. They then reportedly attempted to force their way into union headquarters while workers fought back with stones; three more workers were wounded in the incident. The funeral for Mamani Romero, the worker who had been killed, became an act of protest attended by workers and union and community leaders. Government officials, meanwhile, implied that the police had been attacked by terrorists who had infiltrated the labor movement.

Another incident of violence occurred on October 16, 1989, near the Ministry of Education in Lima. The ministry's workers had been on strike for nearly a month, and some fifty were demonstrating in support of the strike; they were joined by about eighty striking police officers. When police cars and patrol wagons arrived to break up the demonstration, the striking police and the on-duty police exchanged fire, leaving one demonstrator dead and three seriously wounded.

In a communiqué issued in mid-August 1989, at the start of a nationwide strike, the miners' federation stated that between May 1988 and May 1989, more than a thousand of its members had been arrested and a hundred had been wounded by gunshot and that fourteen leaders had been assassinated—eight by Sendero, three by the Comando Democrático Rodrigo Franco death squad, which operates with official tolerance, two by police forces, and one by the armed forces.[14] The suppression of peaceful and legal dissent continued into 1990. On April 24, for example, police officers attacked striking workers of the Health Ministry, beating several seriously. Labor activists were also subjected to other abuses, as described below, because of legal organizing and strikes.

Sadly, the new government has done no better. When an Americas Watch representative visited Peru in May 1991, the daily marches by striking professors and health-sector workers were being dispersed by police with beatings and tear gas and televised nightly. The health care workers had been on strike for over two months without a negotiating offer from the government. Peruvians commented wryly that while the country found itself at the mercy of cholera, the effective paralysis of the health care system had hardly been noticed, so neglected and impoverished had the system become in recent years. But the sight of police beating demonstrators for demands known to be reasonable—indeed, essential for survival—was a painful reminder of Peru's dearth of options.

Loss of buying power led to other strikes in early 1991, among them a peasant strike in Cusco starting March 17 to protest the government's agrarian policy. Confrontations between police and peasants during the first week of the strike left three campesinos dead and seven wounded. The minimum wage at the time was equivalent to sixty dollars a month.

RAIDS AND MASSIVE DETENTIONS

Massive detentions by army, police, and combined forces have long been a feature of the counterinsurgency strategy in zones of emergency, and have occurred in nonemergency rural zones as well. One danger of these operations in the emergency zones is that they often lead to disappearances. Particularly vulnerable are refugees from areas of conflict, who attract the suspicion of the authorities by virtue of their origin.[15] These families commonly flee their homes without identity documents, as Sendero destroys local registries; or the armed forces tear or break or fail to return identity documents when a displaced person is held and questioned. The lack of documents makes them obvious criminal suspects. These destitute citizens are also harassed as a group because anyone coming from a zone of conflict is immediately suspected of sympathizing with Sendero. Many have fled to Lima, where they fare best if they recreate their previous community ties or at least find others from the same province. The displaced thus tend to settle together, and their settlements are easily targeted by the security forces.

An example is the settlement called Justicia, Paz, y Vida (Justice, Peace, and Life) in Huancayo, Junín, which was invaded by some three thousand members of combined police and military forces on April 26, 1989. Fifteen residents were detained for having books and articles on political subjects. To prevent robbery of residents' belongings, which is common in such raids, and to prevent the disappearance of any detainee, community leaders monitored the authorities' progress block by block. The raid lasted from 4:00 A.M. to 4:00 P.M.

In Puno, where the state of emergency was not in force in 1989, police carried out massive detentions. Tensions in the area had been growing, and the police reportedly identified the campesino movement and leaders of leftist parties with the insurgency. Such attitudes have prevailed for years in zones where Sendero is strong. Puno in particular is notable because hostility to popular organizations there is frankly counterproductive: the organized campesino movement is the very thing that has prevented Sendero from becoming established in Puno.

In recent years as insurgent violence has spread to the coastal cities, especially to Lima, the military and police have adapted tactics of counterinsurgency to urban conditions—that is, in the wake of Sendero or MRTA actions, the forces of order have commonly rounded up slum dwellers or students to investigate them for possible links to armed groups. The destruction of personal or institutional property has often accompanied these sweeps. When combined forces of the army and police raided the University of San Marcos and the Enrique Guzmán y Valle–La Cantuta National University in Lima on April 16, 1989, the University Council of San Marcos protested that about three hundred students had been arrested and taken to undisclosed locations, while official forces had destroyed or stolen books, photocopy machines, food, and money from safes in deans' offices. An official communiqué stated that the raids had been based on intelligence of terrorist activity in the universities and that arms and explosive devices had been found there; university authorities and students denied the charges. The official communiqué reported the number of detainees at 518, of whom 30 were held on suspicion of terrorism and the rest released.

On April 25, police raided the San Antonio Abad University, Cusco. On June 6, for the second time in 1989, the National Central University, in Huancayo, Junín, was raided, and in spite of a dean's protest that no evidence of terrorist activity had been found even after several such raids, a third took place on July 21—with more than fifty students arrested—and a fourth around the time of the November 12 municipal elections. In the tense period surrounding those elections, universities were raided in Huamanga (Ayacucho), Huancayo, Callao, and Lima.

At San Marcos University in Lima, university authorities protested the violence with which soldiers and police had detained some fifty students and the disappearance of one of the detainees. Even in Arequipa—a southern department not under state of emergency at the time—police raided San Agustín University on December 6; after failing to find subversive material here, however, the police made no arrests.

On June 6, 1989, in Lima, some four hundred persons were detained after a police sweep through Villa El Salvador, a highly organized slum neighborhood. The purpose of the raid was to find subversives. Villa El Salvador has a history of leftist sympathy and has been a focus of Sendero efforts to find an urban base, but until the end of the García administration the neighborhood effectively resisted Sendero attempts to infiltrate its community organizations. In a similar raid carried out by the army, on June 16 in the Huaycán settlement in Lima, eight hundred persons were detained.

Sweeps during 1989 were concentrated in November, in conjunction with the municipal elections. On November 2, the Sendero newspaper *El Diario* was shut down because it had called for the assassination of several public figures and had hailed Sendero executions of municipal candidates. After closing the paper, the armed forces and police raided universities and shantytowns in Lima. On November 9, soldiers and police occupied the Huanta shantytown, in the San Juan de Lurigancho district of Lima, treating the residents violently and destroying their meager belongings. Most people in this settlement were refugees from the emergency zone. More than two hundred persons were detained after a similar operation by combined forces on November 11 in the Huaycán settlement in Lima.

There are Sendero sympathizers and members among students in Peru, and Sendero plays on the disaffection and lack of prospects of Peruvian youth to appeal to them. The universities, as elsewhere in Latin America, are cradles of rebellious thinking of all kinds; Sendero's revolutionary ideology, and its beginnings among intellectuals, make the university a natural place for it to proselytize. The obvious social marginality and frustration of slum dwellers make them targets of Sendero recruitment. But to punish entire communities for the actions of Sendero in their midst—rather than offer support for organizations and individuals that reject Sendero—is a strategy both abusive and counterproductive. It is also disturbing that the Peruvian public has paid so little attention to these developments, as if they have been a necessary cost of the counterinsurgency effort.

In early 1990 massive detentions peaked around the elections of April 8. In response to Sendero actions in Lima the week after the elections, the police detained more than 2,500 persons. After the July 9 mass escape of top MRTA members from the Canto Grande penitentiary, police carried out some 5,000 detentions in the prison's surrounding areas, and residents of the Huanta settlement complained that police not only arrested persons arbitrarily but robbed homes as well. According to the human rights organization CeaPaz (Centro de Estudios y Acción para la Paz), in the first ten months of the year 69 percent of detentions in Lima were "preventive" and just 20 percent "investigatory."[16]

Some of the raids on settlements, such as several in April 1990, were unrelated to the security situation but were characterized by the same gross abuse of authority and impunity. In one raid intended to evict squatters, on April 14, dozens of families living on a former plantation in Bocanegra, Lima, were confronted by police using tear gas and guns; one child was shot to death and more than fifteen other children nearly suffocated from the tear gas. When the families tried to resettle in the same place on April 26, police used tear gas and sticks, seriously wounding some of the squatters.

In another incident on April 20, 1990, police sought to evict ten thousand families from El Naranjal, a plantation on the outskirts of Lima, using tear gas, bullets, and buckshot (the use of which is prohibited), wounding seventy people, mainly women and children, and burning the shanties. According to squatters' denunciations, the judge who ordered the eviction did so after residents refused to meet his demand for a bribe.[17] Interior Minister Mantilla visited the site two days later, accompanied by doctors to tend the wounded. Mantilla announced that there was insufficient evidence of abuse on which to start an official inquiry. Such tolerance of abuse obviously promotes rather than contains disaffection.

If such incidents depict the style of the later García years, another gives a glimpse of the Fujimori style. The president, having determined that Sendero graffiti on the university walls should be covered over, arrived at La Cantuta University in Lima on May 21, 1991, bringing with him members of the army carrying paintbrushes and paint. No one at the university had been given advance notice of the visit, but a group of pro-Sendero students were ready for Fujimori and pelted him with insults and stones. In response he ordered that the whitewashing proceed and that the students' rooms be raided. The following day the police arrested thirty students and passed them to DIRCOTE for questioning as to their presumed links to Sendero. University authorities protested both the violence of the raid and the government's failure to consult them, while supporting aims of the action. On May 23, Fujimori told the press that the government would continue "with a physical cleaning" and "cleanings of other kinds to achieve an academic climate of discipline and seriousness," arguing— for the benefit of those who might cite traditions of university autonomy—that the universities had already lost their autonomy. "Our presence on the university campus has not violated any university autonomy; on the contrary, university autonomy has been lost because there is not freedom of expression or self-government, there is rather a disorder that must be corrected."[18] Protest against the raid was minimal.

TORTURE

The army and police both practice torture systematically in Peru. Persons who "reappear," after a period of unacknowledged detention in army centers, describe extensive torture under interrogation. Persons suspected of terrorism and held by police suffer the same treatment, although in Lima this appears to have diminished in recent years. Street-crime suspects in police custody are commonly beaten under interrogation. When the bodies of "disappeared" persons are discovered, many bear marks of torture. Women and girls who are detained in the emergency zone frequently report being sexually abused.[19] As with other grave forms of human rights violations, the victims are principally campesinos of the emergency zone. In a typical case, Deputy Alejandro Olivera Vila denounced that during the week of February 27 to March 3, 1989, sixty people in Junín were detained and tortured by members of the army. Cases involving victims from other social sectors follow:

- Víctor Taype, president of the National Federation of Mining and Metallurgical Workers—a union that represents eighty thousand workers in a strategic industry, making Taype one of the foremost labor figures in the country—was detained by police on November 20, 1989, in Huancavelica department and tortured throughout that night until early morning the next day. He was later accused of "apology for terrorism." The accusation was widely perceived as an attempt to intimidate the union, which had struck Peru's major mines in the last half of August and had experienced various forms of repression for more than a year.[20]
- On October 5, 1989, hooded men forced construction worker Alberto López Bautista from his home in Ayacucho and took him to the army barracks in Huamanga called Los Cabitos, where he was severely tortured. A local prosecutor ordered his case transferred to Lima on the grounds that in Ayacucho his life was in danger.
- On November 1, 1989, the Federation of Yanesha Native Communities denounced the army's detention and torture of members of the native community of Izcozacín, in Pasco department.
- A doctor, Carlos Reaño, was detained by police in Cajamarca on September 8, 1989, and tortured for several days thereafter. This case became well known because it is one of the few in which the torture of a detainee was medically verified and made public, by representatives of the medical association who visited Reaño in detention. Reaño was hung by his wrists for so long that he suffered permanent damage to his right arm.
- Outside the emergency zone during 1989, in Puno department, the local Vicarías de la Solidaridad of the Catholic church and other human rights organizations reported numerous cases of campesinos detained on suspicion of terrorist association and tortured extensively, then freed for lack of evidence. In Puno in August 1989, a grave was discovered containing the corpses of five persons bearing marks of torture, which local investigators did not believe to be the work of Sendero.

Most cases receive neither judicial nor medical attention. Torture is so frequent a practice—on common-crime suspects as well as those detained on suspicion of terrorism—and the courts have been so ineffectual in responding to denunciations that few cases reach public notice. Even in the case of Víctor Taype, the Instituto de Defensa Legal, a legal aid and documentation group, noted how little attention the media and political leaders paid his torture.

The same was true of torture cases that occurred during the first year of Fujimori's government. Perhaps the most widely publicized of these was the spectacular case of Fidel Intusca Fernández, driver for a mining concern in Ayacucho.

Intusca was told to present himself, on August 6, 1990, at the army base in Puquio, Ayacucho, to answer questions concerning an August 2 incursion by Sendero. In that action, senderistas had attacked a mine site and stolen explosives. Intusca was released after questioning and was returning to the mine site with his wife and son and other miners when their truck was intercepted by six men who, according to a statement Intusca gave the human rights group APRODEH (Asociación Pro-Derechos Humanos), "wore ponchos and ski masks and the shoes and uniforms of the 'milicos' [slang for 'military']." His abductors took him blindfolded to an unknown place, speaking against the military and calling him a spy for the army, using the term *compañero* and other watchwords of the left to give him the impression that they were guerrillas. He became aware that he was near the army base; then he was taken inside, where he was tortured for four or five hours under interrogation about Sendero sympathizers in the mine and the whereabouts of the stolen explosives. In addition to being kicked and beaten, he was blindfolded, and submerged in water with bound wrists and ankles about six times until he lost consciousness. The officer in charge was the same major with whom he had spoken earlier that day; Intusca recognized his voice. That night Intusca managed to escape while his guard slept. Had he not, human rights monitors in Peru believe he would have been killed.

Intusca's union denounced the torture to Congress and provoked an investigation. Although the facts could hardly be disputed, Fujimori's defense minister, retired Gen. Jorge Torres Aciego, sent an army report to the investigating commission in which he claimed that "the Armed Forces have no connection whatsoever with the tortures suffered by the miner Intusca" and called Intusca's denunciation a Sendero ploy to discredit the army.[21] Fidel Intusca was forced to leave his home area for his security.

Three other cases during the first year of the new government demonstrate, by their differences, the wide range of situations in which torture is occurring in Peru. The first involves gross abuse of power by police, without an apparent counterinsurgency motive; the second indicates the lengths to which the army has gone to dispose of torture victims in the emergency zones; the third portrays a range of abuses of the rural population, including torture leading to death.

- Juan Apolinario González, thirty-seven, a trade union leader at a Lima paper factory, was detained on March 10, 1991, in the neighborhood of Paramonga. In reporting on his case, Amnesty International noted that workers at the paper factory had been on strike for approximately two weeks when the detention occurred; this may have been a cause of the harassment he suffered. Police forced him inside a police vehicle, where they beat him. They then transported him to Security Police headquarters, where—supposedly to make him confess to breaking the windshield of the police car—he was beaten, nearly drowned, and given electric shocks. He was released without charges on March 12 and subsequently denounced the torture to the human rights authorities of the government. In making the denunciation, he was risking sustained harassment by the police, as his union supporters pointed out.

- Professor Moisés Tenorio Banda, of the Naranjillo-Rioja community, was detained by the army after a May 10, 1991, MRTA incursion into Rioja, San Martín; in that incursion, the MRTA had taken nine police officers prisoner (see chapter 5). Tenorio was tortured and then thrown from an army helicopter. He survived the fall, severely wounded, and was found by campesinos who took him to the Hospital de Nuevo Cajamarca. The case was immediately denounced to the Fiscalía de la Nación, whose human rights specialist was already in the zone to investigate the MRTA prisoner situation. Human rights monitors in the area feared for the victim's life and planned to move him to Lima at first opportunity.

- Vilcashuamán province, Ayacucho, is the site of the Accomarca military base, installed in 1985. Since the army came to the area, it has required each hamlet to provide a monthly tithe of meat and vegetables for the soldiers. In the hamlets of Pucapaccana and Pacchuahuallhua, in Independencia district, the villagers did not fill their quota during August or early September 1990 because the town official usually in charge of coordinating the goods was away. Apparently as a result of this failure, on September 25 a patrol led by officers with the cover names Moreno and Gitano arrived from the Accomarca base and entered Pucapaccana shooting into the air. They rounded up the villagers in the main square and demanded several head of sheep. At the same time they read from a list the names of a family; sixty-four-year-old Bernabé Baldeón García and two of his relatives were detained, supposedly to carry the sheep to the base. The patrol left about 10:00 A.M. for Pacchuahuallhua, capital of Independencia, and coming across three campesinas along the road, they raped the women and took their sheep. On arrival at the district capital they met other patrols bringing detainees. They locked up the combined detainees in the town council offices, separated the women, and raped them. That night, in a bizarre excess of cruelty, the soldiers forced the detainees to dance naked until they collapsed from exhaustion; then, locking the detainees once more in the council office, the soldiers began to torture them. Three, including Bernabé Baldeón García and two unidentified men, died as a result. Among those who survived the torture were three professors, five villagers, and a local mayor. The next day, taking the body of Baldeón to the base at Accomarca, the patrol's officers claimed he had died of a heart attack. According to the reports of Peruvian human rights organizations, the other two bodies did not arrive at the base and may have been dumped along the way. Other victims of torture were given medical examinations at the base and freed under threat of reprisal if they should denounce their mistreatment. On September 27, Baldeón was buried in Accomarca by soldiers from the base. When Americas Watch took up this case with the Defense Ministry, our representative was shown the results of the army's investigation, which attested that no abuse had occurred.

Americas Watch welcomed the Peruvian government's decision in 1989 to allow the International Committee of the Red Cross unimpeded access to the DIRCOTE (anti-terrorism police) center in Lima; this has apparently diminished the use of torture there. Police cooperation with the ICRC had become erratic by mid-1991, however, and Americas Watch learned that the humanitarian agency's representatives were being permitted to see detainees only after the initial period of preventive detention, up to fifteen days. When this information emerged—during delicate aid negotiations with the United States—the Fujimori government committed itself to resolve the problem. The government also announced its intentions to give the ICRC access to military facilities that serve as detention centers in the emergency zones. If implemented, this would be a crucial step. For until the ICRC is able to visit and inspect army and police holding centers freely throughout the emergency zone, there appears to be little hope of curbing this widespread practice. As for the creative cruelty shown by soldiers in the course of army patrols, away from their barracks, the only effective impediments to this are punishment from above—an option not yet seriously explored in Peru—and relentless publicity from victims and their defenders. Victims are often too terrified to make denunciations, and the courts' ineffectiveness, as well as the limits on press and investigative access to areas of conflict, leave them virtually without defenders. Not only should the ICRC be granted timely and unrestricted access to detention centers, but the presence of prosecutors, judges, journalists, human rights organizations, and congressional representatives from Lima must be strengthened in the zones of conflict. This need is expressed in dozens of seminars and opinion pieces in

Peru every year. How it can be done, in the face of Sendero violence, government corruption, and military resistance, is a question no one has yet answered. A beginning would be the president's taking a consistent, firm position against torture of any detainee under any circumstances, and throwing his support behind congressional and legal investigations that reveal such criminal behavior. Under no circumstances should President Fujimori tolerate a cover-up by his officials, and all feasible efforts should be made—as a matter of policy— to protect victims and witnesses from reprisal by official forces.

DISAPPEARANCES

In 1987 Peru became known internationally for its high number of disappearances; that year, according to U.N. figures, 559 forced disappearances took place worldwide, of which almost one-fourth, 133, occurred in Peru.[22] In 1938 this proportion declined slightly, but Peru remained the nation with the highest number of new disappearances in the world, and in 1989, when the U.N. Working Group on Forced and Involuntary Disappearances registered 975 cases worldwide, Peru had a staggering 440. In 1990 Peru's proportion again was high, more than half the new disappearances registered by the United Nations, but the absolute figure had declined to 232.[23]

Figures released by national human rights' groups tend to be lower than those of the United Nations working group for methodological reasons, but they indicate the same trends.[24] A profile of disappearances during 1989 suggests the range of the phenomenon. That year, Peruvian human rights organizations registered 306 forced disappearances, a slight increase over the previous year, though notably less than the number of cases the United Nations received. Half of these occurred in Apurímac, a department in the central-south of Peru where the state of emergency had lasted for more than six years. Of the 158 disappearances in Apurímac, 87 occurred in the province of Abancay, where the emergency zone PMC is headquartered in the capital city. Next in frequency of disappearances was Ayacucho department, with 87 cases. In other departments, the incidence was as follows: 27 in Huancavelica, 13 in Huánuco, 18 in Lima, 2 in San Martín, and 1 in Ucayali.[25]

Members of the army carried out the overwhelming majority of the disappearances (268). Other official forces engaging in disappearance included the navy's marines (12), the investigative police (7), the combined forces (3), the intelligence services (1), and the regular police (1). Paramilitary groups were responsible for 4 disappearances. The remainder were either carried out by Sendero (3) or the details are unknown. Detainees who disappeared were generally held in army barracks.[26]

Thirty-one of the victims were younger than eighteen.[27] In Ayacucho's capital city, Huamanga, for example, a schoolmate watched as fourteen-year-old Rita Marlene Valer Munalla was forced into an army vehicle and disappeared on October 11. Her brother, Walter Valer Munalla, had been detained by the army in Ayacucho the previous month, and his body, bearing marks of torture, had been found on October 7.

Sometimes entire families have disappeared, such as Victoria Palomino García and four of her children, aged sixteen and under, detained in Circa district, Abancay province, Apurímac, on August 30, 1989.

Labor activists, professionals, and students have been victims of disappearance. On November 6, 1989, the National Miners' Federation denounced the disappearance of ten of its members, detained by the army in the barracks of Marcavalle, province of La Oroya, Junín. The labor movement also launched a campaign to demand the reappearance of Javier Antonio Alarcón Guzmán, professor at the National Engineering University and leader of the National Federation of University Professors of Peru. Alarcón had been on a work-related trip from Lima to the central region of Junín when he disappeared. He left Lima on December 7, intending to stop at several universities, but failed to reach even his first destination.

Most of the disappeared in 1989, however, were adult male campesinos, and disappearances took place in the context of army sweeps or military operations in rural areas. On May 17 in Las Mariposas district, province of Satipo, Junín, a military column of about one hundred soldiers detained more than twenty campesinos; the bodies of eleven—including that of a young girl—appeared the next day on the banks of a nearby river, bearing evidence of torture, and the others disappeared.

Of the 135 persons who disappeared for substantial periods of time and then reappeared, either dead or alive, nearly all (128) had been detained by the army. The "reappeared" are not counted by Peruvian human rights groups among the "disappeared."

These figures are conservative, based on investigations and the testimony of witnesses. Cases denounced in inaccessible areas, where it has not been possible for human rights monitors to follow up, are not included. Such is the case of twenty-five persons whose disappearance was denounced to the government's prosecutor general in October 1989: the disappearances had taken place, according to the prosecutor serving in Tocache, San Martín, between August 14 and 27, 1989, in the hamlets of Ischanga, Acceso Limón, and La Esperanza, and the victims had been taken to the military base in Palma de Espino. According to the prosecutor, Pedro Chimay, the arrests were part of a counter-insurgency operation; the victims were detained in the presence of family members and were taken out of the zone by air force helicopters. (This area of San Martín lies within the Upper Huallaga River zone, the coca-producing area where conflict became markedly more intense during 1989.) Prosecutor Chimay had requested information on the detainees from the PMC commander of the zone, Gen. Alberto Arciniega, without result.

A provincial prosecutor in Ucayali, a neighboring department, described the local situation in these terms: "In Pucallpa [the capital of Ucayali] it is already customary to find, almost every day, the bodies of people who have been cruelly assassinated. As well, from time to time people disappear who have been kidnapped by uniformed, hooded individuals who only act at night."[28]

From January through April 1990, at least 60 persons disappeared in the emergency zones, all but 5 after detention by the army. Another 29—among them 3 dead—"reappeared." The total number of disappearances registered during the year was 204, according to the Coordinadora Nacional de Derechos Humanos, with an additional 98 who "reappeared." The following were among the cases investigated by APRODEH:

- Alfonso Aguirre Escalante, engineer and supervisor of a state project under the Ministry of the Presidency, was taken from his home in Huamanga by soldiers at 2:00 A.M. on February 8. He was first held in Los Cabitos barracks, then was transferred twice, finally to the military barracks in Cangallo. Although the chief of the PMC of Ayacucho agreed to investigate the case, this was not done.
- Benjamín Naupas Astucuri, campesino, was detained by soldiers while herding cows toward the city of Vilcashuamán, in Ayacucho. A woman pointed him out as a subversive element, and he was taken first to the local barracks, then to Los Cabitos in a helicopter. His name had appeared on a police blacklist of ninety-five residents of his town, Huambalpa. The town has been harassed by the army since 1983, forcing the massive emigration of its residents.
- Juan Romero Aguila, campesino, vice-president of the civil defense in his hamlet, Jaucantaucar, in Huancavelica, was detained by the police at a roadblock, date unknown.
- Rafael Antonio Navarro Simerman, student, was detained on March 7 by approximately twelve soldiers, in uniform but wearing ski masks, who broke down the door to his home in La Unión, Huancayo province, Junín, and violently took him away. When his relatives tried to impede the detention, the soldiers left a bomb at the entrance to the house, which exploded, causing extensive damage.

Few bodies of the disappeared are recovered, but Peruvian human rights groups consider disappearances a prelude to assassination.

- Falconieri Saravia Castillo, president of the agrarian federation in Huancavelica, was stopped by a soldier in civilian clothes on March 16, 1990, as he went to a municipal meeting in the city of Huancavelica. His son witnessed the detention and followed his father to the offices of the political military commander of the zone, but the army denied that Saravia was being detained. On April 1 his body was found in a wooded area outside the city, his throat slit.
- Americas Watch learned of a group disappearance in the environs of the antidrug base at Santa Lucía, in the northeastern department of San Martín. According to peasant leaders from the area, on April 8, 1990—the day after several snipers fired on the base from across a nearby river—police entered the hamlet of Nueva Unión, near where the snipers had been situated, and took away a dozen young people as suspected senderistas. A month later, their parents were still unable to locate them. Although police informally acknowledged their detention, they claimed not to know the young people's whereabouts.

Disappearances in 1990 primarily concerned campesinos, but urban disappearances also took place. In chapter 2, we described the case of Ernesto Rafael Castillo Páez, a recently graduated student whose arrest on October 21, 1990, in the street of a Lima slum was amply witnessed but whose relatives' legal denunciation was discredited by the Supreme Court.

In 1991 disappearances continued and, despite the government's celebration of slightly lower figures, did not diminish so significantly as to indicate a change of policy. Dozens of individual cases, as well as groups of persons detained en masse, are known. Two group disappearances have drawn more than usual attention in Peru.

- On March 14, 1991, four residents of Chuschi, in Cangallo province, Ayacucho—Mayor Manuel Pacotaype Chaupin, Gov. Marcelo Cabana Tucno, Council Secretary Martín Cayllhua Galindo, and a resident named Isaías Huamán Vilca—were violently detained before numerous witnesses at a local fair. The army denied their detention, but local groups believed that the action was in retaliation for the community's refusal to form a civil defense patrol. The relatives of the victims received information that they might be held in the army base in Cangallo. Accordingly, the provincial prosecutor of Cangallo went to the base on March 26 with his secretary, the mayor of Cangallo, members of the Technical Police, and relatives of the victims. Told to come back three hours later, they were greeted on their return by the detonation of explosives. Even so, the prosecutor presented his credentials, demanding to see the base commander. After waiting for several hours without result, the prosecutor left to avoid being caught in a torrential rainstorm and was sped on his way by another explosion. When the prosecutor and his group arrived in nearby Morochucos, they were followed by three soldiers, who surrounded them threateningly in the city's main square while another explosion went off. The prosecutor concluded that the army had caused the disappearances in retaliation for the villagers' resistance to forming a patrol as well as their denunciation of the General Police of Chuschi for criminal behavior, including robberies, sexual abuse, and illegal hunting. Peruvian human rights organizations feared for the safety of the prosecutor and those who had accompanied him.

• In the late afternoon of April 19, 1991, five men courageously enrolled as candidates for municipal elections in Huancapi, the capital of Victor Fajardo province, Ayacucho. By this action they were volunteering to be targets for Sendero execution. Such bravery would seem to deserve support from the official forces. Perhaps because these men were candidates for the United Socialist Left (IUS), however, they and two friends became victims of the army. After enlisting as candidates, the group had a few drinks, then dropped off a political colleague, Professor Julio Arotoma Cañahuaray (director of the province's education service), at his home and continued on to another bar. At about 10:30 P.M. they left, shouting IUS slogans in the quiet streets; suddenly they came upon an army patrol. The commanding officer, who uses the cover name Centauro, was well known locally by face, though his identity remained secret. The five candidates—Wilfredo Huamaní Quispe, Zenón Huamaní Chuchón, Napoleón Quispe Ortega, Eleuterio Fernández Quispe, and Luis Amaru Quispe—were not immediately arrested but were kicked and punched, then taken to the street in front of Professor Arotoma's house and told to call him for help. When the professor opened his front door, he was violently detained; when his wife, Honorata Oré, eight months pregnant, sought to help him, she was struck and also detained. Relatives of the detainees now surrounded the army patrol shouting in protest and followed the patrol to the army base of Huancapi. Soon they heard the sound of an explosion from inside the base. When the detainees' wives went to the base the next day to ask when the detainees would be released, authorities at the base denied holding them. Relatives were later told that the detainees had been transferred to the military base in Pampa Cangallo. The provincial prosecutor of Cangallo attempted an investigation but met only denials by the political military chief of the Huancapi base, Lt. Carlos Morgan. Centauro had been transferred by the time the prosecutor investigated the base. The detainees have not been seen since.

Between June and November 1990, the Comité Vicarial por los Derechos Humanos de Pucallpa, a Catholic church office in the capital of Ucayali department, presented complaints on ninety-two killings and thirty disappearances. Then, in mid-November the bishop of Pucallpa himself, Monsignor Martín, sent a denunciation in the office's name to the Fiscalía de la Nación: about 19 miles from Pucallpa, corpses had been discovered in a swamp; five skeletons could be seen, although some six months earlier up to twenty bodies had been reported floating on the surface. The Comité Vicarial believed that disappearances it had denounced had ended in these killings.[29]

In several cases of disappearance during late 1990 and early 1991, there are indications that explosives may have been used to dispose of the bodies. The lawyer for disappearance victim Ernesto Castillo Páez told colleagues in COMISEDH of his belief that the young men had been murdered by dynamite,[30] and human rights monitors have partial evidence from other cases as well. The Chumbivilcas massacre also fits this pattern: a combination of gunfire and explosives was used. This would appear to be an expensive way to destroy evidence, but it suggests that the discoveries of common graves of victims from 1990, and the general effort underway to improve the army's image, may be having some effect.

The army's tendency to blame Sendero for its own abuses must also be noted. This evasion, used in the Fidel Intusca torture case, is used by the Defense Ministry when discussing disappearances generally; Americas Watch presumes this is due to the uncomfortable attention Peru has received from the United Nations and the international press, as well as Peruvian activists, on human rights.

In certain cases it may be difficult to distinguish Sendero from the army, but in general residents of small towns and provincial cities know the members of local army patrols by sight, and as numerous denunciations attest, even when armed men dress in civilian clothes, civilians can tell who they are by their weapons, boots, and deportment. Although Sendero is capable of such tactics, it tends toward public rather than hidden displays of cruelty. Forced disappearance remains a policy pursued above all by the army.

It is therefore urgently required that the International Committee of the Red Cross be given access to all army posts, since many of the disappeared are first taken to these facilities. In this way the ICRC can verify unacknowledged detentions in their earliest stages and prevent mistreatment and clandestine execution.

EXTRAJUDICIAL EXECUTIONS

Sendero Luminoso is not known to disguise its fighters as the army, but the reverse is not true. There is evidence that soldiers pose as members of Sendero when in the field; the Fidel Intusca torture case is one indicator of this. Another, recounted in chapter 2, is the conduct of soldiers during the week of abusive behavior in Chumbivilcas. So, too, is the following account, published in a Lima newsmagazine.[31]

The article describes an incident of September 10, 1990, in which soldiers posed as senderistas and entered the districts of Caiminto and Maronilla, near Aucayacu in Huánuco department. They reportedly called a village "rally" and threatened residents with reprisals if they did not attend. Once all had gathered, the "senderistas" called on their "delegates" to come forward.

It must be understood that Sendero drafts these "delegates" by threat if none volunteer; it is not necessary for a town to support Sendero to have Sendero "delegates," nor for a person to support Sendero to become one. The "delegates" must report to Sendero on village activities; if they refuse they are murdered. When called forward here, dozens who showed themselves to be Sendero "delegates" were reportedly then taken away and machine-gunned, their bodies burned to destroy the evidence.

A similar incident cost the lives of six villagers in Humaya and Chambara, district of Sayán, Huaura department, on May 3, 1991. Huaura is an area of intensifying Sendero activity. In this incident, men with their faces covered by ski masks entered the communities and, after selecting their victims, shot them in the head. Witnesses identified the attackers as soldiers from the army base in Andahuasi, dressed as guerrillas. The case was denounced to the Ministerio Público by the local human rights committee of Huacho.

It is impossible to assess how frequently the army murders civilians in the emergency zone because neither the press nor human rights monitors have regular access to areas of conflict and the army controls information from those zones. But there are enough documented incidents of extrajudicial executions— both targeted assassinations and group killings of villagers—to establish the pattern. Cases like three corpses discovered with marks of torture and bullet wounds, in Colpa, Huancayo district, Junín, on December 13, 1989, are the outcome of disappearances. Similarly, a case reported by Amnesty International concerned the vice-rector of the University of Huancayo, in Junín, Jaime Cerrón Palomino, and his driver, Armando Tapia Gutierrez, who disappeared after being abducted by heavily armed men on June 8, 1990, while driving to the university. Ten days later they were discovered dead under a cliff, their bodies bearing marks of torture. The May 17, 1989, army raid into Las Mariposas, in Junín (described above), involved a combination of disappearances with outright executions.

As was noted in chapter 1, human rights organizations in Peru question the army's definition of some persons killed in emergency zones as "subversives." Human rights organizations especially fear that when the army reports on battles without offering information on wounded or detainees, this may indicate that noncombatants or wounded combatants have been extrajudicially executed.

The events of April 28, 1989, in the hamlet of Los Molinos, near Jauja, Junín, illustrate this problem. About two hundred elite members of the army's airborne division, traveling along a road near the settlement, reportedly came upon a column of the MRTA in two trucks. When a firefight ensued, some MRTA fighters escaped in a truck, and the army gave pursuit, killing an unspecified number. The official number killed was sixty-two, but none were identified. When President García and Defense Minister López Albújar flew to the site in a helicopter, they invited the state television and channel 5 to film their visit.[32] When other media, including Reuters and the national magazine *Caretas*, attempted to visit and report on the incident, the PMC prevented them from doing so. President García stated that the dead "are the same ones who assaulted Juanjuí a year and a half ago," thereby supporting without question the army's version of events.[33] This, though among the dead were old people, women, and children. The MRTA recognized forty-seven of the dead as its combatants.

As noted earlier, the military's attitude toward the civilian population has advanced through phases during the past decade. First there was Belaúnde's one-note repression; then, until the Cayara massacre of May 1988, the García administration appeared to be convincing the military to spare civilians; since Cayara, there have been no such illusions. At the same time, treatment of the civilian population also depends, in any given area, on the character and personal philosophy of the zone commander, as well as on the role that his area plays in any current crisis.

Especially notable during 1989 was the increase in politically related deaths in the north-central Upper Huallaga River valley, which includes Leoncio Prado province in Huánuco and Tocache province in San Martín. Deaths rose dramatically between May and July of that year, coinciding with an all-out counterinsurgency campaign by the newly established PMC for the Upper Huallaga. A study on numbers of deaths for the first seven months of the year, by department and province, shows that Huánuco held second place in the nation, with 290 deaths—of which the greatest number, 166, occurred in Leoncio Prado. San Martín occupied fourth place with 220 deaths—of which 195 occurred in Tocache.[34] The study does not break down the deaths, but, as elsewhere in Peru, it is likely that a large portion were civilians.

Political violence during 1990 shifted somewhat, becoming concentrated in Junín. There, 719 Peruvians died for political reasons, over half of them civilians. In Ayacucho, next highest with 686 deaths, the proportion of civilians was even greater. The departments of Huánuco (556) and San Martín

(467) were third and fourth in the number of political killings, while the department of Lima (317) was fifth.[35]

The use of bombardment as a combat tactic increased the probability of civilian casualties. The Upper Huallaga region was bombarded frequently during 1989. On July 6, army helicopters bombarded the community of La Morada, Huánuco, killing twenty supposed subversives. When questions arose about possible civilians deaths, Gen. Alberto Arciniega, then PMC commander of the zone, did not deny the possibility. He justified the action in *Sí* magazine: "It was the residents of La Morada who warned a column of Sendero Luminoso of the presence of a military patrol near the hamlet."[36] Whatever the residents may or may not have done, they were not legitimate targets for retaliation but noncombatants whose rights must be respected under international humanitarian law. In Ucayali, near the departmental capital of Pucallpa, an army bombardment and strafing of a settlement in the Quebrada de Espinal on October 20, 1989, left four dead, one wounded, and two disappeared, according to a survivor who denounced the attack. Among the four dead were a woman and her young daughter.

During the second half of 1990, troops seeking out Sendero in the Upper Huallaga were supported by armed helicopters. There is no information that any village was strafed in that period, although on at least one occasion troops accompanied by helicopters attacked and killed civilians along with senderistas (see chapter 9).

Another problem in the Upper Huallaga region was that the army sometimes announced large numbers of dead and wounded after a battle but failed either to produce the wounded for their families to identify or to turn over the bodies of the dead. This and other facts—such as the disproportionately small numbers of arms reported captured from dead "subversives"—contributed to a growing concern that the civilian toll was being camouflaged.

In early September 1989, about twenty corpses, many decapitated and missing hands and feet, were found floating down the Huallaga River near the antidrug base at Santa Lucía, San Martín. For obvious reasons, it was not possible to identify the bodies or to determine who was responsible for their deaths, although there was public speculation that the army had in this way disposed of some drug traffickers and attempted to intimidate others. Americas Watch does not endorse any theory about these executions but considers it indicative of the army's reputation in the emergency zone that it should be suspected of such barbarity.

A 1991 case shows that the army continued to camouflage civilian killings after the change of government. In Chillutira, a tiny community in Puno, four armed men commandeered four villagers' bicycles on May 19 and took the four villagers with them to the neighboring hamlet of Huancatira, where the armed men presented themselves as Sendero fighters. There, through a tense chain of events, two villagers were wounded, two of the strangers fled, and the hamlet's residents beat the two remaining senderistas to death. The following day police were notified; police and soldiers soon arrived to take away four of the villagers, as well as the bodies of the two senderistas. Some two hundred people saw the four live detainees taken away with the two corpses. On May 21, the next day, Radio Ayaviri announced that in a Sendero-army clash in Orurillo, six presumed subversives had been killed. The wives of the four detained villagers identified their husbands' bodies and gave sworn statements as to their condition. All had been slashed and shot; the head and face of one, Francisco Atamari Mamani, had been virtually destroyed. By contrast, the bodies of the senderistas killed in anger by the villagers bore fewer wounds.[37]

The defensiveness that marked the late García government has also characterized President Fujimori's first year in office. The president's attempts to legislate impunity for the armed forces in the emergency zone, though blocked by Congress, set a certain tone. While the justice minister accused human rights groups of creating obstacles to counterinsurgency operations, the Defense Ministry was denying army involvement in abuses. The military was uncooperative in an early 1991 congressional investigation into a carnival of abuses—including torture, rape, and group murder—in Chumbivilcas province, Cusco (the case is described in chapter 4).

Yet in many cases the evidence has been overwhelming. Two young Cusco students, Marcelino Valencia Alvaro and Zacarías Pasca Huamani, were arrested on September 24, 1990, by police in Santo Tomás, and when townspeople forced police to open the station five days later, the bodies of the youths were found buried, marked by atrocious torture. Two large army massacres—of twelve and eighteen peasants, respectively—in Ayacucho in August and September 1990 were further proof that the advent of the new government had not altered the military's performance. Those killings are discussed in chapter 8, because they involved civil patrols along with soldiers, but in both cases army officers organized and ordered the actions. In the case of Chilcahuaycco, Huamanga district, where eighteen campesinos were shot to death on September 22, 1990, the noncommissioned officer responsible was one Jhonny Zapata Acuña, better known as Centurión, who had been repeatedly denounced for extortion and kidnapping.

Two cases involving police during June and July 1991 were so obvious and shocking that they incited legislation to restructure the force. That these incidents occurred while the U.S. Congress was taking up the Bush administration's proposals for military aid to Peru may also have contributed to the attention they received.

On the morning of June 21, police exchanged gunfire with a group of armed robbers in Miraflores, a relatively prosperous neighborhood of Lima. Soon thereafter, officers in a patrol car detained two minors, the brothers Emilio and

Rafael Gómez Paquiyauri, and a young medical student named Fredy Rodríguez Pighi in Callao. By chance, reporters from channel 5, who had been filming the shoot-out and subsequent police operations, caught the detentions on video; the two brothers were stuffed into the trunk of the police car, whose license plate was legible on the videotape, and Rodríguez was also taken away.

All three young men were shot to death at close range before they arrived at a police precinct.

The videotape, broadcast on national television, combined with the fact that the abuse occurred in Lima and the affluence and high social position of Rodríguez's family, made this case exceptional: five police officers were removed from the force and charged before a civilian court (although military courts immediately prepared to contest jurisdiction); senior police officials were also implicated.

Recipients of U.S. antinarcotics assistance were the offenders in the second case. These murders were not, strictly speaking, politically motivated, but they are relevant to the concerns of this book because the police officers involved belonged to the antidrug force in the Upper Huallaga and because their gross misconduct was initially concealed by high government officials.

On July 9, a detachment of police in Bellavista, San Martín, were drinking heavily to celebrate one colleague's return and another's leaving. Being ill-paid and in need of more liquor, the police stopped cars and demanded money from the drivers; this sort of illegal "toll" is common police practice. The officers also attempted to shake down a plane readying for takeoff at the Bellavista airstrip with pilot, co-pilot, and fifteen passengers aboard, but the pilot refused them entry. Soon after the plane was airborne, the drunken police opened fire and shot it out of the sky, killing all those on board. After informing the rest of the police contingent in the hamlet, the culprits and their colleagues went to the wreckage and proceeded to search the dead for valuables.

The local prosecutor, who is reportedly known as an ally of the police, issued a statement claiming that MRTA fighters had shot down the plane. Later the interior minister issued a communiqué describing the police as sober and the circumstances as a patrol action carried out in the mistaken belief that the plane carried drugs. Investigators quickly discovered the true nature of the crime, however, learning from Bellavista residents that the plane was a regular service, its pilot was well known, and the police were fully at fault. Yet the interior minister, an active-duty army general, did not offer his resignation, nor did President Fujimori demand it. The local prosecutor was fired, not by the executive but by the Fiscalía de la Nación. And four policemen were removed from the force.

In these two cases efforts were made to punish those directly responsible, but some in Peru remain skeptical as to the importance of that effort. The prestigious newsmagazine *Caretas* commented dryly in an article about the murder of the three young men by Callao police that it would be healthy indeed "if they [the military command] acted with the same speed when those involved did not belong—as in this case—to the National Police but to the ranks of the Armed Forces wherein, to date, no one has been sanctioned, let us not say drastically, but not even with the petal of a rose."[38]

PARAMILITARY GROUPS

In Peru, freedom of expression and association is guaranteed and generally respected by the state. Indeed, these freedoms prevent Peru from falling into unqualified crisis. They are not always secure freedoms—witness the pressure on trade unions described above. As the economic crisis has sharpened, moreover, and as the security situation has exposed the fragility of the state's legal apparatus, paramilitary groups have emerged with a mission to suppress the resulting debate and dissent. The Bernales Commission found that 164 murders had been committed by paramilitary groups during 1989, of which 153 were attributed to unidentified groups and the remainder to the most formal and self-advertising group, the Comando Democrático Rodrigo Franco.

The Comando Rodrigo Franco, whose activity is usually dated from 1988, was responsible for at least eleven killings during 1989, as well as for bombings and innumerable threats against persons it considered sympathizers of Sendero or the MRTA. Among the victims of CRF assassinations were two members of the Chamber of Deputies, Eriberto Arroyo Mío and Pablo Li Ormeño, whose deaths prompted the formation of a special chamber commission to investigate paramilitary violence. That commission reviewed evidence of links between the CRF and the ruling APRA party, but could not reach unanimous conclusions, as described in chapter 4.

The CRF is also suspected in the murder of radio journalist Guillermo López Salazar. López was shot to death in his home in Tingo María on April 19, 1989, in front of his family, by eight men. Shortly before his death, López had told foreign journalists that the CRF had attacked his house and that the military and police had threatened him after Sendero had forced him to play a cassette containing propaganda on his radio program. It is unclear whether López was murdered for his journalism work or for his activities as a local official of the United Left party.

Two paramilitary executions that caused great public concern and were widely attributed to the CRF (though this was not proven) were those of Saúl Cantoral, president of the important and combative Mine, Metallurgical, and Iron Workers Union, and union adviser Consuelo García Santa Cruz, a teacher and labor activist specializing in women's rights. Cantoral had received threats from the CRF on several occasions. He was visiting Lima to negotiate with the government and to prevent, if possible, the renewal of a national miners' strike. The two were abducted in Lima during the evening of February 13, 1989, and their bodies were found a few hours later in the Lima district of Canto Grande. Pinned to both bodies were placards suggesting that Sendero Luminoso was responsible for the executions, but observers familiar with Sendero messages of this kind did not consider these authentic. Cantoral had been shot; forensic tests suggested that a silencer had been used. García's skull had been crushed, and forensic tests revealed tire marks on her body, suggesting that she had tried to flee and had been run over by a vehicle.

On June 5, 1989, the press reported on threats against several priests of the Instituto Español de Misiones Exteriores, in Ica department, by the paramilitary group calling itself Manuel Santana Chiri. In the meantime, several human rights activists received threats from the Comando Rodrigo Franco (see chapter 7).

Whether or not the CRF itself took credit for an action, paramilitary activity evidently enjoyed at least the tolerance and at times the active support of official forces. On September 20, 1989, in Lima, for example, residents of the settlement Rodrigo Franco charged that 250 hooded paramilitary agents, accompanied by a contingent of police, had attempted to evict them by burning their shanties, destroying their meeting houses, and wounding fifteen residents. As the special commission of the Chamber of Deputies concluded in a preliminary report in August 1989, the utter failure of the police to track down and arrest members of the CRF indicated either a lamentable inefficiency or a conscious decision not to investigate.

The Bernales Commission report for 1990 made evident that the problem of paramilitary activity had persisted; there were 284 deaths attributed to "unidentified groups" throughout the year—heavily concentrated in Lima, with lesser concentrations in Junín and Ayacucho.[39] The CRF was credited with just five killings during 1990. Some observers, reflecting their suspicion of former interior minister Mantilla, speculated that the decline in CRF activity was due to the political decline of APRA generally and Mantilla's sector in particular. It is also possible that the members of the so-called CRF, whoever they are, were acting under different names. Finally, it is possible that President Fujimori's early purging of reportedly corrupt and APRA-connected police officers—some 250, including senior officers, were forced into retirement in August 1990—may have had the desired effect, if not on paramilitary activity as a whole, at least on this manifestation of it.

Clearly, however, death squad activity continued into 1991, and although the various paramilitary groups did not appear to be coordinated, they continued to enjoy the tolerance and even the participation of members of the security forces. One emerging group, for example, the Comando de Liberación Anti-terrorista, based in Huanta, Ayacucho, was known to be led by an army sergeant named Jhonny Zapata Acuña, or Centurión, the same noncommissioned officer charged with the mass killings at Chilcahuaycco (see above). The Comando de Liberación Antiterrorista was responsible for threats against two Ayacucho journalists in June 1991 and for the murder of another journalist, Luis Antonio Morales, on July 13 in Huamanga; Morales had been investigating local paramilitary activity.

Each victim whose name appears here left behind people damaged by his or her death, or survived horror to return home damaged, or could not return home. Computations of the social cost of political violence, such as the figures of the Bernales Commission, do not take into account the multiplied effect of a single death or case of torture, let alone the social psychosis created by living with several thousand political deaths a year. The sample here is small; Peruvian newspapers carry such stories every day, and after eleven years of violence it is sometimes difficult for Peruvians to be shocked. In recent years, moreover, Sendero's abuses and its growth have so frightened the population that army and police abuse have seemed to many a necessary evil. Nor do critics of the counterinsurgency tactics necessarily consider themselves antimilitary. But it is openly acknowledged by both military and civil authorities that even apart from its almost unimaginable social cost, the strategy to date has been a failure. The military's hopes at present would seem to reside, to a great degree, in Peru's civil patrols.

7

THE ROLE OF
CIVIL DEFENSE PATROLS

The long indifference of the central government to Peru's Indian communities has led these communities, in some parts of the country, to form village patrols for protection against strangers, robbers, cattle rustlers, and neighboring communities with a score to settle. *Rondas campesinas* have existed in the northwest of Peru for many years as an expression of community self-government.

As early as 1982 in Ayacucho, there were signs that the military was using this model of self-protection to enlist peasants in the counterinsurgency campaign. At first the PMC denied organizing peasant militias, but in August 1984 the policy became public. The first patrols were organized by the navy in the highlands of Huanta and in the Apurímac River valley. Under Gen. Adrián Huamán Centeno of the army, in 1984 patrols in Huanta, Huamanga, and La Mar—all provinces of Ayacucho—began to represent part of the counterinsurgency strategy; General Huamán emphasized the need for social and economic solutions while forcing unwilling campesinos to give, in effect, unpaid military service to contain Sendero.

Because these militias differ so greatly from traditional rondas campesinas, they are perhaps better distinguished by the name *montoneras,* or, as the campesino population nicknames them, *montos.* Another colloquial name for them is *defensistas.* The military has adopted the ronda terminology to create an impression of continuity and communal autonomy that is not accurate with regard to the counterinsurgency patrols. Americas Watch therefore uses the other available terminology.

Montoneras instructed by the military in the early 1980s did not receive weapons, but their leaders reported regularly to the PMC. They were also immediately implicated in killings. The deaths of eight journalists in Uchuraccay, Huanta province, Ayacucho, in 1983, a landmark case, happened where frequent killings by patrollers had been reported and where the journalists had gone to confirm those reports. Examining the last year of Belaúnde's government, in 1985 Americas Watch described the montoneras in the following terms:

> Human rights organizations have obtained testimony showing that those who refuse to serve [in the patrols] are suspected of senderista sympathies; they may be jailed for a few days or forced to work in the camps established by the rondas. Males from age twelve and up to fifty or sixty are inducted into the patrols. In some cases women also are made to join; the prominent Lima weekly newsmagazine *Caretas* has published photographs of women and children marching in columns.
>
> Both the Army and the Navy promote the formation of these patrols. . . . The reasons for their creation, their structure and training may vary, but it appears that, by and large, they are not allowed to use firearms, and that security forces appoint chiefs and group leaders. The rondas sometimes consist of 200 to 300 persons, and their training camps are designed to accommodate several rondas at a time.[1]

Forced membership and forced unpaid labor—both violations of the right to free association—have been features of the civil patrols in most though not all cases. Moreover, the patrols' conduct sometimes reflected local conditions rather than any issues related to the insurgency. Such was the case of the communities Ccaccamarca and San Cristóbal de Manzanayoc, neighboring hamlets in Concepción district, Cangallo, Ayacucho, with a long history of disputes over land rights. As described in legal complaints to the Fiscalía de la Nación in 1984 and 1985, harassment of Manzanayoc began with arbitrary arrests by an army contingent in January 1983; two prominent village residents were arrested and subsequently died in custody. Four months later, another community member died in army hands, and in December there were further detentions. Then, in July 1984, the community was invaded by civil defense patrols from Ccaccamarca and other villages, led by the army. The twenty-four Manzanayoc residents detained in that attack included the local authorities, four minors, and at least two elderly persons. All were mistreated, and the women raped and abused. They were deprived of food and water, and forced to "confess" by being hung from trees or pushed into wells of dirty water. Eighteen of the prisoners were eventually released. The bodies of the other six, including the *teniente gobernador* (senior local authority) and two minors, were found by relatives near a road, but the army did not allow the families to retrieve and bury the corpses.[2]

As this case shows, the examination of the civil defense patrols often involves reporting on army abuses undertaken with the help of patrollers. The army officers exercise command, but the soldiers and defensistas are often equally responsible for violence.

At its outset, the García government did not appear to promote the formation of montoneras; campesinos who wished to return full-time to their crops were allowed to do so. But this posture gradually changed, and in 1989, García openly called on the rural population to form village self-defense patrols as part of the counterinsurgency effort. It was not made clear how these poorest of Peruvian citizens were to survive and plant their meager fields while serving in the patrols, which sometimes involved operations of several days away from their home villages. But García himself went to La Rinconada Baja, a community in La Mar province, Ayacucho, on December 8, 1989, to officiate at a ceremony in which arms were distributed to the local civil defense committees under the leadership of a Comandante Huayhuaco. Calling the work of the patrols "democratic insurrection," the president asked rhetorically, "They always say that if we give arms to the campesinos maybe they will use them badly, I say: Why must we distrust them?"[3]

In the public debate that surrounded this event, some sectors of opinion praised the efficiency of the patrols in La Mar, while others argued that they would not be militarily effective and simply militarized civilian communities. The secretary general of the Confederación Campesina del Perú, Juan Rojas Vargas, accused the montoneras under Comandante Huayhuaco of killing and threatening peasants. Soon thereafter, two national magazines, *Caretas* and *Sí*, published findings that the comandante had been convicted of trafficking in drugs and that he should still have been serving his ten-year sentence.

The patrols in La Mar had been formed at the urging and with the tutelage of the navy's marines. And well before the controversy over Comandante Huayhuaco, these and similar montos had been organized in the Ayacucho emergency zone, both in the highlands and in the rain forests. They were formed by sectors, each with a certain number of hamlets grouped under a single command, and that command selected or at least approved by the local military, which was responsible to the PMC. Men, women, and even children were pressed into service in the patrols, which had shifts round the clock, and though by this stage the patrollers were "armed," the arms they carried were rudimentary, often made by the peasants themselves. Preferential training and treatment—for example, slightly better weapons—went to those in a community who had done their military service. These *licenciados* were also, in some cases, put in charge of the community's self-defense, reordering the communal authority structure without regard to tradition.

In some areas of Ayacucho, villages reportedly organized spontaneously during 1989 to ward off Sendero; generally, however, even when a certain will to organize patrols existed, the patrols were not left autonomous by the PMC, and in many cases the PMC urged, or imposed, the patrols on peasant communities. In part for this reason Sendero Luminoso targeted the montos or used the existence of a civil patrol as an excuse to execute villagers (see chapter 5). Sendero's technique, which is always to encourage militarization and exhaust the state's reform options, is adaptable to conditions in which the state's representatives—the enemy—are "the people" the revolution seeks to represent. Moving into its "strategic equilibrium" offensive, Sendero regarded the civil patrols as an obstacle and in some cases a military threat.

The PMC commander in Ayacucho during 1989, Gen. Howard Rodríguez, took the position that to accept civil patrols "would be to recognize the state's inability to defend itself through the mechanisms established in the Constitution."[4] But his was a minority voice. His successor, Gen. Petronio Fernández Dávila Carnero, expanded the Ayacucho patrols; in late 1990 and early 1991, Sendero was systematically attacking montos in the northern Ayacucho provinces and reportedly decimating them. Patrols were also constituted in the central rain forests of Peru, mainly in Junín, in 1990 and failed to curb violence there. Indeed, in part because of Sendero reprisals against patrols, Junín became the department with the most political killings that year. The patrols also contributed to the body count: according to the Bernales Commission, of 719 dead in Junín during 1990, "campesino organizations" (civil patrols) were responsible for 101. (All 101 are described, by official sources, as Sendero.) By contrast, the army killed only 79 in the department.[5] Considering the relative sizes of the two forces, the patrols are an evident bargain. It is perhaps not surprising, then, that the Fujimori government determined to fortify the patrols, as his defense minister announced in January 1991. A congressional commission, meanwhile, examined the possibility of creating urban self-defense patrols, while the defense minister expressed support for the concept of self-defense patrols in mining areas, which are inaccessible to the army because of hard terrain and subversive activity.

In 1991 the newest idea in counterinsurgency was passing out arms to civil patrollers; 450 shotguns with ammunition were reportedly distributed in the Mántaro River valley east of Lima in April.[6] In early June, Fujimori announced his intention to travel to an unnamed zone of conflict to oversee arms distribution to peasant patrols. But arming the patrols does not necessarily increase members' security: on July 13, two weeks after receiving arms from the president's hands, the leader of the civil patrols of Alto and Bajo Tulumayo, Concepción, Junín, was executed by Sendero. And this begged the question of how abusive tactics by montoneras were to be curbed.

There are other issues as well. At least in some areas, campesinos have been forced to buy their weapons—for 40 million intis (about fifty-five dollars) apiece, according to an Ayachucho campesino leader.[7] Defensistas also complain of the lack of compensation for their labor and lack of reparation to the families of those who have fallen in battle.

Two types of abuse arise from the creation of the civil defense patrols: abuse directed at the patrollers by Sendero and MRTA or the military, and abuse the patrollers carry out themselves. To note the heavy toll of Sendero attacks is not to consider them illegitimate in all cases. Under international law, a paramilitary agent is a legitimate target for attack if he or she is armed and engaged in military activity. These definitions remain clear so long as the scenario is direct confrontation in the field, and no doubt Sendero does kill some defensistas in battle situations where both sides are capable of defending themselves; unfortunately, it is impossible to gather precise data on skirmishes like these. The legal and ethical lines become more subtle when one considers the situation of a village guarded by active, armed patrollers but containing, like any village, noncombatants, including the sick and children. Certain facilities in the village, for example those contributing economically to the adversary's war effort, like an energy source or a major factory, are also legitimate targets. When assaulting these targets, the attacking force must take adequate care to protect the lives of the civilians present—for example, by discriminating between a building in which arms are kept and the day care center or clinic. A civilian home is a legitimate target if it contains an active combatant, but burning that home after the conclusion of battle, or killing persons in the hut other than the combatant, when that can be avoided, is not permissible under international law. Civilians who die in the course of an otherwise legitimate attack may be "collateral" casualties; their deaths do not constitute a violation of the law of war. Nevertheless, under all circumstances, the attacker is under an affirmative duty to minimize harm to the civilian population. Civilian objects can be seized or destroyed only if such action is an imperative military necessity. This standard, known as the rule of proportionality, determines whether damage to civilian objects and risks to civilian population are legitimate or illegitimate under the circumstances.[8]

In Peru, where the military has "drafted" not only men but women and even children into the patrols, the normal lines between civilian and combatant would be extremely difficult to draw if a village were attacked. In practice, Sendero kills many of its campesino victims outside the context of battle, when they are clearly not legitimate targets. But according to Bernales Commission figures, patrols were responsible for 259 deaths in 1990, mainly of presumed senderistas. Most, though probably not all, of these would be battle fatalities, which suggests that in the most dangerous areas the patrols are very active. By comparison, the MRTA was credited with just 68 killings during 1990 and the army, parent organization to the patrols, with only 849.[9]

Americas Watch does not discount Sendero's violent pressure on peasant communities, which lack adequate police and military protection and therefore may see the patrols, imposed or not, as a possible step toward safety. But to draw civilians into an irregular conflict through identification with the military authorities—indeed, to demand that civilians make this organized identification, as the PMCs frequently do in the emergency zones—is to invite further violence against them, to avoid responsibility for their protection, and implicitly or explicitly to encourage violence on their part.

A case in point is Naylamp de Sonomoro, Satipo province, Junín. During 1989, Sendero's presence in this part of Pangoa district had been growing; the town of Cubantía, near Naylamp, had been attacked several times by Sendero beginning in August 1989.[10] Peasants in the area, who are predominantly indigenous, approached the police for protection and found that the police preferred that they organize a patrol. The PMC, in a bit of civic action, began to offer courses in carpentry and other skills. Montoneras were formed throughout Satipo as of February 1990, encouraged by the PMC but not necessarily imposed by it. Communities eager to establish patrols pressured their neighbors to follow suit or be suspected of Sendero sympathies.

Naylamp, relatively prosperous by rural standards, did not wish to form a patrol, preferring to stay out of the conflict. But to protect themselves in part from Sendero and in part from neighboring communities with grudges, Naylamp's residents organized a patrol in March. On March 28, 1990, in an incident that a newspaper based in Lima reported as a confrontation between Sendero and the police, the "monto" of Naylamp entered the town of Cajiriari and killed residents of the town with machetes and old hunting rifles, while a contingent of police followed them in. Among those captured by the patrollers and police were two children who have not been seen again. The press described the six dead as Sendero leaders in the zone, probably on the basis of a police communiqué.

Alejandro Quispe, patrol leader of Naylamp, opposed violence by the patrol and represented the original community opposition to involvement in the conflict. But Quispe was away from the community when patrollers committed the crime that would bring Sendero down on them.

In April, the patrollers detained a family from Centro Sanibeni, a nearby center of Sendero activity. One son was a known member of Sendero; a daughter had been arrested on suspicion of membership in Sendero but had been released. Naylamp patrollers detained the family as it was preparing to leave the area. When they reported the detentions to the local police post, asking for instructions, they were told, "Be men, don't come to us." They took this as an instruction to eliminate the family but were reluctant to kill their captives and went back to the police a second time. The response was even more vehement. Though some members of the patrol refused to participate, the "self-defense patrol" of Naylamp then violently murdered the family with machetes and guns and threw their bodies in a river. The daughter who had been arrested earlier survived this atrocity and informed Sendero. On April 12, 1990, as described in chapter 5, Sendero entered Naylamp in force and committed an atrocity of its own, killing thirty-five villagers—including patrol leader Alejandro Quispe—and wounding twenty-six more.

As this example demonstrates, militarization of peasant communities calls forth local rivalries, overrides nonviolent tendencies within a community, and encourages abuses by patrollers. Nor does the military offer patrols any protection from the inevitable reprisals of Sendero. The army may deny responsibility for abuses by self-defense patrols—or profess horror, as the military command at Mazamari did after this family was murdered—but "deniability" is also convenient for the authorities. The patrols are trained by and accountable to the military and police, and in the incidents described above they simply did what they were told.

Because a community that organizes a civil defense patrol submits to the military's tutelage, its local structure of authority is weakened or destroyed. Even when the army deals with communal authorities without replacing them, militarization alters the priorities of village life and makes old leadership skills unimportant. In the case of Naylamp, the head of the patrol had prior authority as a community leader, but in his absence the logic of police authority swayed some members of the community to break the most basic rules.

The example described next concerns abuse of power by armed civilians with what appears to have been covert military support. It shows, even more clearly than the Naylamp incident, how intercommunity grudges—in this case, the resentments of an isolated indigenous group toward whites and another indigenous group—may be used to accomplish the military's dirty work. These incidents grew out of MRTA activity, which led to militarization in the environs of Constitución, Pasco department, starting in mid-1989. This area comprises the Pichis and Palcazú rivers, where Ashaninka and Yanesha indigenous peoples live.

After the MRTA assassinated a long-established leader of the Ashaninka indigenous community, Alejandro Calderón, in December 1989, the victim's sons mobilized a force of Ashaninkas to "clean out" the MRTA from the Pichis River valley. According to sources familiar with the zone, the army and navy gave their blessing to the Ashaninka revenge campaign. That campaign, which extended into January 1990, left dozens dead in the Pichis River valley and Constitución.

In early February 1990, an Ashaninka force of about two hundred crossed the Pichis River from their communities and attacked the settlement of Iscozacín, which contains some white farmers but is mainly occupied by about five thousand Yaneshas, another ethnic group. The history of distrust between the two indigenous peoples may have played a part in this attack; so, too, may have envy, as the Yaneshas inhabit a more fertile area than the Ashaninkas and have historically been more integrated into the local economy. It is also relevant that the Yaneshas had denounced the army the previous November after soldiers entered Iscozacín and detained and tortured residents. The Yaneshas have a self-governing democratic organization and did not wish to militarize. In any case, the Ashaninkas arrived with a list of MRTA suspects—not something they were likely to put together by themselves—and imprisoned the bulk of the Yanesha population in a municipal building. They then forced Yanesha detainees to execute five Yaneshas and nonindigenous residents to murder others of their own kind.

The Ashaninkas remained in the town for the rest of February 1990, forcing the residents to feed and support them and to do ronda duty for their protection. They also banned Yanesha organizations and ordered the Yaneshas to militarize in self-defense patrols. According to sources close to the Yanesha community, however, the MRTA had already been quite effectively excluded by the Yaneshas, who wanted no part of the insurgency. The Yaneshas may have been victimized, at least partially, because of their reluctance to enter the conflict on the military's side.

In April, Gen. Manuel Delgado Rojas, PMC commander of the zone, praised the paramilitary activities of the Ashaninkas, calling them "an example of how the population should defend itself against terrorism" with the support of the armed forces.[11] In early May, after the Yanesha community published a protest against Ashaninka abuses in a Lima newspaper, they were threatened with a return of the Ashaninkas; fortunately, this did not occur. Yet there are signs that the Ashaninkas' paramilitary activity was not solely the emotional response of an isolated indigenous people to its leader's assassination or a local feud between indigenous communities but something caused by more pragmatic forces.

The classic scenario for abuse by montoneras is the raid performed under military leadership. In August and September 1990, two horrendous massacres in Ayacucho were the result of joint operations of the army and local rondas. On August 22, 1990, in Iquicha, province of Huamanga, Ayacucho, twelve campesinos were killed, another three disappeared, and several days later another was murdered by the army and the patrollers of three neighboring villages—Ccentabamba, Choque, and Ccano. It was a massacre of revenge—the victims, frightened and not wishing to die, had not joined the neighboring patrols in an August 19 clash with Sendero. The detainees were accused of Sendero sympathies and tortured, then cruelly killed with blows to the head by heavy sticks and rocks. Relatives were not permitted to recover the bodies. A local judge attempted to make identifications on September 6, but the army refused to permit it. Once the judge left the village, patrollers from other towns unearthed the remains and burned them in the central plaza to destroy the evidence. Days later, when journalists arrived accompanying relatives of the victims, only bits of bone were left; the one identifiable cadaver, that of elderly Juana Lapa Huachaca, had been disfigured by multiple blows to the head with stones.[12]

The second group killing provoked a congressional investigation. It took place on September 22, 1990, in the high sierra town of Chilcahuaycco, where a month later eighteen bodies were unearthed in three common graves, all the victims naked and shot in the head with 7.62-millimeter bullets, the kind used by army-issue FALs (fusil automático liviano, or light automatic rifles), or 9-millimeter pistol ammunition such as army officers use.

The chain of events began on September 21, when at least fifty self-defense patrollers from Jollpa, Chanchara, and other nearby hamlets cooperated with the army in a sweep through this portion of Huamanga province. Responding to a Sendero attack on the civil defense committee of Cangari, in Huanta, the combined forces made their way from Santiago de Pischa toward Orccohuani, killing two minors (twelve and fifteen years old) on the way and detaining three campesinos as presumed Sendero sympathizers. Arriving in Orccohuani, they detained some local residents and mistreated their captives throughout the night.

More detentions, including those of two female minors, occurred the next day, September 22. Entering Pongoyocc, the ronderos and approximately twenty-five soldiers spread out, beating villagers and burglarizing their houses. Eleven adults and five children were detained and locked up with the others. Old people and children were later separated from the rest as the patrol moved into Chilcahuaycco, in the district of San Pedro de Cachi. There the detainees were ordered to undress and were then shot to death. The killers burned the victims' clothing where they buried the bodies.

The special Senate commission that investigated the events in Chilcahuaycco had harsh words for the civil-patrol strategy—among them, that communities that do not bow to pressure to form patrols are often victimized in revenge by the army and other ronderos; that militarization of communities severely undermines traditional communal authority; that to give arms to patrollers may facilitate criminal or political violence; that the patrols generate intercommunal conflict, as between militarized villages and those unwilling to do so; and that, as in the case of Chilcahuaycco, tragedy is often the result.

National campesino leaders also criticize the government's promotion of civil patrols. Juan Rojas, secretary general of the Confederación Campesina del Perú (CCP) stated in a recent interview: "The general law on peasant communities does not say that the army has the obligation—or the faculty—to organize communities in self-defense, or anything like that. We say they are violating communal autonomy."[13] The national organizing secretary of the

Confederación Nacional Agraria (CNA), Walter Sacayco, went further: "The peasant federations . . . maintain that this is not the appropriate way to pacify the country. The only road is through an agrarian policy favoring development in the countryside."[14]

Unfortunately, just as in other countries where civil defense patrols have been part of a counterinsurgency strategy, in Peru the formation of such patrols tends to create paramilitary forces that function principally to punish other civilians—on the theory that this "drains the sea" in which subversives swim like fish—and in the process, local forms of democracy are ruptured, the most violent members of a community benefit, and even when abuses are committed by patrols independently of the military, it is not in the military's interests to punish those abuses, because that would mean dismantling a patrol. In Peru there is hardly a need for another force to prey upon the rural civilian population.

Even recognizing Peruvians' desperation to find effective means of containing Sendero, and even acknowledging that villagers themselves may regard local militias as necessary for self-defense, Americas Watch believes that the creation of the patrols must take into account the substantial human rights risks they imply, both to the patrollers themselves and to other civilians whom they may be pressured to intimidate, detain, and execute. If the state is to support the formation of self-defense patrols, these should be trained and oriented only for self-defense activity, such as the protection of residents and property from attack, by means of regular and democratic distribution of guard duty in the manner chosen by the villagers themselves. Patrols should be used neither for aggressive actions in any circumstances nor as a replacement for traditional village authorities. No community should be forced to organize a patrol if it does not want one, no community should be punished and considered subversive for its reluctance to militarize, and no individual should be forced to be part of a patrol.

Given the isolation of many areas under state of emergency and the lack of oversight of military training for the patrollers, these necessary limits on patrol actions may be unenforceable. If so, then the formation of the patrols should be discontinued as a matter of policy. If communities wish to form patrols, they should be permitted to do so strictly for defensive purposes and without subservience to the military authorities, so that they do not enter the wider conflict.

8

THE PERSECUTION OF
HUMAN RIGHTS MONITORS

The controversy over U.S. aid to Peru, and recent egregious cases of abuse, provoked public debate about human rights in August and September 1991. But such debate about human rights has otherwise decreased perceptibly over the past few years. In a 1988 report Americas Watch noted that the government's tolerance of abuses was largely responsible for a growing public tendency to consider abuses inevitable. In spite of this disturbing trend, impressive human rights organizations in Peru continue to document and publicize human rights violations by the insurgents, the paramilitary groups, and the armed and police forces. These organizations condemn abuses by, and thus encounter hostility from, all sides.

Conditions for investigating human rights abuses in Peru are extremely difficult in areas under state of emergency. In rural areas especially, human rights monitors work under a multitude of constraints and at great personal risk. Delegations from the Lima headquarters of human rights organizations are able to travel to some emergency zones and gather testimony, but in others the lack of security and the army's attitude do not permit this. The provinces of the Upper Huallaga valley in particular are so dangerous that little human rights information is available.

Where it is not possible for human rights monitors to work, the civilian population is completely at the mercy of abuses by either side, and Americas Watch is concerned that the growing difficulties of human rights monitoring in Peru, in addition to posing greater risks for the monitors themselves, may indirectly contribute to a further rise in abuses.

In a survey of conditions for human rights organizations from December 1988 through December 1989, Americas Watch registered nineteen cases of persecution of Peruvians engaged in the defense of human rights, either as members of formal human rights organizations, as witnesses, or as the legal representatives of victims of repression.[1]

A few examples follow:

- Carlos Escobar Pineda, the prosecutor who investigated the massacre at Cayara (see chapter 4), worked on behalf of the surviving witnesses of the massacre after being fired from his post in August 1989. After the principal remaining witness was killed that September, Escobar publicized the execution in the Peruvian media. In late September he received three telephone death threats and noticed being followed. He had been receiving threats sporadically since August 1988. The new threats forced him to leave Peru for the United States on November 8.
- Dr. Coqui Samuel Huamani Sánchez, a lawyer and director of the Comité de Derechos Humanos (CODEH) in Cerro de Pasco, a community-based organization, was found dead on August 23, 1989, some hours after being seized in his home by armed men believed to be members of the security forces. He was the first human rights activist killed in the region.
- Dr. Wilfredo Saavedra, a lawyer and president of CODEH in Cajamarca, was detained on September 19, 1989, by members of the investigative police after being asked to accompany them to their headquarters supposedly to identify a detainee. He was reported to have been severely tortured in order to force him to confess to collaboration with the MRTA and was charged under the antiterrorist law.
- Four witnesses to the May 14, 1988, army massacre of at least twenty-nine peasants in Cayara, Ayacucho, were murdered between December 1988 and September 1989. Three, Antonio García Tipe, Fernandina Palomino Quispe, and Justiniano Tinco García (mayor of Cayara), were shot dead at an army roadblock on December 14, 1988. The fourth, Marta Crisóstomo García, received death threats for several months in 1989 and was executed on September 8 by men who entered her home in Huamanga and whom witnesses identified as military. She was the ninth witness to the Cayara massacre to be the victim of disappearance or extrajudicial execution.
- Cecilia Olea, member of the women's rights organization Flora Tristán, received repeated telephone threats and, on May 10, 1989, a note signed by the Comando Democrático Rodrigo Franco accusing her of being a "communist."
- Fernando Mejía Egocheaga, a legal adviser to peasant communities and shantytown dwellers, leader of the Oxapampa Bar Association and president of the provincial committee of the United Left, was

found dead on June 18, 1989, after being seized in his home on June
15 by military personnel in Oxapampa, department of Pasco. His
body bore signs of severe torture and bullet wounds.

Also during 1989, presumed paramilitary agents in Lima bombed the homes
and offices of Rodolfo Calderón and Andrés Ascencio, lawyers who defend
persons accused of terrorism, on March 22. Paramilitary agents were also
responsible for the murder of labor and women's rights activist Consuelo
García Santa Cruz on February 13 in Lima. The Instituto de Defensa Legal, a
legal aid and documentation group, noted that in Junín, lawyers engaged in
human rights cases reported being "permanently threatened and each time there
are fewer [legal] professionals to take those cases due to the threats and
mistreatment."[2]

Although a section on the press is not included here, several journalists have
been killed in recent years and are discussed in various contexts. It is not always
possible to determine whether journalists have been killed simply for being
journalists or more specifically for reporting on human rights. But in addition to
the cases mentioned elsewhere, the case of Hugo Bustíos, of the weekly magazine *Caretas,* should be emphasized. *Caretas* has frequently focused on the
human rights situation in Peru, and Bustíos was murdered while on his way to
investigate a double murder.

Hugo Bustíos and a colleague, Eduardo Rojas of the daily *Actualidad,* were
traveling in Huanta on November 24, 1988, when they were shot from the side
of the road. Bustíos was killed, Rojas wounded. Both had reported on the
conflict from this area. The military authorities had twice denied them permission to investigate the murders at the crime scene. The day of the attack, Bustíos
had sought permission to investigate from an army lieutenant colonel in the
Castropampa military base, who questioned Bustíos about his possible ties to a
recently captured Sendero leader. The ambush took place after the journalists
left the army post, when only the army and Bustíos's wife knew their route, and
just seconds after they had been waved through an army roadblock. The military has attempted to impede the investigation of the case, and soldiers have
detained and threatened Bustíos's widow, Margarita Patiño, and Rojas, as well
as six witnesses. One witness, Alejandro Ortíz Serna, was murdered on May
27, 1989.

In early May 1990, the U.S.-based Committee to Protect Journalists filed a
complaint against Peru on the Bustíos case before the Inter-American Commission on Human Rights of the Organization of American States (oas), asking
immediately for special precautionary measures ("medidas precautorias") to
protect the lives of Patiño, Rojas, and the witnesses. On May 16, 1990, the
commission issued a special request for protection to the Peruvian government,
as well as an urgent appeal to the Inter-American Court of Human Rights to

issue similar preventive measures. On June 5, 1990, the president of the court, Héctor Fix Zamudio of Mexico, ordered Peru to protect the lives of the witnesses and to refrain from actions against them. A court hearing was set for August 7, 1990, in San José, Costa Rica, to hear all parties on the issue of appropriate precautionary measures while the case is being processed. The court then ratified the president's order and asked Peru to report what measures were taken to protect the lives of the witnesses. Peru reported in late 1990. Though these powers of the commission and the court are contemplated in the American Convention on Human Rights and in their respective regulations, this is the first time that they have ever been put to use. The case on its merits is now before the commission.

In March 1991, after the local prosecutor denounced the killer as a soldier with the nickname Ojos de Gato, the judge ruled that without a precise identification no trial could go forward, and the case was stalled again. It remained for *Caretas*, rather than the courts, to identify Ojos de Gato as Amador Vidal Sambento, who evidently acted on the orders of his commanding officer, an army colonel calling himself Comandante Landa Dupont, whose real name is Víctor la Vera Hernández. On June 4, the home of Judge Moisés Ochoa Girón, who was in charge of the case in Huanta, was raided by soldiers whose commanding officer, a captain calling himself Tauro, responded to Dr. Ochoa's protests by citing superior orders, claiming to be seeking "supposed subversives." This attempt to intimidate Dr. Ochoa increased fears for his safety and that of the provincial prosecutor on the case, Maximiliano de la Cruz Hinostroza.

Some of the other recent persecutions of human rights monitors are listed below:

- On February 16, 1990, while Dr. José Burneo, director of CeaPaz, an organization associated with the church, was away attending a session of the United Nations Human Rights Commission, his home was visited by men who refused to identify themselves. This had also occurred in September 1989, when a man armed with a pistol or revolver knocked heavily on Burneo's door after midnight but refused to identify himself. A third intimidatory visit was paid to Burneo's house on March 16, 1990, while he was still away.
- On February 18, 1990, at 3:30 A.M., a bomb exploded in the Lima offices of the Andean Commission of Jurists, an international human rights organization. Staff members of the commission and of CeaPaz had noted surveillance of their homes in the days preceding the bombing.
- A few minutes later, another bomb exploded in the Lima offices of the International Committee of the Red Cross.

- On February 27, 1990, Angel Escobar Jurado, vice-president of the CODEH of Huancavelica, was kidnapped by five men in civilian clothes, and has disappeared. His name reportedly had been included on a CRF death list in 1989.
- On March 1, 1990, persons identifying themselves as members of the CRF made telephone threats to Francisco Soberón, coordinator of the Asociación Pro-Derechos Humanos (APRODEH), which documents human rights abuses in the emergency zones.
- On March 4, 1990, at 2:30 A.M., a high-powered bomb greatly damaged the Lima offices of Amnesty International. According to the antiterrorist unit of the national police, DIRCOTE, the bomb was "of high potency and sophisticated manufacture."[3]

None of these cases has been adequately investigated. The Interior Ministry's investigations into the three bomb attacks were superficial and unsatisfactory. It remains unknown whether the bombings were orchestrated by the MRTA (as the Interior Ministry concluded), by the CRF, or by the intelligence services of the armed forces. The timing and targets of the bomb attacks suggest that, at a moment when the United Nations was studying the situation of human rights in Peru, international human rights organizations with expertise on Peru were being warned to act with care.

At the moment of the 1990 presidential elections, two new cases were reported.

- On June 9, 1990, a bomb was planted in the house of Rosa Mandujano, in Huancayo, Junín, according to Amnesty International. Mandujano worked as human rights secretary of the Huancayo Defense Front.
- Amnesty International reported the detention of a human rights monitor in Ayacucho on June 10. Guadalupe Ccallocunto Olano was reportedly detained by armed men in civilian dress at 2:30 A.M. When her family approached the military authorities about her detention later that morning, they were told that the authorities had no record of it. Her relatives believe that the army was responsible, because Ccallocunto had been threatened by members of the army in recent months. She had also been detained twice in earlier years. Ccallocunto had been active in the association of the relatives of the detained and the disappeared in the emergency zone since her husband's disappearance in 1983. She had also recently been working with the international human rights organization Servicio Paz y Justicia (SERPAJ) in Ayacucho.[4] Americas Watch called on the government of Peru to ensure that, if she were in custody, her detention be acknowledged,

that she be guaranteed due process, and that her physical integrity be respected. The case also generated concern in the U.S. Congress, reflecting a growing recognition of the Peruvian human rights crisis. She has not reappeared, however.

Slightly more than a month later, on July 19 and 20, two human rights lawyers in Ayacucho were assassinated. Máximo Rico Bazán was taken violently from his home in Huamanga by a group of hooded men. The following day, Fernando Colonio Arteaga, legal adviser to San Cristóbal National University in Huamanga, was dragged from his home and shot in the head. These killings, which suggested some complicity between the death squad and military authorities, were part of a wave of attacks in Huamanga, many of them apparently targeting the university. They drew some international attention. So, too, did the May 13, 1991, execution of Porfirio Suni Quispe, leader of the Federación Departamental de Campesinos de Puno and president of the human rights commission in the regional parliament. In 1988 Suni had been imprisoned for ten months on suspicion of terrorism, then released for lack of evidence. His murder, however, appears to have been at Sendero, not military, hands. Two men in civilian clothes dragged Suni from his home and shot him four times, the final shot a coup de grace.

The killing of Porfirio Suni, though not acknowledged by Sendero, was followed quickly by an editorial in the June 18 edition of the insurgents' organ, *El Diario,* in which the work of human rights organizations was described as an "escape valve" for the frustrations of the people; "human rights are based in a bourgeois conception of the world that is centered on the individual and conceives of humanity as a family, in order to deny class struggle."[5]

The most widely publicized case of an attack against a human rights monitor during the first year of the Fujimori administration, meanwhile, was the near-fatal bomb attack on human rights lawyer Augusto Zúñiga Paz, on March 15, 1991. Zúñiga Paz, the only full-time staff lawyer at COMISEDH, was representing the family of disappeared student Ernesto Castillo Páez, whose case was described in chapter 2. Having just been defeated in a historic habeas corpus action in that case, Zúñiga was planning to pursue the perpetrators through other charges. In his mail on March 15 was a large envelope, hand-delivered and bearing what looked like a government stamp, addressed to the "Legal Department" of COMISEDH, presumably himself. The envelope was a sophisticated bomb of a kind not used before in Peru; when Zúñiga opened it, the explosion took off his left forearm.

The U.S. Department of State protested this attack in a cable to the Peruvian government, and unanimous condemnation was voiced in Peru. Yet the new government's attitude toward human rights organizations has been ambivalent.

Fujimori has indicated a certain openness to human rights activists, for example in appointing representatives of several well-known human rights groups to serve on the special pardon commission he established to benefit unconvicted prison inmates. Yet his justice minister, the representative of his government who would logically serve as liaison with the human rights community, has taken a public stance so hostile and at the same time so graceless that relations are, at best, uncomfortable. Minister Antoniolli has accused human rights organizations of "creating obstacles to police and armed forces' intervention in zones affected by subversion."[6] He has spoken of "eternal defenders of human rights who, instead of supporting the forces of order, limit themselves to denouncing apparent excesses and thus, only contribute to a climate of demoralization" among those forces.[7] The characterization is untrue: human rights activity in no way affects the conduct of the counterinsurgency campaign in emergency zones—though arguably it should—and human rights organizations have always noted abuses by all parties. Furthermore, such an attitude on the part of the nation's highest law-enforcement official might well be taken as a license to threaten or attack human rights monitors, whether or not intended as such.

The minister's remarks, in short, are unacceptable. Americas Watch urges the Fujimori government to make a gesture of reparation to the country's human rights groups by offering them strong and unequivocal support. In documenting a bleak situation, Peruvian human rights organizations are careful and rigorous, and their consistent condemnation of violence by Sendero and the MRTA, as well as by official forces, leaves no doubt of their sincerity in advocating respect for human rights for its own sake.

9

THE ROLE OF THE
UNITED STATES

The United States government's relation with Peru has become thoroughly determined by its antinarcotics program in the Andean region. Of the three nations affected by that program, Peru has been the most vociferously unhappy with U.S. premises and goals, and the one in which U.S. programs have most obviously fallen short. A May 1991 framework agreement between the United States and Peru acknowledged that "the actions developed thus far in combating narcotics trafficking in Peru have not had the desired results."

The fertile, mountainous Upper Huallaga River valley is exceptionally well suited to the cultivation of coca, which can be harvested up to four times annually on the slopes there. Coca plants grown in the Upper Huallaga's acidic soil are also exceptionally suited for processing into cocaine, because they possess a higher alkaloid content than plants grown elsewhere. This region produced more than half the world's coca leaf in 1989 and was the point of origin of nearly half the cocaine and "crack" consumed in the United States that year. Because Peru is the world's largest producer of coca leaf, the failure to date of the U.S. strategy places enormous pressure on American antidrug officials, and through them on the Peruvian government, to do more, do it better, and do it fast.

Although Peruvian leftist parties take a nationalist position about U.S. aid, fearing it will mean inordinate American influence in national affairs, other Peruvians welcome the prospect of aid that may reduce drug-related corruption and violence and—for there is no mystery about U.S. intentions—restrain the expansion of Sendero. But Peruvians do not view the drug problem through the same lens as U.S. politicians. An economic activity that brings the nation one billion dollars annually, or about 30 percent of Peru's foreign-exchange earnings, coca is the nation's "informal" life-support system; as Peru's finance minister told a U.S. congressional subcommittee in January 1990, "The elimination of coca from Peru's economy would . . . be nothing short of devastating."[1] In 1989 the coca-production economy employed 26,000 agricultural workers in the north-central Upper Huallaga valley and permitted the economic survival of 60,000 small-farm owners and their families there, a total of about 200,000 people.[2] On a larger scale, the laundering of coca revenues contributes indispensably to stabilizing the price of the dollar, which otherwise would have spiraled out of control in recent years; this stabilization, combined with the actual revenues generated by coca, have enabled Peru to attempt repaying its foreign debt.

Evidence is surfacing that the Peruvian drug trade has become more sophisticated, with Colombian-financed laboratories for cocaine refinement being built in the rain forest. Peru's indigenous coca traffickers are far from being a cartel, however, and Peruvians think of coca primarily in terms of the growers, who are peasants barely supporting themselves. Coca, moreover, is a traditional drug in Peru, chewed by campesinos or brewed in a tea and associated with medicine and ethnic custom rather than addiction. The drug crisis in the consuming country means little to the producer nation, which has crises of its own. And although drug-related violence is rising, the eradication of coca is widely perceived in Peru as a favor to the United States, which should share the burden of solving the problem its consumers created.

Negotiations between the United States and Peru have been especially difficult given these differences of perspective. The framework agreement of May 1991 is careful to use language that implies the resolution of these differences. Actual conditions in the Upper Huallaga, and within the Peruvian army and police, suggest otherwise, however, and amid the many and complex problems facing antidrug policy in Peru, Americas Watch remains deeply concerned about the human rights impact of U.S. strategy.

PROPOSED MILITARY AID, 1989–90

In September 1989 the director of national drug control policy for the United States, William E. Bennett, announced a plan to curb the production, processing, and commercialization of narcotics in Colombia, Bolivia, and Peru. Accompanying that plan was a request that the U.S. Congress release $125 million in military aid for the three Andean countries for Fiscal Year 1990. How these funds would be spent was not explained until March 1990 and did not satisfy some members of Congress, who demanded that human rights concerns receive more emphasis and that the administration provide written assurance of the objectives of this aid: members of the House Foreign Affairs Committee, for example, insisted that aid must go only for counternarcotics training and equipment, not for counterinsurgency.

The administration provided such assurances, and for FY 1990, $35.9 million in military aid was appropriated for Peru, as well as $19 million for the Peruvian police and $6.8 million to the U.S. Drug Enforcement Administration (DEA) to support DEA liaison with the Peruvian military once the military aid was accepted. The package also contained $4 million in economic support funds tied to the counternarcotics program.[3]

The García government did not approve the counternarcotics package for FY 1990, except for the portion for police; as García's term ended, Peru had not signed the agreement to disburse the remaining funds—$46.7 million. This FY 1990 aid awaited acceptance or rejection by the new government of Alberto Fujimori.

The most controversial item in the package was the military aid, which represented an immense increase over U.S. military aid in the past and the first time that the Peruvian military would receive training for counternarcotics activity.[4] According to press reports and U.S. officials in Lima, the aid would be used to train five battalions of the Peruvian army and one battalion of marines (navy), the primary military force deployed in the Upper Huallaga; to provide motor launches for actions along the rivers of coca-producing areas, as well as replacement parts for surveillance aircraft; and to outfit this force with such basic equipment as uniforms, ammunition, and weapons. The package reportedly also contained some $8 million for the construction of a new military training base in the Upper Huallaga, but the construction project appeared to have been abandoned or postponed; it was unclear how those funds would be used if the base were not constructed.

If the new Peruvian government approved this U.S. initiative, training was expected to begin as early as September 1990. On the ground in the Upper Huallaga valley would be an undisclosed number of U.S. Green Berets acting as trainers—one source said as many as twenty-four[5]—as well as a small group of support personnel, coordinated by the military group attached to the U.S. embassy in Lima. Members of Congress questioned U.S. officials closely about reports, including one in a military magazine, that the Green Berets would be involved in combat operations, and Pentagon officials stated that the trainers had been prohibited from any combat role.

In spite of the earlier assurances given to Congress, it was evident that the military training would include counterinsurgency tactics. Melvyn Levitsky, assistant secretary of state for international narcotics matters, told a subcommittee of the House Foreign Affairs Committee on June 20, 1990, "Where the insurgency and the drug traffickers are inextricably bound together, we have to deal with them together. . . . We have an interest in helping them [the Peruvian military] fight that insurgency."[6] More pungently, an unidentified U.S. military official told *Newsweek*, "We're going back to what we know best—how to fight the commies."[7]

Aspects of the human rights situation, and how it is deteriorating, in the Upper Huallaga have already been described. In brief, human rights violations in the Upper Huallaga by uniformed agents of the military and police forces in recent years have included disappearances, army bombardment of villages, and police abuse of civilians during drug searches. There is also circumstancial evidence of army killings of noncombatants in situations other than the bombardments of inhabited areas (see chapter 6).

These facts should have been sufficient to disqualify the Peruvian army and navy for U.S. military assistance under Section 502(b) of the Foreign Assistance Act, which states that a government may not receive such assistance if it "engages in a consistent pattern of gross violations of internationally recognized human rights." Although Americas Watch does not believe that the García government deliberately pursued a policy of human rights violations, the abuses described here reveal that a "consistent pattern" of human rights violations took place during the García administration, reflecting at least an official acceptance of abuses and a refusal to confront or curb them. What is more, the requirements of Section 502(b) pertain to human rights conditions in a country as a whole; even were the Peruvian military blameless in the climbing incidence of abuses in the Upper Huallaga, their overall performance would disqualify them for aid to fight there.

United States officials were aware of this, just as they were aware of the extent of human rights violations in Peru. Although U.S. officials in congressional hearings sought to downplay the human rights situation in Peru, the Department of State's *Country Report* on human rights in Peru during 1989 was an excellent profile of that situation, sparing neither the military nor the police. The counternarcotics aid package, therefore, was proposed in full knowledge that the requirements of Section 502(b) could not be satisfied in Peru.

The legislation under which the counternarcotics aid was requested, the International Narcotics Control Act of 1989, also contains human rights language; it makes Section 502(b) conditions applicable to all assistance appropriated for the antidrug campaign. This reiteration of human rights standards for countries that receive aid was also ignored.

Similarly, the $19 million in police aid already appropriated for FY 1990, and accepted by the García government, had been passed through the U.S. Congress only by waiving the relevant human rights legislation, Section 660 of the Foreign Assistance Act. That legislation prohibits the use of U.S. aid "to provide training or advice, or provide any financial support, for police, prisons, or other law enforcement forces for any foreign government." The legislation was drafted specifically to prevent U.S. assistance to abusive police forces, of which Peru's unfortunately is one. Sound policy cannot be made by waiving human rights laws, which were developed to avoid the repetition of bitter past experience.

Given the intense pressure in the United States for initiatives against international drug traffic, and given that the United States government has defined the war on drugs as a matter of national security, arguments based on human rights legislation may not convince those who argue for military aid. Sendero Luminoso and the drug traffic do pose real dangers for the stability of the Peruvian state, and there is a great need for the efficient military confrontation of Sendero.

But the Peruvian government, as desperate as its situation was in 1989, viewed the problem differently, and despite Alan García's plummeting popularity, this different view was widely held in Peru. García pursued a multilateral response to the drug traffic through discussions with Colombia and Bolivia and through demands that U.S. and European governments take responsibility to discourage drug consumption while helping these Andean nations find viable alternatives for economic development. In a letter to García in December 1989, as a prelude to the February 1990 Cartagena summit meeting of the presidents of the United States, Bolivia, Colombia, and Peru, President George Bush wrote that, while attacking the problems of consumption and production, "we must, at the same time, provide legitimate alternatives to peasants who live in the countries where coca is cultivated."[8] García's objections to the FY 1990 U.S. aid proposal centered on its small economic component, which did not bode well for a long-term developmental strategy as agreed upon in Cartagena.

For FY 1991, the Bush administration requested for Peru an increase of military aid to $39.9 million, the same amounts of police and DEA assistance as in FY 1990, and a substantially larger allotment of counternarcotics economic aid, $63.1 million, which was intended for balance-of-payments support; the local currencies generated would be used for counternarcotics activities. This did indicate substantial economic aid for the counternarcotics effort, but it was aid for budgetary support, not for development or crop substitution, as the Andean governments had envisioned. And the economic support funds were contingent on Peru's acceptance of the military portion of the package. The administration's linking of economic aid to the Peruvian government's acceptance of military aid was explored and criticized at House and Senate hearings in June 1990.

In addition to raising objections based on Sections 502(b) and 660, Americas Watch has raised questions about the destination of U.S. aid in a region under military control where the civilian government presence is decreasing and human rights abuses are multiplying. It is highly debatable whether a military response to coca cultivation can substitute for a coherent regional political, military, and economic program, coordinated and supervised by the Peruvian government. It is also reasonable to ask whether militarization as the United States proposes it—that is, a combination of antinarcotics and counterinsurgency campaigns—

may actually inhibit the development of such a coherent program, for reasons explained below.

There are, moreover, valid concerns that the proposed U.S. aid package might commit the United States to a strategy that could not succeed without further infusions of military aid over time and without wholesale human rights violations. Those who judge that a combined war on drug traffic and Sendero Luminoso in the Upper Huallaga valley can be won quickly, with what pragmatists may regard as an acceptably selective loss of civilian life, are, Americas Watch believes, mistaken.

Conditions in Peru are such that a military approach to narcotics control must victimize small growers, peasants who have no part in the processing or sale of cocaine but who also lack viable alternatives to planting coca. To evaluate the full implications of this approach for human rights, it is important to take stock of the history of Sendero Luminoso and coca cultivation in the Upper Huallaga region, as well as the failure to date of U.S. programs for drug eradication.

THE UPPER HUALLAGA AND U.S. DRUG PROGRAMS

The Upper Huallaga river valley is a loosely defined rain forest area comprising the provinces of Marañón and Leoncio Prado in the northern half of the department of Huánuco and the province of Tocache, which occupies most of the southern half of the department of San Martín. These areas are joined by a highway that runs from the city of Huánuco north through the town of Tingo María and then northwest through the center of San Martín department. It is a fertile area capable of producing fruit, grains, palms, and sugar. The population of the area is roughly estimated at 300,000.

Colonization of the Upper Huallaga was promoted by Belaúnde's first government (1963–68), under a program to develop the jungle. The military governments of 1968–80 paid no attention to the region, however, leaving campesinos without adequate commercial roads and other services for development. The increase in coca cultivation resulted in some measure from the state's failure to provide development options to people who, inspired by the promises of the Belaúnde government, had moved to the area to improve their quality of life.

Before the mid-1970s, some coca was produced for local consumption by the campesinos, who traditionally chew the leaf. After 1975, however, in response to the international demand for cocaine, and in the context of government inattention to peasants' economic needs, the area of cultivation increased from about 2,500 acres (1,000 hectares) to 15,000 acres (6,000 hectares) in 1980 and, by 1989, an estimated 500,000 acres (200,000 hectares).[9] Tens of thousands of peasants later migrated to the Upper Huallaga to plant coca. These are people defined less by their identification with the area than by their immediate interests in survival and who thus tend to make alliances with whatever force is dominant in the zone.

American antinarcotics programs in the area date from the beginning of the 1980s. By the time Belaúnde was returned to power in the 1980 elections, coca cultivation had become a serious international problem, and the Belaúnde government combined the establishment of a special police unit, Mobile Rural Patrol Unit (UMOPAR), with two U.S.-financed programs for coca control. One of the American programs, run by the Agency for International Development (AID), was a long-term agricultural development project; the other was explicitly aimed at drug eradication. In this context, DEA agents were sent to work with the Peruvian police.

The police made little headway—in part because many officers were corrupt, a situation that persists today. Peasant growers of coca found themselves pressured both by the eradication program and by police who demanded bribes, as well as by the traffickers, who violently opposed any organizing to defend peasants' interests. In this situation, both Sendero Luminoso and the MRTA established a presence in the zone, claiming to represent the interests of the small growers.

Sendero had more success than the MRTA, taking on the police, the paramilitary organizations of traffickers, and the MRTA where the two groups competed. By 1988 Sendero was operating in most of the Upper Huallaga and acting as an intermediary between the cocaleros and the agents of the Colombian traffickers who buy the coca leaf or its first-stage refined product, coca paste (*pasta básica*). Sendero offered the peasants protection and bargained with the traffickers for higher prices.

The governments of Belaúnde and then García faced a two-sided problem: either they could give priority to the drug eradication effort, as the United States wished to do, and thereby alienate the peasants by destroying their livelihood without offering them an alternative; or they could pursue Sendero first, seeking support from the local population through development programs, and deal with coca production in a more gradual fashion. If drug eradication were to take priority, the police would be in charge of operations and the issue would be defined as criminal activity. If Sendero were the prime target, the army would take charge under emergency authority.

Belaúnde decided to make Sendero the first priority and ordered the suspension of drug eradication efforts in the zone. Under a state of emergency declared in July 1984, the army focused on confronting Sendero and explicitly guaranteed the population that it could continue to plant coca. The United States opposed this strategy, however, and convinced the Peruvian government to allow limited renewal of its eradication efforts, which were unpopular among the peasants. Then in December 1985 the new García administration lifted the state of emergency. Sendero took advantage of the unpopularity of the U.S. programs to kill workers with the programs. It took advantage of the army's withdrawal to attack the police.

In July 1987, García reimposed the state of emergency, which has been in force since then. He did not, however, immediately install a PMC in the Upper Huallaga, as has been the practice elsewhere. Instead, a sort of in-between state of emergency authority resided with the police.

The DEA continued its programs and had some success at interdiction in the last months of 1988. But the U.S. initiatives were constantly under attack by Sendero, and it was evident that the police could not operate securely. These are the conditions that prompted the United States to turn to the Peruvian military, proposing to "solve" the narcotics problem by eradicating coca and Sendero together.

MILITARY CONTRADICTIONS AND HUMAN RIGHTS ABUSES, 1989–90

During 1989 Sendero increased its activity in the Upper Huallaga. For the first time senderistas were prepared to fight in open confrontations. As it became more difficult for antinarcotics agents to operate safely—and given the local population's lack of cooperation—the United States promoted the use of an herbicide, Tebuthiuron, popularly known as Spike, to eradicate coca plantations from the air. Use of the chemical has serious environmental consequences; it reportedly kills trees and shrubs and, in the mountainous Upper Huallaga region, could have increased problems of erosion by destroying vegetation indiscriminately.[10] The political effects of this spraying could be equally serious, in terms of its potential propaganda value to the insurgency. The government's proposals to use Spike met strong opposition from local campesino organizations and were dropped, although one "experimental" application was made in March 1989.[11]

In the meantime, the absence of a clear strategy for confronting Sendero in the region led to national scandal. Sendero's late March 1989 attack on the Uchiza police post in San Martín revealed the government's lack of military preparedness and flexibility, as ten policemen were killed and another fourteen wounded while the government was helpless to send reinforcements (see chapter 5). The incident provoked widespread criticism of the emphasis on drug eradication in the Upper Huallaga, because it was perceived that Sendero was the greater danger.

The controversy produced a change of direction, an all-out campaign against Sendero. In April 1989, Gen. Alberto Arciniega was named chief of military operations in the security zone comprising Huánuco and San Martín departments, which includes the Upper Huallaga, and in May 1989 the armed forces were given control of internal order in the zone with the formation of a PMC. Arciniega prepared to confront Sendero while also seeking popular support for the counterinsurgercy effort.

Arciniega's civic action strategy was to win over Sendero's social base, the cocaleros, by permitting them to continue planting coca while urging that the government help them to substitute other crops. He was also publicly critical of DEA's programs and methods. "We have to make a distinction between the peasant grower and the narcotrafficker," noted Arciniega. "The first must be brought out of his marginality, the second must be repressed. What the DEA does is to repress the two equally. And if we do that, that is if we repress fifty thousand cocalero peasants, in a short time we have fifty thousand recruits or collaborators of Sendero. We cannot corner them like wounded beasts, we must give them an opportunity to change."[12] Arciniega thus supported such initiatives as the formation of the Cooperativa Agraria del Alto Huallaga, an organization dedicated to promoting projects of crop substitution and agricultural development.

Arciniega beat back Sendero militarily for three months, until the insurgents decided to retreat from open engagement in the zone. The culminating battle took place in late July 1989, when Sendero attacked a military base in Madre Mía, where materials were being stored for the construction of the antidrug base in Santa Lucía. After four hours of battle, according to Arciniega, there were sixty subversives and nine army personnel dead; eight enemy rifles were recovered. Such direct confrontations, combined with engagements in villages and the active pursuit of Sendero cadres, gave the army its first significant victories over Sendero in the region.

The human rights cost of the strategy appears to have been high, however. The Upper Huallaga is the most difficult area in Peru in which to gather human rights data because of the security situation and the problems of access, but a study of politically related deaths throughout Peru shows that such killings rose dramatically in the Upper Huallaga between April and July 1989.[13] Some of the dead were certainly combatants, but Arciniega's own declarations suggest that many unarmed civilians may have died because the army considered them sympathizers of Sendero.

It is sufficient here to mention the bombardment of La Morada, in Huánuco, on July 6, 1989 which Arciniega sought to justify by saying, "It was the residents of La Morada who warned a column of Sendero Luminoso of the presence of a military patrol near the hamlet."[14] Twenty people died in that army attack, though as civilians the residents of La Morada were not legitimate targets. While the Interior Minister was estimating a total Sendero presence in the Upper Huallaga of one thousand combatants, General Arciniega was claiming to have eliminated more than seven hundred.[15] And he was registering virtually no wounded. Nor were the publicized numbers of recovered arms so large as would be supposed had all the dead been combatants.

When Sendero shifted tactics after Madre Mía and settled into the use of selective terrorism that typifies its method elsewhere in Peru, the army responded as it does elsewhere, with disappearances, torture, and arbitrary arrests. This shift, like the human rights abuses that accompanied the earlier confrontational strategy, highlights the enormous dangers attendant on a policy of purely military response to Sendero.

The civic-action component of Arciniega's strategy was not backed by any long-term government initiative for the development of the zone. Equally important, it was not backed by consistent official support for the formation of broad peasant organizations that could act, over the long term, as the peasants' own political representatives with the government or the traffickers. So long as Sendero could represent itself as a benefactor to the cocaleros (who have no other), the army regarded that population as suspect, and so long as the army and police represented contradictory government strategies, Sendero could use that contradiction to maintain some measure of popular support. The peasants, whose interest is less in cultivating coca than in cultivating whatever will permit them to live safely and sell their crops at reasonable prices, are targets from four sides: the traffickers, Sendero, the police, and the military.

General Arciniega was transferred in December 1989, well before his year-long appointment expired. He had been accused by Melvyn Levitsky, U.S. assistant secretary of state for international narcotics matters, of colluding with the traffickers, a charge that was not publicly supported with evidence and that was interpreted by some Peruvian observers as politically motivated. Like so many accusations in Peru, this one has not been investigated. Its timing and results, however, led to speculation that Arciniega's demise was due to his having criticized the DEA's program and objectives.

Arciniega's successor was more comfortable with the DEA presence in the region. But his tenure was brief precisely because one of his subordinates was caught colluding in a drug shipment. The next chief of the PMC, Gen. Mario Brito, assumed the post in March 1990 and remained until October 1990, when the MRTA attempted to assassinate him. He was seriously wounded and was transferred. In a less publicized fashion, Brito shared Arciniega's perspective: "If we attack drug trafficking, we will convert the local population into our enemy. . . . Then instead of one enemy, Sendero, we will have three: Sendero, the local population who will then support Sendero, and the drug traffickers, who will then provide resources to Sendero."[16]

In the meantime, the Cartagena summit, which brought together the presidents of Peru, Bolivia, Colombia, and the United States in February 1990 to coordinate a strategy on drugs, encouraged many Peruvians in that its final document referred not only to repression of the drug traffic at its source but also to controlling consumption and seeking economic alternatives. But the attitude of U.S. representatives on the ground in Peru apparently did not echo this broad conception of the problem. In a letter to President Bush following the Cartagena summit, the Cooperativa Agraria del Alto Huallaga based in Uchiza, the most important regional grouping of peasants organized for crop substitution, stated, "We have spoken with many of your representatives. It seems that they do not faithfully transmit our intentions, which leads us to sense that they wish the problem to continue." The peasants' disgust was perhaps due to their having labored for three years to build a hope of development solutions among their neighbors and to their fear that without timely support these efforts would be vitiated as violence took over the zone.

Peasants arguing for crop substitution programs were seeking an initial state investment in infrastructure, seeds, and other basic goods and the promotion of adequate conditions such as roads for the marketing of their crops. In the isolated Huallaga, coca is the only crop for which marketing and transport are not problems; they are handled by the Colombians. The farmers also argued that this was the time to make a commitment to crop substitution, for economic as well as political reasons: the price of coca had fallen dramatically, and Sendero had been unable to affect the price.

After September 1989, the price of coca leaf declined to 40–50 cents per kilo, about half the peasants' cost of production. This was compared to a past price of $2 to a maximum $3 per kilo, which permitted the peasants to live at slightly better than subsistence level.[17] The price reached its nadir in early 1990; then it began to rise slightly, in what some observers believed to be a response to poor harvests in Bolivia, but for much of the year it remained below the cost of production.

In early 1990, Sendero attempted to enforce a united front among the cocaleros such that they would refuse to sell until higher prices could be negotiated, but the economic desperation of the small growers led many to defy Sendero and sell. The price remained low, and Sendero lost face. These conditions, argued development specialists in the Upper Huallaga, were propitious for the launching of a crop substitution program. Estimates on the cost of such a program varied widely, and the potential for embezzlement of funds is always great in Peru. But projects underway, assisted by the United Nations Development Program, had laid the basis for at least a limited substitution plan and possible oversight.

This opportunity was not seized, although some of its lessons appeared in the language of the May 1991 U.S.-Peru framework agreement: an emphasis on finding alternative economic strategies, an awareness of the peasants' need for help with marketing licit crops. In the meantime, the U.S.-built antidrug base at Santa Lucía went into operation in January 1990.[18] An April 7 attack on the base by a large contingent of senderistas severely damaged three of the nine helicopters used in interdiction by UMOPAR and the DEA and, for the first time, drew DEA agents into a battle. (The attack also exposed serious deficiencies in security and evacuation measures; as a U.S. congressional report noted, procedures for evacuating American personnel had been developed, but Peruvians working at the base were expected, in the event of an attack, to "open the gates and head for the hills"—a patently callous instruction, given Sendero's treatment of its captives. In the event, the April 7 attack proved that the helicopters would be the first targets—thus leaving Americans stranded and at the insurgents' mercy along with local personnel.)[19] News of the attack on Santa Lucía was not released at all in Peru; national media learned of it only through U.S. coverage.

At the same time, drug interdiction efforts were repeatedly associated with abuses of peasants' rights. It is well known in Peru that police, whose regular wages earn them barely enough to live, bribe their superiors in order to be assigned to the Upper Huallaga because of the opportunities for personal enrichment there. While the traffickers can afford to pay off police, the peasants cannot. According to peasant representatives from the Upper Huallaga interviewed by Americas Watch in May 1990, the police working with DEA "totally confuse[d]" the civilian population with the traffickers. Peruvian television news on May 6, 1990, carried interviews with residents of Uchiza who spoke of DEA agents as participating in police abuses such as violent raids on homes and physical mistreatment. United States officials strongly questioned these statements, and Americas Watch is not aware of any formal accusations against DEA agents. Nonetheless, it was evident that, in the local perception, the DEA was identified with abusive and unpopular police practices.

The logic of the U.S. military aid proposal in 1989 was that, without eliminating or at least controlling Sendero, it would not be possible to pursue the drug traffickers efficiently, and without U.S. training, the army might do no better than it had in the past. This logic might have made sense in a counterinsurgency context, but combined with an antinarcotics objective it had serious flaws.

The first was that coca eradication in the Upper Huallaga is not a purely military problem, just as Sendero's existence and expansion are not purely military problems. The only areas of Peru where Sendero has been successfully excluded, or where it is now penetrating with most difficulty, are areas where the population is autonomously organized around economic interests, has voluntarily assumed self-defense, and has sufficient political influence—through campesino federations and other such organizations—to achieve economic advances. This is the case, for example, in the departments of Puno and Cusco. The Upper Huallaga valley, as an immigrant area, lacks a history of strong local organization. It is arguable, however—and organizations like the Cooperativa Agraria del Alto Huallaga argue tenaciously—that local initiatives can be strengthened if the government of Peru, and foreign governments like that of the United States, assist peasants in organizing around economic issues and follow up with aid to facilitate the marketing of alternative crops. Militarizing the situation, as the United States proposed to do it, would undermine the political advances achieved by peasant organizers and make further advances extremely difficult, if not impossible.

A second flaw in the U.S. strategy, especially regarding the presence of Green Berets in the Upper Huallaga, was that the direct involvement of U.S. personnel would permit Sendero Luminoso to claim that its war against the Peruvian state was also a war of national sovereignty, an anti-imperialist war. The unpopularity of the DEA's past efforts had played into Sendero hands; equally or more so would the presence of Green Berets engaged in antidrug training. The U.S. military personnel would themselves become preferred targets of Sendero, as DEA program workers had been. Indeed, there were signs that Sendero had wished for some time to provoke just this situation and expected to gather support from it. These considerations made it likely that, in the scenario proposed by the United States, the civilian population of the Upper Huallaga would be viewed as suspect by the Peruvian military. In such conditions, which the U.S. presence would partially define, Americas Watch was deeply concerned that peasants would be victimized, and in large numbers.

CONTEXT FOR THE CONVENIO, 1990–91

By 1991 Sendero was taking protection money from traffickers in the Upper Huallaga. That is, it regulated a crucial aspect of commercial activity in a zone where over 90 percent of the economy is based on coca production and related "services"; its control over landing and takeoff rights and effective collection of taxes on those rights gave Sendero additional bargaining power as the cocaleros' self-styled protector and, not incidentally, made the insurgents immensely richer—by as much as $20 or $30 million a year.[20] Although Sendero did not openly confront the army as it had in 1989 and had suffered setbacks in its attempt to control peasant growers' price negotiations, it remained a force throughout the Upper Huallaga. As coca cultivation spread northward into the Central Huallaga—into the San Martín provinces of Lamas, Rioja, Moyobamba, and others, to escape military pressure—Sendero followed it, even into areas where the MRTA was the more established of the two groups. In the meantime, the price of coca was recovering.

In the months following the July 1990 change of government, press reports indicated that the army had stepped up pressure in the Upper Huallaga, killing a substantial number of presumed subversives. The Bernales Commission's year-end report also noted that the high point of political violence related to increased conflict in the coca-growing regions, both Junín and the Huallaga, although it placed that intensification earlier, in June.[21] Although such figures must be taken with caution, given the difficulties of verification, it is impressive how high the Upper Huallaga departments rank in relative violence while also being areas from which violence is seriously underreported. For the number of deaths due to political violence in 1990, Huánuco with 556 ranked third in the nation—after Junín and Ayacucho—and San Martín ranked fourth with 467, according to the Bernales Commission. For killings by Sendero, San Martín ranked second—after Ayacucho—and Huánuco stood with Huancavelica in third place.[22]

For killings by the armed forces, the statistics are even clearer: Huánuco and San Martín represented by far the areas of most intense activity.[23] As in the account that follows, some of those killed as subversives in this period were civilians.

On September 24, 1990, an army column supported by helicopter gunships made a surprise attack on Merced de Locro, Huánuco. Surrounding a building where senderistas were among about 250 people having a party, the soldiers killed 85 senderistas, according to an army communiqué. Witnesses who gave statements to the prosecutor's office in Leoncio Prado, however, said the soldiers entered firing indiscriminately. According to these witnesses, though some fifty of the dead had been senderistas, the others had simply been villagers attending the party. News media investigating the incident found these statements convincing.

The difficulties of gathering information in the Huallaga region are such that even the most careful investigators must be guided by press accounts, and these are incomplete at best. It would appear from media reports that Sendero was somewhat damaged by the army's offensive in the latter half of 1990, but on December 10, Sendero destroyed the installation of Mobil Oil's subsidiary SEREAL in Barranca, San Martín, a major operation and one that exposed the army's inadequacy. Some 180 senderistas took over the surrounding hamlets, occupied the exploration camp on December 1, and controlled it completely for ten days, before setting fire to its buildings, hangar, and exploration equipment and causing some $3 million in damages. During the occupation senderistas killed five villagers. During the occupation, too, residents and SEREAL workers informed the army and the nearest police post of the Sendero presence but received no help whatsoever. Only days after the insurgents had withdrawn did the army begin to search the area for subversives. Contrary to statements by the minister of defense of the new government, a congressional investigative commission found that the army had sufficient knowledge to have prevented the December 10 attack; the commission found the PMC of the Huallaga negligent. The PMC commander was removed, but the commission's other recommendation, the ouster of the defense minister, was not followed.

United States relations with the Defense Ministry, and the military generally, had by this time become tense for other reasons. The army's hostility to police antinarcotics operations and the DEA appeared to go beyond competition for operative seniority in the Huallaga; military corruption was another obstacle to the drug interdiction program. In March 1990, police investigating drug flights from a landing strip near the Ramal de Aspusana military base reportedly were fought off by soldiers so that a small plane could be loaded and take off unexamined. The same month, near the same army base, police found a clandestine landing strip where soldiers were overseeing the loading of a drug shipment. Two captains and two lieutenants were denounced, retired from the service, and submitted to trial.[24]

The army acted rapidly to discipline the culprits in that case, but incidents later in the year—including one case in which twenty to twenty-five soldiers allegedly prevented DEA and police agents from entering a storage facility for semiprocessed cocaine—led the DEA to suspend operations in Peru as of November, citing "interference." A November 25 article in the *Washington Post* widely publicized in Peru contained charges that high army officials were passing traffickers information on planned operations by the DEA and Peruvian police.[25] (Because the area was under PMC authority, police were required to notify the army command twenty-four hours before an operation. This prior-notice requirement was later rescinded.)

Denying the allegations, the military charged police and the DEA with fabricating them to undermine the army's seniority in the Upper Huallaga and excuse their own inefficiency. But Prosecutor General Pedro Méndez Jurado said in June 1991 that the leaks were real: "The information we have is that they [the narcotraffickers] are told from the moment the helicopter leaves . . . Santa Lucía and they are informed all along the route."[26] Meanwhile, according to a U.S. embassy official who traveled in the coca-growing region in early 1991, even some local prosecutors, who are required to be present when the air force searches an interdicted plane, were turning a blind eye to military corruption. And under pressure to produce results, the police-military tension continued.

So did difficulties at a higher level. President Fujimori had rejected the U.S. aid package for FY 1990 in September, taking U.S. officials by surprise. He did so with the agreement of the army, whose relations with the new government were close. Fujimori emphasized that the economic component of the aid did not satisfy Peruvian requirements for developing long-range alternatives. In October, he announced a program to grant land titles to coca growers and deregulate markets for legal crops, as incentives for crop substitution. And in a November 26 speech he enunciated what was called the "Fujimori doctrine," advocating an effective anticoca campaign but stating, too, that crop substitution was "imperative."

The Bush administration was not completely happy with Fujimori's policies or progress in the fight against the drug trade. And promises were implied in a March 1991 announcement by the Bush administration that it was certifying Peru for its efforts to curb the drug industry. At the same time, however, the Bush administration also announced that it was withholding the FY 1991 aid, more than $90 million, because the administration was unable to determine that Peru was carrying out an effective counternarcotics program, was respecting human rights, and was in control of its armed forces and police. The two apparently contradictory announcements were interpreted as a means of pressuring Peru into accepting the U.S. antinarcotics aid on American terms; if Peru refused, it would not be eligible for the economic aid it desperately needed.

As independent as Fujimori may have wished to seem, Peru requires U.S. support in the multilateral banks that hold its debt; the price of such support was evident. In keeping with Fujimori's rather abrupt, autocratic style, a framework agreement between the two countries was signed and announced in Lima on May 14, 1991, without significant prior public discussion. The *convenio* demonstrates that U.S. officials have recognized the pitfalls they face with both the U.S. Congress and the Peruvian public, for the document is more than anything a statement of good intentions, not tied down by dangerous specifics. It offers only broad suggestions of how aid might be spent, gives no hint as to whether or how many trainers might be assigned to the Upper Huallaga; mainly, it sets out some ideals to be pursued, a few of which follow.

- "[T]he effort to combat narcotics trafficking is understood as a task for both countries, a joint venture as envisioned in the Declaration of Cartagena." Nowhere in the document, however, is any measure to which the U.S. commits itself regarding control of consumption. The entire agreement is devoted to measures to be taken in Peru, by and primarily affecting Peruvians.
- Key to implementation of the agreement is the creation of "an autonomous authority at the highest political level, reporting directly to the President of the Republic, with the objective of achieving efficient

coordination with a decision-making authority at the equivalent high levels in the U.S. G[overnment]." This is intended to reduce "division and overlapping of authority." The problem in Peru, however, as explained above, is more than administrative; it involves the determination of the United States to force mutually exclusive strategies to coexist. The agreement states without irony that the Peruvian government "may also set policies for the coordination among the Peruvian National Police, the Army, the Navy and the Air Force so as to achieve prompt results" regarding antidrug actions; this belies real conditions in Peru, including interservice competition and corruption. It also belies the logical effect of the aid itself, which will be to strengthen military over civilian authority.

- Regarding human rights, the agreement "reiterate[s] the importance of carrying out this battle within the context of internationally developed standards of human rights such as the U.N. Declaration on Human Rights and the Geneva Conventions." It also calls for "actions such as unrestricted access for the International Committee of the Red Cross." American officials have emphasized human rights concerns to the Peruvian government during aid negotiations. President Fujimori has himself made laudable statements on the subject, though his policies have often been inconsistent with those statements. ICRC access is a measure Americas Watch strongly supports. At the same time, U.S. officials told Americas Watch that they had not advised the ICRC of their intention to include the organization's name and activities in the framework agreement. Such lack of communication is an unhappy precedent, and not the only one: on the same day the agreement was signed, the Peruvian Defense Ministry refused to permit the ICRC to receive nine prisoners from the MRTA in the Central Huallaga (see chapter 6). The incident was an example of how the military misreads the role of the ICRC. As for an overall policy commitment to respect human rights, nothing could be more worthy of support or, under current conditions, more elusive.
- "[T]here must be efficient judicial and administrative systems to which all citizens can turn . . . above all when this is the result of arbitrary and abusive actions on the part of the state or other organizations," says the agreement. To this end, U.S. aid has been earmarked for administration of justice programs.
- "In order to achieve the objectives set forth in this Agreement, it will be necessary to establish a framework of justice, respect for human rights, order, security, and peace in all the zones linked to drug trafficking and related activities." This, in paragraph 23, is followed, in

paragraph 25, by an explanation of the strategy for justice and peace, whose "central features are based on . . . (a) The need to feed, equip, train, provide with uniforms and adequately support the armed and police forces who will be fighting against narcotrafficking and those who support and encourage it." This is as close as the agreement comes to mentioning U.S. training and counterinsurgency intentions.

The convenio also briefly addresses protection of judges, eliminating corruption in detention facilities, offering better salaries to antinarcotics police, and protecting the environment, among other important matters. Finally, the United States agrees to work with Peru "to mobilize timely and effective support for Peru in multilateral and economic institutions in the framework of sound economic policies and effective programs against drugs." This language suggests that Peru will receive crucial U.S. support only so long as it pursues the Bush administration's antidrug plan.

Implementing agreements on each of the main policy areas—law enforcement, military assistance, and economic assistance—were to be developed within six months, in consultation with affected sectors of the population. FY 1991 aid was to be released on signature of the implementing agreements: this was expected to be $34 in military aid, $60 million in Economic Support Funds (for balance-of-payments and some as yet unspecified projects), and slightly under $1 million for military training.[27] For FY 1992 the aid request for Economic Support Funds was expected to rise significantly.

It is early to gauge the effects of the Convenio. Its provisions reflect a multifaceted understanding of the drug and security problems in Peru, and in isolated areas it may be the forerunner of genuine improvement. But U.S. aid is not to be dedicated to the social or developmental challenges outlined in the convenio, with the exception of the minor allotment for development assistance. As a framework for aid, the convenio's central meaning is to ratify at least three contradictions imposed on Peru by U.S. needs. One of these is beyond the scope of this book; it involves the nation's reliance on coca revenues to pay its foreign debt, as mentioned at the beginning of this chapter. The other two, however, bear directly on the human rights situation in the coca-growing regions.

- An antidrug strategy alienates the coca-growing peasants unless a truly viable economic alternative is presented; a counterinsurgency strategy requires these peasants' support if it is not to be a war against the population. The two strategies are, for human rights purposes, in conflict.
- To the extent that an antidrug strategy is backed by the army, as the U.S. plan would have it, Sendero develops a natural alliance with the

traffickers and uses this mutual antagonism to the army to make financial deals with the traffickers that benefit Sendero enormously, thus aiding its expansion and generating further violence.

Americas Watch is concerned that widening violence and militarization in the zone are likely to increase its isolation, leaving peasants even more vulnerable to abuses by both sides in the absence of monitoring by the press and human rights organizations. Access by the ICRC is necessary but not sufficient; because the ICRC's findings are confidential, shared only with the government, they cannot perform the essential function of providing Peruvians with information. Already the Upper Huallaga is largely inaccessible to the press. Foreign reporters can take a U.S.-sponsored air trip to the Santa Lucía antidrug base, where they are treated to dramatizations of how coca is dried and converted into paste, in a scenario described by *Caretas* as "Cocalandia, the Disneyland of the war on drugs."[28] But neither foreign journalists nor their Peruvian counterparts can travel safely outside major towns like Uchiza.[29] News of abuses in isolated areas, although it does often reach the press, tends to arrive slowly, so that it is too late for human rights groups or official investigators to gather fresh evidence or to check the military's version of events. Human rights monitors already find the Upper Huallaga the most difficult zone in which to gather information on abuses by either side.

Where military abuses are concerned, the state of military justice in Peru offers no prospect of effective prosecutions or redress for victims. And past experience shows that impunity encourages the continuation of abusive practices. Moreover, as elsewhere in Peru, further militarization would tend to reduce the presence and independence of civilian authorities, such as judicial personnel who are capable of pursuing human rights complaints. A complaint of disappearances made during 1989 by a local prosecutor from the Upper Huallaga area has been noted (see chapter 6). Such initiatives are rare and courageous enough under current conditions. Unless the new government can protect and build up the legal system in the Upper Huallaga, that system will have even greater difficulty in criticizing the army under the high-stakes conditions of a war pursued with international aid.

The United States could not hope to remain aloof from abuses committed by the forces it trains and equips. Defense Department official Daniel Fisk told a congressional committee in June 1991 that trainers "are required to teach respect for human rights in both formal classroom lectures/discussions and in practical hands-on instruction."[30] But given the nature of the counterinsurgency and antinarcotics efforts to date, and the difficulties of monitoring in isolated areas, serious abuses will continue to occur. The United States would become an indirect party to those abuses.

Finally, Americas Watch is concerned that the widening war in the Upper Huallaga—and soon too, it would seem, in the Central Huallaga—will force the dislocation of peasants there and swell the population of internal refugees. Peasant organizers from the Uchiza area told Americas Watch in May 1990 that, when the military expected Sendero attacks in the environs of the Santa Lucía antidrug base around the time of the April 8 first-round presidential vote, residents of the area were advised by the army to leave and stay away for two weeks before the elections and two weeks after. Residents did not leave because they could not afford to, and one result was the disappearance of about a dozen young people from a hamlet across the river from the base, on April 8, 1990 (see chapter 6). Evacuations, either "suggested" or forced, are likely to multiply as the war widens, creating social upheaval and placing the Peruvian military authorities in charge of yet another unmanageable crisis. Depending on the military's treatment of the displaced population, which to date has been poor in other areas of the country, the United States could be implicated in abuses that come under international humanitarian law.

These dangers are outlined not with the intention of painting the worst picture but of presenting a realistic one. Although U.S. officials have sought to convince Congress that human rights abuses by the Peruvian military and police are not serious, the facts are otherwise. Nor is it acceptable to make excuses for brutality, as did Assistant Secretary of State Melvyn Levitsky in June 1991, when he explained the "extrajudicial violence" of the Peruvian military as part of their "trying to defend the Peruvian Government from two of the world's most violent terrorist groups as well as narcoterrorists."[31] To engage the military in the counternarcotics "war" is to force a confrontation with civilians whose security and economic development are necessary to win the counterinsurgency war. Those civilians have already been victimized from many sides. And there are serious questions to be asked about potential conditions like massive displacement—or for that matter, military promotion of civilian self-defense patrols—where these could involve troops equipped and/or trained by the United States. American human rights law, which is being waived or ignored in the campaign for military and police aid to Peru, was drafted with good reason. As one U.S. official has said of the military aid plans in Peru, "I don't think any of us really knows how complicated this will be."[32]

10

SUMMARY AND RECOMMENDATIONS

Internal armed conflicts tend to punish first the poorest and their leaders and defenders. In Peru, both insurgent and official forces have an interest in removing what for the other would be valuable assets; as a result, in the zones of conflict, it is the most experienced campesino organizers, the traditional village leaders, the most active unionists, the candidates for municipal office, and the mayors who have most consistently been the targets of repression. For Sendero, preexisting organizations, no matter how broadly supported, represent the "old" order. The armed forces, for their part, think of popular organizations as the "sea" in which subversives swim. In assessing the damage that more than a decade of conflict has done this nation, one must consider the loss that such people represent for their communities.

In Ayacucho, for example, where there has been some examination of internal displacement patterns, local leaders such as mayors and communal authorities were among the first to be forced out. Replacing this leadership is a task that becomes harder each time it is undertaken, and each time there are fewer members of a community to lead. In 1990, the human rights organization Comisión de Acción Social (CEAS) estimated an internally displaced population of some 75,000 nationwide, based on cases attended by the church, and calculated that in thirty-two Ayacucho communities the population had fallen by half between 1981 and 1985 because of repression and migration.[1] The CEAS estimate is undoubtedly conservative, however, and the displaced may number as many as 200,000.[2]

About half of the displaced make their way to Lima, where they are not visible in Peruvian media or political debate; they have lost their value in the society. Only now, after more than a decade, are government statisticians beginning to assess their numbers. Meanwhile, for those who lack documents, the exercise of certain rights is not possible; they are less than citizens. Indeed, they are lucky if, having fled Sendero, they are not harassed by the police in Lima. As time goes on, if present trends do not change, their numbers will increase and their plight will become increasingly extreme.

141

These people must fend for themselves. And they are emblematic, for every year, displaced or not, more Peruvians must simply fend for themselves; the state can neither protect nor provide for them. Peruvians who remain in the conflict zones, who seek to stay neutral in the conflict or take up weapons in their own defense, are living without the benefits of a government. As August 1991 municipal elections approached in Junín, few candidates had come forward, and the president of the Provincial Elections Jury of Huancayo stated that the mayors elected previously had "not even assumed their duties" for fear of Sendero.[3] In the meantime, Sen. Raúl Ferrero Costa made public the staggering fact that fifty-one police stations had been closed in Ica, Huancavelica, and Ayacucho; for obvious reasons, the number of candidacies in these areas was also low.[4] The receding state asks Peruvians to defend it, to believe in the system it represents when that system, a democracy deeply flawed and economically crippled, can do little even to protect their lives. And in the meantime, the army, like Sendero, targets their neighbors and colleagues, and may force them to leave the land and culture they know.

The cost of the repressive strategy has been more than 23,000 lives, the overwhelming majority of them civilian; some 3,500 disappeared, who must also be presumed dead; and a habit of impunity which the new government seems unwilling to break, though it fosters further abuse. Since 1988, after an interval of less spectacular abuses, the army has again engaged in killing large numbers of civilians together, often combining murder with inhumane treatment and humiliation. Sendero's practices are equally brutal, and the MRTA has also violated the law of war; those insurgents responsible for gross abuses should be tried and severely punished. The state's repressive policy, however, feeds a chaos that favors the rebels, because the logic of repression is polarizing.

In matters on which the state's authority rests, such as the legal system and law enforcement, a combination of scarce resources, military and police influence, corruption, and political confusion has prevented far-seeing reform, endangering persons on both sides of the bench: terrorism suspects do not enjoy adequate due-process protections, criminal suspects may expect abuse and delays, judges trying terrorism cases are exposed to violent reprisals. The Fujimori proposal to let military courts try civilians accused of terrorism in secret proceedings was only the most recent expression of a tired and unconstitutional idea. Yet military courts do try human rights cases, because the Supreme Court habitually and controversially awards them jurisdiction; some of the results are reported here, in such crucial cases as Lurigancho and Cayara. Trial delays, judicial corruption, indiscriminate "preventive" arrests, hellish conditions of confinement—these are what citizens experience of the state's legal and law-enforcement system. And those outstanding judges, prosecutors, and lawyers who provide exceptions, in particular those who take up human rights cases, are at risk; after a brief period of promoting such activism in the mid-1980s, the state withdrew its support for tenacious legal investigation.[5] It is encouraging that congressional commissions perform part of this task, but political entities like these, important as they are, cannot substitute for impartial legal inquiry and full prosecutions.

There is also reason for concern about the proposed role of the United States, and its antidrug strategy, in the Upper Huallaga valley. Grave abuses have accompanied the militarization of the Upper Huallaga. Americas Watch holds that U.S. involvement in training and equipping the Peruvian police and military will not eliminate these abuses and may contribute to their increase. We do not discount the seriousness of the Sendero threat in the Upper Huallaga—and the MRTA in the Central Huallaga—but both the insurgents and the production of coca have evolved from conditions that are not addressed by militarization. We are concerned that providing military assistance will involve the United States in a complex and protracted conflict, the civilian casualties of which would become, in part, the United States's responsibility.

Americas Watch urges the Fujimori government to work to create a national consensus on the issues of security and human rights, such that the counter-insurgency program based on repression may be reexamined and that nonviolent means of fortifying the Peruvian state may be seriously explored. We urge that civilians who expose themselves to reprisals for ethical reasons—such as judges trying terrorism cases, human rights monitors receiving threats, and witnesses to human rights abuses who are willing to testify—be protected by the state and that their commitment to human rights be echoed and validated by the president. We urge that the legal system be fortified by attention to first principles, including the right to due process of all detainees and the right of victims to obtain redress. We urge that the state provide political support for endangered popular organizations, unions, and humanitarian organizations who retain the trust of their members and communities and thus can be crucial allies; we urge in particular that the representatives of these groups not be victimized by official forces, including when they engage in peaceful public dissent.

Finally, Americas Watch urges that the government cease to tolerate killings, disappearances, and torture by official forces or by civil defense patrols or other paramilitary groups. Oversight by the International Committee of the Red Cross can play a valuable role, and we believe that the ICRC should have unrestricted access to military bases as well as prisons. But this is not sufficient. The president is responsible for sustaining public sensitivity on these issues;

past experience suggests, also, that a strong presidential stance does affect military performance in the field. If the state is to have credibility, and therefore to survive, it must embody values superior to those of the insurgents. Alberto Fujimori gave voice to the disaffection of many citizens in his campaign. As president, he can represent them first and foremost by ensuring that their basic rights are respected.

NOTES

PREFACE

1. Gorriti, "Líos in Cocalandia," p. 92.

INTRODUCTION

1. Paper prepared for the Instituto de Estudios Peruanos, Seminario-Taller sobre Liderazgo y Concertación Democrática, April 23–27, 1990, Lima.
2. Ibid.
3. *Cambio,* the organ of the Movimiento Revolucionario Túpac Amaru (MRTA). The organ of Sendero Luminoso, *El Diario,* was shut down in November 1989 after it advocated assassinations of public figures; it now publishes erratically and clandestinely.

CHAPTER 1: THE SOURCES AND SCOPE OF VIOLENCE IN PERU

1. Thais, *Pobreza en el Perú,* p. 9.
2. Ibid., pp. 15, 18.
3. Instituto de Defensa Legal (hereinafter IDL), "Informe Mensual No. 7," p. 5.
4. IDL, *Perú 1990,* p. 10. Underemployment is a truer reflection of actual conditions because a significant part of the workforce is engaged in "informal" economic activity, as noted below.
5. Coordinadora Nacional de Derechos Humanos, "Informe Síntesis"; Inter-Church Committee on Human Rights in Latin America, *1989 Annual Report,* p. 4.
6. "Fujishock," *Economist,* October 12, 1991, p. 42.
7. Andean Commission of Jurists, "Informativo Andino," November 12, 1990, p. 7, citing report of APRODEH.
8. In 1988, President García stated that income from the drug trade—in Peru, primarily the growth of coca leaf and its initial refinement into coca paste, *pasta básica*—amounted to $30 million a month, or $360 million a year (all dollar figures are in U.S. dollars). In June 1989, Minister of the Economy César Vásquez Bazán said on television that narcotics annual income was approaching $1 billion. The fluctuating price of coca has affected these figures, however. According to research by the Andean Commission of Jurists, there was a fall in national income from the production of pasta básica and cocaine (cocaine being a small proportion of the total) between 1989 and 1990: from the equivalent of $458 million to the equivalent of $152 million. A U.S. Department of State study also found a decline, although its figures are higher for both years.

9. De Soto et al., *El Otro Sendero*. The "informal" economy of Peru, made known in the United States primarily through the writings of Hernando de Soto, director of the Instituto Libertad y Democracia (ILD), is activity that takes place outside the law or government regulation, including small enterprises in poor neighborhoods, peddling, the black market, the multitude of jobs that the underemployed take on to supplement their incomes, and outright illegal activity such as drug trafficking, as well as much commercial activity that is legal but is conducted "off the books."

10. Nash, "Fujimori in the Time of Cholera."

11. See Degregori, *Qué Difícil es Ser Dios,* pp. 10–19.

12. Ibid., p. 23, quoting the Sendero Luminoso document "Desarrollar la Guerra Popular Sirviendo a la Revolución Mundial," p. 20. The quotation is translated from the Spanish by Americas Watch.

13. There were, in addition, 687 Sendero killings of campesinos, some unknown proportion of whom were members of civilian self-defense patrols. The figures of the Bernales Commission, described in detail below, do not include a category of victims for these patrollers—one indication of the anomaly of their position in the conflict, as is explored in chapter 6.

14. Comisión Especial de Investigación y Estudio sobre la Violencia y Alternativas de Pacificación (hereinafter Bernales Commission), *10 Años de Violencia,* p. 19.

15. Centro de Estudios y Promoción del Desarrollo (hereinafter DESCO), *Violencia Política,* pp. 348–49, listing of supreme decrees declaring states of emergency.

16. See figures of the Bernales Commission, cited below.

17. Under Decree 46, a person was considered terrorist if he or she was deemed guilty, for example, of adversely affecting international relations or the security of the state, or of speaking out publicly in favor of terrorism or a terrorist.

18. Andean Commission of Jurists, "Informativo Andino," March 11, 1991, p. 6; citing, with regard to Ayacucho provinces, a study of thirty-two communities in the provinces of Cangallo, Victor Fajardo, Huamanga, Huanta, and Vilcashamán conducted by the Universidad Nacional San Cristóbal de Huamanga.

19. Between forty and sixty-nine villagers of all ages and both sexes were murdered in Accomarca in August 1985, evidently by an army patrol. In Pucayacu, where a clandestine grave containing fifty corpses had been discovered in 1984, seven persons were killed just days after Accomarca; they were held in the local military headquarters before their executions. Both cases were investigated by military tribunals, with officers facing such minor charges as negligence and eventually being acquitted.

20. Figures released by the Bernales Commission for May 1991 (see below); total deaths were 526.

21. Bernales Commission, *Violencia en el Perú,* p. 40.

22. Bernales Commission, *10 Años de Violencia,* p. 55.

23. Without detracting from the commission's findings, which we consider sound and which are widely quoted in Peru, it is relevant to note a methodological observation made by DESCO, which has published a thorough study of violence in Peru, 1980–88. In its discussion of "terrorist attacks," DESCO notes that official sources generally offer figures twice as high as those of the national press on terrorist attacks, while official figures for numbers of victims are generally 20–25 percent lower than those reported in the press. DESCO, *Violencia Política,* p. 23. Such are the discrepancies that the Bernales Commission attempts to resolve.

24. Bernales Commission, *10 Años de Violencia,* p. 24.

25. Ibid., p. 17.
26. Andean Commission of Jurists, "Informativo Andino," May 7, 1990, p. 5.
27. Bernales Commission, *10 Años de Violencia*, pp. 9–10.
28. Ibid., p. 20.
29. Ibid., p. 22.
30. Ibid.
31. COMISEDH, *Informe Estadístico*. The figure for 1986 includes 115 inmates of the San Juan Bautista (El Frontón) prison whose whereabouts were not clarified after the June 1986 riot there. In the zone of emergency that year, 99 persons disappeared.
32. Amnesty International, *Peru: Continuing Human Rights Violations*.
33. COMISEDH, *Informe Estadístico*.
34. Americas Watch interview with Gen. Alberto Arciniega, Ministry of Defense, Lima, May 22, 1991.

CHAPTER 2: THE JUDICIARY

1. Americas Watch, *Tolerating Abuses*, p. 30.
2. This special court sentenced Morote—reputedly Sendero's second in command—to twenty years' imprisonment in November 1990.
3. Quoted in IDL, *Perú 1989*, p. 141.
4. See, e.g., the Cayara massacre investigation by prosecutor Carlos Escobar Pineda, in chapter 4, and the human rights complaint filed by local prosecutor Pedro Chimay of Tocache, San Martín, in chapter 6. Also César San Martín Castro, judge of the Twenty-first Investigation Court of Lima, who granted a petition for habeas corpus in November 1989 after an arbitrary detention by police, rejecting the government's claim that the state of emergency barred the remedy of habeas corpus; see Human Rights Watch, *Persecution of Human Rights Monitors*, p. 225.
5. Flavio Núñez Izaga. See IDL, *Perú 1989*, p. 137.
6. Quoted in IDL, *Perú 1990*, p. 232.
7. The new law regulated habeas corpus and amparo (protection); the cancellation of Decree 171 was just one of its many provisions. The constitution allows sixteen days for the president to promulgate or block a measure passed by Congress. After the president did not act for well over a month, Congress promulgated the new law.
8. *Sí*, December 2, 1990.
9. Andean Commission of Jurists, "Informativo Andino," December 10, 1990.
10. Further details on the legal history of this case may be found in Americas Watch, *Human Rights in Peru after President García's First Year*, pp. 93–94.
11. For a detailed description of these events, see ibid., pp. 99–112, and Americas Watch, *Tolerating Abuses*, pp. 61–68.
12. See Americas Watch, *Abdicating Democratic Authority*, pp. 24–25, 27.
13. A special commission investigating the suppression of the riots, chaired by Sen. Rolando Ames, could not reach a unanimous conclusion on the culpability of civilian officials, but both the majority and the minority (with whom Ames associated himself) coincided in their reports on the involvement of President García and members of his cabinet, as well as the director of the National Penitentiary Institute (INPE), in the events that led to the massacres. For details of the Ames Commission's investigation and findings, see Americas Watch, *Tolerating Abuses*, pp. 61–65.

14. IDL, *Perú 1989*, p. 147.

15. Patricio Ricketts Rey de Castro, in an editorial for *Expreso*, a Lima daily; quoted in IDL, "Informe Mensual No. 21," p. 11.

16. Law 23,506, enacted in 1982.

CHAPTER 3: PENAL CONDITIONS

1. Of the approximately 450 security-related prisoners held in Canto Grande in early 1990, both men and women, some 80 percent were associated with Sendero. Later in the year, this proportion would rise further, as the bulk of MRTA prisoners, forty-nine at once, tunneled out to escape.

2. IDL, *Perú 1990*, p. 184, citing National Penitentiary Institute (INPE) figures for June and August 1990 on capacity and population in each prison, and p. 193, citing President Fujimori on overpopulation percentages.

3. Ibid., p. 185, referring to Wilder Vidal Ramos, director of INPE, who resigned in January 1990.

4. Americas Watch, *Human Rights in Peru after President García's First Year*, p. 78.

5. Ibid., p. 195.

6. Andean Commission of Jurists, "Informativo Andino," October 9, 1990, p. 6.

CHAPTER 4: CONGRESSIONAL INVESTIGATIONS OF HUMAN RIGHTS ABUSES

1. At the women's prison of Santa Bárbara, the military confrontation was brief and casualties were light: two prisoners dead and six wounded. The conduct of the authorities in putting down the riot in Santa Bárbara has not been seriously questioned.

2. Goldenberg, "El Frontón." See Americas Watch, *Certain Passivity*, pp. 49, 50.

3. Amnesty International, "Peru: 'Disappearances,' Torture and Summary Executions." See Americas Watch, *Certain Passivity*, pp. 49, 50.

4. Transcripts published as part of the Ames Report, contain details from his remarks. He praises the Joint Command of the Armed Forces "for the efficient compliance with the orders of the government. It is also pointed out that, according to Law 24,250 which regulated states of exception, jurisdiction in this matter lies with military courts; therefore it was decided that civilian judges would not be allowed to enter the prisons nor the nearby premises, starting that same afternoon; the prisons are declared Restricted Military Zones, and access to civilians is thus prohibited." Cited in Americas Watch, *Tolerating Abuses*, p. 64.

5. *La República*, June 30, 1988. See Americas Watch, *Tolerating Abuses*, p. 67n.

6. Quoted in IDL, *Perú 1989*, p. 148.

7. Ibid.

8. In a May 1991 conversation with Americas Watch, the Defense Ministry's spokesperson on human rights, Gen. Alberto Arciniega, contended that Escobar had been removed from his post for embezzlement. Elsewhere, such an accusation might successfully foster doubts, if repeated often; but in a nation where embezzlement is the hobby of so many functionaries and routinely goes unpunished, the accusation runs against common sense. Were Escobar an embezzler, he would likely be enjoying the rewards of conformity, rather than confronting a life of exile.

9. See Americas Watch, *Tolerating Abuses,* p. 52.

10. Quoted in IDL, *Perú 1989,* p. 164.

11. Ibid.

12. A police investigation also established that the perpetrators of the massacre were Army personnel, as did an investigation by the provincial prosecutor of Chumbivilcas.

13. Peru, Senate, "Informe Final," Senate of the Republic, Lima, 1991, pt. 1, sec. 4.

CHAPTER 5: VIOLATIONS OF THE LAWS
OF WAR BY INSURGENTS

1. Protocol II of 1977, which is a more detailed instrument covering internal conflicts or civil war, contains rigorous requirements as to control of population and territory by an insurgent force. Essentially, Protocol II requires that the insurgents replace state authority in the areas they control and function as an alternative state.

2. Americas Watch telephone interview with Gustavo Gorriti, August 15, 1991.

3. Author telephone interview with Gustavo Gorriti, October 7, 1991.

4. With regard to Sendero's attitude toward traditional indigenous culture: a denunciation by the ashaninka organization CECONSEC, in September 1990, noted that Sendero "threatens us [saying we must] parcel up our land . . . saying that the native community [of property] is part of the old state which is no longer useful, like our leaders and culture." IDL, *Perú 1990.* p. 170. With regard to the pyramidal structure, see Degregori, *Qué Difícil es Ser Dios.*

5. Americas Watch interview with Gustavo Gorriti, Lima, May 22, 1991; IDL, *Perú 1990,* p. 167; information gathered by APRODEH on a visit to Junín in early 1991.

6. See, e.g., the Los Molinos incident, described in chapter 6.

7. COMISEDH, "Violencia Política en el Perú," pp. 12–13.

8. Andean Commission of Jurists, "Informativo Andino," November 9, 1989, p. 7.

9. Reuters News Service, August 11, 1991.

10. Grupo de Trabajo de la Coordinadora Nacional de los Derechos Humanos, "Boletín Informativo," pp. 2–3.

11. COMISEDH, "Violencia Política en el Perú," p. 12.

12. Some rondas are imposed by the military, while others are organized by the communities themselves; see chapter 6.

13. Americas Watch has received various reports of Sendero kidnappings of young boys and of Sendero "columns" that have included many young boys. In conjunction with these reports, we note the presence of children in the Sendero column that attacked Naylamp de Sonomoro, as described above.

14. IDL, *Perú 1989,* p. 65.

15. Quoted in Andean Commission of Jurists, "Informativo Andino," May 7, 1990, p. 5.

16. These incidents are cited from Instituto de Defensa Legal, *Idéale,* Lima, August 1991, pp. 31–34.

17. "Agosto, Récord Fatal," *Sí,* August 24, 1991, p. 32.

18. Bernales Commission, *10 Años de Violencia,* p. 24.

19. The violent eviction of some ten thousand families from El Naranjal is described in chapter 6.

20. Recognition of a fighting force as a belligerent is a formal diplomatic decision that is made by the enemy government or by other foreign governments. It does not alter

the humanitarian obligation of the insurgent group and has bearing only on its capacity to negotiate an end to hostilities.

CHAPTER 6: HUMAN RIGHTS VIOLATIONS

1. U.S. Department of State, *Country Reports on Human Rights Practices for 1989*, p. 708.

2. Bernales Commission, *10 Años de Violencia*, pp. 46–49. In the case of Puno, the department had been declared under state of emergency once before, in 1983.

3. U.S. Department of State, *Country Reports on Human Rights Practices for 1990*, p. 736.

4. Precise figures: 55.86 and 39.26 percent, respectively. CeaPaz, citing its own Banco de Datos and the statistical almanac, "Peru en Números, 1990," of Cuanto S.A.

5. IDL, *Perú 1990*, pp. 232–33.

6. Simons, "Peru Adopts Severe Tactics."

7. Simons, "Peruvian Military Fights Terrorists with Terror."

8. This lack of uniformity, of course, is due in part to the differences between such sharply contrasting regions as the highlands of Ayacucho and the Junín rain forest. It is also due to lack of resources and inadequate coordination at the highest levels.

9. Americas Watch interview with Gen. Alberto Arciniega, Defense Ministry, Lima, May 22, 1991.

10. The population of metropolitan Lima was about 6.7 million in 1991. According to official INE estimates, although no census has been taken since 1983 (when the figure was some 4 million for the department as a whole). The precise figures offered by Colonel Torres were: 49,720 operations and 2,459,040 persons *intervenidas*. Colonel Torres was chief of the Comité de Apoyo y Asesoramiento de la 7ma. Sub-region de la Policía General, and offered these figures at a forum on individual liberty and democracy, sponsored by CeaPaz, the Comisión Andina de Juristas, and Alternativa, on November 14–15, 1990, in Lima.

11. Bernales Commission, *10 Años de Violencia*, p. 27. One province of Junín, Yauli, had been placed under state of emergency twice in 1983 and then again in 1985, but the department as a whole did not become an emergency zone until October 1988.

12. Coordinadora Nacional de Derechos Humanos, "Carta Circular no. 15," Lima, August 1991, front page.

13. Exact figure: 49.8 percent. National Statistics Institute (INE), cited in IDL, *Perú 1989*, p. 14.

14. IDL, *Perú 1989*, p. 189.

15. During 1989, in Ayacucho and Huancavelica alone, the ICRC assisted 4,872 persons displaced by the conflict, homeless persons, widows, and orphans. Human rights organizations and the Catholic church in Peru estimated, by early 1991, that the total number of persons displaced by political violence exceeded 50,000.

16. Figures from CeaPaz, presented to forum on individual liberty and democracy sponsored by CeaPaz, the Comisión Andina de Juristas, and Alternativa, November 14–15, 1990, in Lima.

17. The judge was subsequently assassinated by MRTA; see chapter 5.

18. *El Comercio*, May 24, 1991.

19. See, e.g., in chapter 4, a chronicle of abusive army behavior, including cases of rape.

20. Taype's predecessor as president of the federation, Saúl Cantoral, was murdered by men believed to be members of the Comando Rodrigo Franco on February 13, 1989; see below.

21. IDL, *Perú 1990*, p. 239.

22. United Nations, Economic and Social Council, Report of the Working Group on Forced or Involuntary Disappearances, app. I, pp. 101, 116.

23. Ibid. Precise figures for 1988 are: 992 worldwide, 230 in Peru. World total for 1990: 434.

24. National human rights organizations use more conservative criteria on disappearance than does the United Nations. They do not include cases that are not in some measure corroborated or are not denounced directly to them and examined by them; and they do not include as disappeared—in yearly figures—those whose disappearance has been resolved either by release from custody, acknowledgment of detention, or discovery of the victim's body. When given a choice, Peruvian human rights organizations tend toward underestimating a phenomenon rather than risk overstating it. Their figures should therefore be regarded as a reliable base minimum.

25. All figures, COMISEDH, *Informe Estadístico*.

26. Ibid.

27. Ibid.

28. Dr. César Montalván, of the provincial prosecutor's office of Coronel Portillo, Ucayali, quoted in IDL, *Perú 1989*, p. 71.

29. IDL, *Perú 1990*, pp. 242–43.

30. *Sí*, March 24, 1991.

31. *Sí*, cited in IDL, *Perú 1990*, p. 123. The article estimated eighty victims.

32. Channel 5 is owned by Alan García's friend, Héctor Delgado Parker; see chapter 5.

33. IDL, *Perú 1989*, p. 97.

34. There were 450 deaths in Ayacucho and 297 in Junín. COMISEDH, "Violencia Política en el Perú," pp. 8–10.

35. Figures from the Bernales Commission's report on 1990, as broken down by CeaPaz.

36. Cited in IDL, *Perú 1989*, p. 70.

37. Information gathered by Comisión de Derechos Humanos-Puno (CODEH-Puno) and the Vicaría de la Solidaridad de Puno, disseminated by APRODEH.

38. "Histeria Criminal," *Caretas*, July 1, 1991, p. 35.

39. The possibility exists that some of this activity is attributable to narcotraffic, in Junín in particular. But the heavy concentration of paramilitary activity in counterinsurgency zones where drugs are less important suggests that it is due, more often, to the same elements as in the past, operating with official tolerance.

CHAPTER 7: THE ROLE OF CIVIL DEFENSE PATROLS

1. Americas Watch, *New Opportunity*, pp. 12–13.

2. Ibid., p. 15.

3. IDL, "Informe Mensual no. 9," December 1989, p. 9.

4. IDL, *Perú 1990*, p. 140.

5. Bernales Commission, *10 Años de Violencia*, app. 4, p. 62, and app. 8, p. 66.

6. InterPress Service, "Fujimori Will Continue Distributing Arms."

7. Juan Asto, president of the Liga Agraria de Huamanga, quoted in Peru, Senate, "Informe Final de la Comisión Investigadora."

8. Common Article 3 to the Geneva Conventions of 1949; Articles 48–54, Protocol I Additional (1977).

9. Bernales Commission, *10 Años de Violencia,* app. 2 (MRTA), app. 4 (Las Organizaciones Campesinas), and app. 8 (Fuerzas Armadas).

10. According to agricultural specialists familiar with the area, Cubantía was bearing the brunt of Sendero attacks through April 1990, but these had not been investigated by the authorities.

11. *El Comercio,* April 3, 1990, p. A15.

12. APRODEH, "Masacre de Campesinos en Iquicha."

13. IDL, "La Opinión de los Dirigentes Campesinos," p. 15.

14. Ibid., pp. 15–16.

CHAPTER 8: THE PERSECUTION OF
HUMAN RIGHTS MONITORS

1. Human Rights Watch, *Persecution of Human Rights Monitors,* pp. 221–26.

2. IDL, *Perú 1989,* p. 91.

3. InterPress Service, March 5, 1990, quoted in Americas Watch, "Wave of Violence," p. 2.

4. SERPAJ is the organization whose leader is Nobel Peace Prize winner Adolfo Pérez Esquivel.

5. EFE cable, reprinted in *La Epoca* (Santiago, Chile), August 7, 1991.

6. Quoted in *Sí,* December 2, 1990.

7. Andean Commission of Jurists, "Informativo Andino," December 10, 1990.

CHAPTER 9: THE ROLE OF THE UNITED STATES

1. Figures and statement by Finance Minister César Vásquez Bazán (as summarized in report, not directly quoted) are from: U.S. House of Representatives, Committee on Government Operations, "Stopping the Flood of Cocaine with Operation Snowcap," pp. 20–21.

2. Ibid.

3. The United States gives food grants and loans and developmental aid to Peru as well, a total of $57.2 million for FY 1988, with $41.2 million requested for FY 1989 and $42.3 requested for FY 1990. For FY 1991, the United States appropriated some $10 million in developmental assistance (part of it carried from FY 1990), $84 million in food grants, some $19 million in emergency food, and—left over from the shorter-than-expected Gulf War—$20 million in Operation Desert Storm surplus food.

4. In FY 1988, total U.S. military training aid to Peru was $400,000 for the International Military Education and Training program.

5. The Department of State refused to give Congress any figure for the number of Green Berets to be sent as trainers. The figure twenty-four was given in Anderson, "Next Nasty War?" p. 36, quoting a U.S. diplomat in Lima.

6. "Peru Drug Fund Used in War, Aide Says," *New York Times,* June 21, 1990.

7. Anderson, "Next Nasty War?" p. 37.

8. IDL, *Perú 1989*, p. 77. The Spanish was translated by Americas Watch.

9. IDL, *Perú 1989*, p. 58.

10. See House Committee on Government Operations, "Stopping the Flood of Cocaine with Operation Snowcap," p. 23.

11. Some Peruvian analysts have suggested that the Sendero attack on the police post in Uchiza—described below—was a response to this "experimental" application.

12. Quoted in IDL, *Perú 1989*, p. 72.

13. COMISEDH, "Violencia Política en el Perú," pp. 8–10. In Leoncio Prado province, Huánuco, there were 166 deaths, concentrated in June. In Tocache province, San Martín, 195 deaths occurred, the vast majority in July.

14. IDL, *Perú 1989*, p. 70, quotation taken from an article in *Sí*. This case is also mentioned in chapter 6.

15. Ibid.

16. Youngers, "War in the Andes"; quotation from Youngers interview with General Brito.

17. The falling price appears to have been due mainly to the advances that the United States and Colombian governments had made in disrupting Colombian drug cartel operations, which in turn disrupted the operations of the Colombians' middlemen in Peru.

18. The base is located about thirty kilometers north of Uchiza, Mariscal Cáceres, San Martín.

19. See Committee on Government Operations report, p. 28.

20. American officials identify Sendero with the traffickers, an analysis contested by Peruvians familiar with both the insurgency and the Upper Huallaga. Sendero has historically had an adversarial relationship with traffickers, reflecting the peasants' own ambivalence. Recently, though not directly involved in the drug trade, Sendero has been profiting from it, as described below.

21. IDL, *Perú 1990*, p. 118.

22. Killed by Sendero: 497 in Ayacucho; 140 in San Martín; 107 in Huancavelica; 106 in Huánuco. Other departments lagged well behind these four, none experiencing more than 40 killings. Bernales Commission, *10 Años de Violencia*, app. 1, p. 59.

23. Army killings in 1990: Huánuco 371, of which 355 were registered as Sendero, 1 was listed as MRTA, and 15 were called narcotraffickers; San Martín 195, of which 183 were presumed senderistas and 12 were presumed MRTA. By comparison, Junín, in third place, had 79 killings registered, and other departments had far fewer. Ibid., app. 8, p. 66.

24. This incident ended the interval between Arciniega and Brito in the PMC zone. General Luis Chacón was removed.

25. Isikoff, "Peru's Military Said to Tip Off Drug Dealers."

26. Powers, "Peru's Coca Industry Grows More Sophisticated."

27. Nineteen million dollars in police aid and and at least $9.7 million in development assistance are already available for Peru and are not contingent upon the antinarcotics agreement.

28. Gorriti, "Líos en Cocalandia," p. 16.

29. See in chapter 5, e.g., the murder of American freelance journalist Todd Smith.

30. In Peru's case in 1991, the DOD was training police only. Testimony of Daniel Fisk, deputy director for Counternarcotics for Inter-American Affairs, Department of

Defense, before the House Select Committee on Narcotics Abuse and Control, June 11, 1991.

31. Testimony of Assistant Secretary of State for International Narcotics Matters Melvyn Levitsky, before the House Select Committee on Narcotics Abuse and Control, June 11, 1991.

32. Anderson, "Next Nasty War?" p. 36.

CHAPTER 10: SUMMARY AND RECOMMENDATIONS

1. In towns like Accomarca, Umaru, Huambalpa, Cayara, and Julcamarca, the study showed that from a total of 6,057 families in 1981 the population had fallen to 2,940 families in 1985. CEAS Legal Department, "Problemática de los Migrantes por Motivos de Violencia Política," Lima, 1990; cited in Schiappa-Pietra, *Apuntes sobre el Desplazamiento Violento de Poblaciones en el Perú,* p. 16.

2. Project Counselling Service for Latin American Refugees, "Situation of Internally Displaced People," p. 19.

3. Andean Commission of Jurists, "Informativo Andino," June 10, 1991, quoting María de la Cruz Camacho.

4. Ibid.

5. See changes in the role of the prosecutor, chapter 2, and the Cayara case, chapter 4.

BIBLIOGRAPHY

Americas Watch. *Abdicating Democratic Authority: Human Rights in Peru*. New York: Human Rights Watch, 1984.

———. *A Certain Passivity: Failing to Curb Human Rights Abuses in Peru*. New York: Human Rights Watch, 1987.

———. *A New Opportunity for Democratic Authority: Human Rights in Peru*. New York: Human Rights Watch, 1985.

———. *Human Rights in Peru after President García's First Year*. New York: Human Rights Watch, 1986.

———. *In Desperate Straits: Human Rights in Peru after a Decade of Democracy and Insurgency*. New York: Human Rights Watch, 1990.

———. *Tolerating Abuses: Violations of Human Rights in Peru*. New York: Human Rights Watch, October 1988.

———. "Wave of Violence against Peru's Human Rights Community." *News from Americas Watch*. March 18, 1990.

Amnesty International. "Peru: 'Disappearances,' Torture and Summary Executions by Government Forces after the Prison Revolts of June 1986." London: Amnesty, 1987.

———. *Peru: Continuing Human Rights Violations, 1989–90*. London: Amnesty, 1990.

Andean Commission of Jurists (Comisión Andina de Juristas). *Coca Cocaina Narcotrafico: Laberinto en los Andes*. Edited by Diego García-Sayán. Lima: Comisión Andina de Juristas, 1989.

———. "Informativo Andino." Lima, various issues, especially November 9, 1989, May 7, 1990, and June 10, 1991.

Anderson, Harry. "The Next Nasty War?" *Newsweek,* May 21, 1990.

Asociación Pro-Derechos Humanos (APRODEH). "Masacre de Campesinos en Iquicha (Huanta, Ayacucho) 22 Agosto 1990." Lima, January 23, 1991.

Centro de Estudios y Promoción del Desarrollo (DESCO). *Violencia Política en el Perú, 1980–1988*. Lima, 1989.

Colegio de Periodistas del Peru. *Sendero de Violencia*. Lima: Colegio de Periodistas del Perú, 1990.

Comisión de Acción Social (CEAS). "Problemática de los Migrantes por Motivos de Violencia Política." Lima, 1990.

Comisión de Derechos Humanos (COMISEDH). *Informe Estadístico sobre la Desaparición Forzada de Personas en el Perú, 1983–89*. Lima, January 1990.

———. "Violencia Política en el Perú, Enero a Julio de 1989." Lima, October 1989.

Comisión Especial de Investigación y Estudio sobre la Violencia y Alternativas de Pacificación (Bernales Commission). *10 Años de Violencia en el Perú: Informe 1990*. Lima, January 1991.

————. *La Violencia en el Perú: Informe 1989*. Lima, January 1990.

Coordinadora Nacional de Derechos Humanos. "Carta Circular no. 15," Lima, August 1991.

————. "Informe Síntesis sobre la Situación de los Derechos Humanos en el Perú durante 1989." Lima, December 31, 1989.

Cotler, Julio. *Clases, Estado y Nación en el Perú*. Lima: Instituto de Estudios Peruanos, 1978.

Degregori, Carlos Iván. *Los Origenes de Sendero Luminoso*. Lima: Instituto de Estudios Peruanos, 1989.

————. *Qué Difícil es Ser Dios: Ideología y Violencia Política en Sendero Luminoso*. Lima: El Zorro de Abajo Ediciones, 1989.

de Soto, Hernando, with Enrique Gneusi, Mario Ghibellini, and the Instituto Libertad y Democracia, *El Otro Sendero: La Revolución Informal*. Lima: Compendio Técnico y Estadístico, 1986.

"Fujishock." *Economist*, October 12, 1991.

Goldenberg, Sonia. "El Frontón y la Historia Oficial." *La República*, July 9, 1986.

Gorriti Ellenboguen, Gustavo. "Líos in Cocalandia." *Caretas*, September 23, 1991.

————. *Sendero: Historia de la Guerra Milenaria*. Lima: Apoyo, 1990.

Grupo de Trabajo de la Coordinadora Nacional de los Derechos Humanos. "Boletín Informativo." Lima, October 1989.

Human Rights Watch. *The Persecution of Human Rights Monitors, December 1988 to December 1989: A Worldwide Survey*. New York: Human Rights Watch, December 1989.

Instituto de Defensa Legal (IDL). "Informe Mensual No. 7." (Also Nos. 9, 21). Lima: Centro de Estudios y Promoción del Desarrollo (DESCO), October 1989.

————. "La Opinión de los Dirigentes Campesinos." *Ideále*, Lima, August 1991.

————. *Perú 1989: En la Espiral de Violencia*. Lima: DESCO, March 1990.

————. *Perú 1990: La Oportunidad Perdida*. Lima: DESCO, 1991.

Instituto de Estudios Peruanos, Seminario-Taller sobre Liderazgo y Concertación Democrática, April 23–27, 1990. Lima, 1990.

Inter-Church Committee on Human Rights in Latin America. *1989 Annual Report on the Human Rights Situation in Peru*. Toronto, January 1990.

InterPress Service. "Fujimori Will Continue Distributing Arms to Peasants." June 13, 1991.

Isikoff, Michael. "Peru's Military Said to Tip Off Drug Dealers," *Washington Post*, November 25, 1990.

Matos Mar, José. *Desborde Popular y Crisis del Estado: El Nuevo Rostro del Peru en la Decada de los 80*. Lima: Instituto de Estudios Peruanos, 1984.

McClintock, Cynthia, and Abraham F. Lowenthal, eds. *The Peruvian Experiment Reconsidered*. Princeton: Princeton University Press, 1983.

Nash, Nathaniel C. "Fujimori in the Time of Cholera." *New York Times*, February 24, 1991.

Peru. Senate. "Informe Final de la Misión Investigadora de los Sucesos de Chumbivilcas y San Pedro de Cachi (Cusco-Ayacucho)." Lima, 1991.

Powers, Mary. "Peru's Coca Industry Grows More Sophisticated, Official Says." Reuters, June 9, 1991.

Project Counselling Service for Latin American Refugees. "The Situation of Internally Displaced People in Peru." San José, May 1991.

Samanez, Alvaro Rojas. *Partidos Politicos en el Peru*. Lima: Centro de Documentación e Información Andina, 1989.

Schiappa-Pietra, Oscar. *Apuntes sobre el Desplazamiento Violento de Poblaciones en el Perú, 1980–1990*. San José: Instituto Interamericano de Derechos Humanos, 1990.

Simons, Marlise. "Peru Adopts Severe Tactics to Combat Guerrillas." *New York Times*, August 18, 1984.

———. "Peruvian Military Fights Terrorists with Terror." *New York Times*, September 2, 1984.

Thais, Luis. *La Pobreza en el Perú*. Caracas: PNUD, 1990.

United Nations, Economic and Social Council. *Report of the Working Group on Forced or Involuntary Disappearances*. (E/CN.4/1991/20.) New York: United Nations, January 17, 1991.

United States Department of State. *Country Reports on Human Rights Practices for 1989: Report Submitted to the Committee on Foreign Affairs, House of Representatives, and the Committee on Foreign Relations, U.S. Senate by the Department of State*. Washington, D.C.: Government Printing Office, February 1990.

———. *Country Reports on Human Rights Practices for 1990: Report Submitted to the Committee on Foreign Affairs, House of Representatives, and the Committee on Foreign Relations, U.S. Senate by the Department of State*. Washington, D.C.: Government Printing Office, February 1991.

United States House of Representatives. Committee on Government Operations. "Stopping the Flood of Cocaine with Operation Snowcap: Is It Working?" Washington, D.C.: Government Printing Office, 1990.

———. Testimony of Daniel Fisk, Deputy Director for Counternarcotics for Inter-American Affairs, Department of Defense, before the House Select Committee on Narcotics Abuse and Control. Washington, D.C.: Government Printing Office, June 11, 1991.

———. Testimony of Melvyn Levitsky, Assistant Secretary of State for International Narcotics Matters, before the House Select Committee on Narcotics Abuse and Control. Washington, D.C.: Government Printing Office, June 11, 1991.

Youngers, Coletta. "The War in the Andes: The Military Role of the U.S. International Drug Policy." Washington, D.C.: Washington Office on Latin America, December 14, 1990.

INDEX

ABOUT HUMAN RIGHTS WATCH

Human Rights Watch conducts systematic investigations of human rights abuses in some sixty countries around the world. It addresses the human rights practices of governments of all political stripes, geopolitical alignments, and ethnic and religious persuasions. In internal wars—such as those in Afghanistan, Angola, Cambodia, and El Salvador—it documents abuses by governments and rebel groups. Human Rights Watch defends freedom of thought and expression, due process of law, and equal protection of the law; it denounces murders, disappearances, torture, arbitrary imprisonment, exile, censorship, and other abuses of internationally recognized human rights.

With a staff that includes more than thirty country specialists, Human Rights Watch annually carries out over one hundred investigative missions to gather current human rights information. In country after country, this ongoing effort makes a difference—saving lives, stopping torture, freeing prisoners, and helping to create the space for citizens to exercise their civil and political rights. Human Rights Watch reports are unique, up-to-date, firsthand sources of human rights information worldwide.

Human Rights Watch began in 1978 with the founding of Helsinki Watch by a group of publishers, lawyers, and other activists and now maintains offices in New York, Washington, D.C., Los Angeles, London, San Salvador, and Hong Kong. Today it includes Africa Watch, Americas Watch, Asia Watch, Helsinki Watch, Middle East Watch, and the Fund for Free Expression. Human Rights Watch is an independent, nongovernmental organization supported by contributions from private individuals and foundations. It accepts no government funds, directly or indirectly.